British History in Persp
General Editor: Jeremy

Please note that a sister series, *Social History in Perspective*, is available
covering the key topics in social and cultural history.

British History in Perspective
Series Standing Order:
ISBN 0–333–71356–7 hardcover
ISBN 0–333–69331–0 paperback

You can receive future titles in this series as they are published by placing
a standing order. Please contact your bookseller or, in case of difficulty,
write to the address below with your name and address, the title of the
series and the ISBN quoted above.

Customer Services Department, Macmillan Distribution Ltd
Houndmills, Basingstoke, Hampshire RG21 6XS, England

The Radical Right in Britain

Social Imperialism to the BNP

ALAN SYKES

First published 2005 by
PALGRAVE MACMILLAN
Houndmills, Basingstoke, Hampshire RG21 6XS and
175 Fifth Avenue, New York, N.Y. 10010
Companies and representatives throughout the world

PALGRAVE MACMILLAN is the global academic imprint of the Palgrave Macmillan division of St. Martin's Press, LLC and of Palgrave Macmillan Ltd. Macmillan® is a registered trademark in the United States, United Kingdom and other countries. Palgrave is a registered trademark in the European Union and other countries.

ISBN 0–333–59923–3 hardback
ISBN 0–333–59924–1 paperback

This book is printed on paper suitable for recycling and made from fully managed and sustained forest sources.

A catalogue record for this book is available from the British Library.

Library of Congress Cataloging-in-Publication Data
Sykes, Alan 1942–
   The radical right in Britain : social imperialism to the BNP / Alan Sykes.
      p. cm. – (British history in perspective)
   Includes bibliogaphical references and index.
   ISBN 0–333–59923–3 (cloth) – ISBN 0–333–59924–1 (pbk.)
   1. Radicalism—Great Britain—History—20th century.
2. Fascism—Great Britain—History—20th century. 3. British National Party (1982–) I. Title. II. British history in perspective (Palgrave Macmillan (Firm))

HN400.R3S95 2005
320.52'0941'0904–dc22   2004056199

10   9   8   7   6   5   4   3   2   1
14   13   12   11   10   09   08   07   06   05
Printed in China

Contents

v

Acknowledgements

The Radical Right is a controversial subject which arouses strong feelings, mostly of hostility towards it. There are obvious difficulties in writing about people who are still alive and in active politics. Some of them may well feel that they or their organizations should not be included in a study of the Radical Right, or be associated with other groups under that umbrella label. I hope that the book will explain why this has been done, and that they will accept my apologies where they cannot accept my arguments. I have met with nothing but courtesy and cooperation from the various organizations and individuals on the 'Radical Right' that I have contacted in the process of securing permission to quote from their material, even when they anticipated that what I have written would be biased against them. Apart from requesting permissions, I have not contacted organizations or interviewed individuals.

I am grateful to the following for assistance in securing permission to quote or for permission to quote from copyright material: Mr Andrew Anthony, the British National Party, Final Conflict (www. politicalsoldier.net), the Freedom Party, the Friends of Oswald Mosley (www.oswaldmosley.com), Professor Roger Griffin, Mr Derek Holland, Mr Tom Holmes and the National Front, the House of Lords Record Office, Mr David Kerr, the Liberal Nationalist Party, Lobster, Mr Donald Martin, Searchlight Magazine, Mr Troy Southgate, Mr Martin Walker, the White Nationalist Party, the Baron Willoughby de Broke. Every effort has been made to contact the holders of copyright. I hope that anyone whose copyright has been inadvertently infringed will accept my most sincere apologies, and the publisher will be pleased to make the necessary arrangement at the first opportunity.

Any survey of a long period such as this would be impossible without pre-existing monographs. I am grateful also to the authors of these, few though they are. My editors at Palgrave, Terka Acton and Sonya Barker have been models of patience, generous with time and sound advice. My former colleagues at St Andrews, Michael Bentley and Hamish Scott, have continued to provide much needed encouragement. So too have those various friends, Wilf and Sabina Prest, Peter Burns, Peter Bruce, Adrian Berry, Tom Jaine, Simon Phillips, Jonathan Harfield, Prem Singh, Richard and Monique Paice, Mike and Sue Broers, and Ken and Sandra Duncan who have down the years provided shelter from the storm. I am grateful to Sue for providing an environment in which this book could be written and enduring the frequent crabbiness of its author. My greatest debt, as ever, is to my children, Tasha, Tom and Claude and their respective partners.

List of Abbreviations

BF	British Fascisti
BM	British Movement
BNP	British National Party
BPP	British Peoples Party
BSP	British Socialist Party
BUF	British Union of Fascists
BWL	British Workers League
BWNL	British Workers National League
C18	Combat 18
EEC	European Economic Community
EFL	Economic Freedom League
ENM	English Nationalist Movement
IFL	Imperial Fascist League
ILP	Independent Labour Party
ITP	International Third Position
GBM	Greater Britain Movement
LEL	League of Empire Loyalists
LRC	Labour Representation Committee
NAR	Armed Revolutionary Nuclei (Italy)
NATO	North Atlantic Treaty Organisation
NCA	National Credit Association
NDP	National Democratic Party
NEW	New English Weekly
NF	National Front
NLP	National Labour Party
NP	National Party

NRF	National Revolutionary Faction
NSA	National Socialist Alliance
NSL	National Service League
NSM	National Socialist Movement
NUM	National Union of Mineworkers
NUPA	'Nu-Party' (Youth Organisation)
RPS	Racial Preservation Society
SNDC	Socialist National Defence Committee
TUC	Trades Union Congress
TUTRA	Trade Union Tariff Reform Association
UDA	Ulster Defence Association
USRC	Unionist Social Reform Committee
WDL	White Defence League
WDU	Workers Defence Union
WNP	White Nationalist Party

Introduction: Some Pointers Towards a Definition

As long ago as 1977, Martin Walker argued: 'to think of National Front (NF) members as Fascists in the classic sense is silly'.[1] In 1981 Nigel Fielding thought it necessary to justify writing about the National Front, concluding that to ignore it was 'absurd'.[2] A quarter of a century later, little has changed. Most of the movements here considered as the 'Radical Right' are still labelled 'fascist', and there is still little published about them beyond studies of anti-Semitism and histories of the British Union of Fascists (BUF). I have, wherever possible, avoided using the term 'fascist'. This is not another book on race relations.[3] There is little here on street violence or even major riots, and less still on infiltrators, moles and 'spooks'.[4] There are no 'infamous international extremists'[5], no shadowy figures who criss-cross Europe like a fifth aeronaut of the apocalypse, not even the scent of a beautiful spy.

The focus is on the ideas, leaving aside the question of hidden agendas, which are not, by definition, susceptible of historical analysis. The object is twofold: to provide through a survey of its history some clarification of the characteristic attitudes of the Radical Right, even if a full definition is impossible, and to draw out the continuities in a political outlook that has, of necessity, changed its priorities and emphases in response to changing circumstances. This means accepting from the start that irrespective of the complexities of the label, there was in reality a British 'Radical Right' whose outlook can be broadly described and distinguished; that it is not simply a form of, or euphemism for, the extreme or 'Far Right'. The emphasis is on the radical component of the 'Radical Right' because its 'right-wing' or 'conservative' aspects, seeking to preserve

1

the British empire, the British nation and/or race, and more recently in the context of American led globalization the very idea of nationalism and national identities, are more obvious.

The concept itself does present difficulties as the description of a distinct political outlook. At best a paradox, it is frequently linked with such phrases as 'constructive conservatism', 'radical imperialism', 'Tory Socialism', 'reactionary modernism' and several others that are used as synonyms, but are themselves paradoxical and explain little. Much of the problem arises from the origin of the term as a compound of two normally conflicting elements in the conventional left-right political spectrum. As the 'Radical Right' itself is well aware, its outlook does not fit within that polarity. It is not some kind of 'authoritarian centre'[6] between left and right, nor just a variant of the 'Far Right', but a 'third alternative', a 'third way' or 'third position', standing outside, 'beyond' or 'transcending' liberalism and the liberal political spectrum in its entirety.

The edges are, of course, blurred. In Britain, the Radical Right was neither a political party, nor a single, unified political movement nor a completely coherent ideology. It was never large enough to shape the political agenda, and its salient attitudes were sometimes virtually indistinguishable from mainstream Conservatism or the Far Right. Occasionally it attempted to identify itself with the Far Left; very rarely it even secured some support from that quarter. Its outlook varied from the authoritarian state to varieties of anarchism, from the de facto nationalization of property to absolute ownership as the only defence against the 'servile state'.

Nevertheless, that outlook revolved around a core of ideology and there are some initial generalizations, necessarily broad, that can be made about even so diffuse a concept. The Radical Right was intensely nationalist, or 'hyper-nationalist'. The nation was the starting point of its political thinking and the nation's interests the objective of its policies. It was elitist in terms of an elite within the nation which should lead, and for the most part of an elite amongst nations. It was purposive, seeking the regeneration of existing society through the transformation of its political and socio-economic structure, and the regeneration of the individual physically, mentally and morally. A new, better society required a new, 'higher type of man'. It was restorative in the sense of looking back to a mythical golden age, although it sought to restore the values, not the physical conditions, of that past age. It thus rested on an ethical perception of man and history.

It was organicist in its belief that society was not an aggregation of disparate individuals who took precedence over it; society was itself an organism and the individual within it part of the greater whole. It was evolutionary. There was no revolutionary breakthrough into utopia, no 'dawn of universal happiness'.[7] Both progress and the struggle to achieve it were continuous, challenging yet honing the individual. It was accordingly both dynamic and catastrophic. Progressive evolution was an upward incline. Failure to meet the demands of progress did not mean stasis, but ever accelerating decline from which there was no recovery unless it was reversed early by exceptional effort. For the Radical Right, catastrophe, the point at which decline became irreversible, was always visible on the horizon.

With such an outlook, the Radical Right was opposed to almost every aspect of existing society and its political system. It was anti-materialist, anti-individualist, anti-liberal, anti-democratic and anti-internationalist. It opposed the institutional expressions of liberal internationalism from the League of Nations between the wars to the United Nations after the Second World War. It was opposed to the materialist and internationalist doctrines of socialism and capitalism, which the Radical Right regarded as two sides of the same international financial conspiracy, often Jewish, against which national autonomy was the only secure defence. But the crucial rejection was the selfish, materialist individualism upon which it believed the entire liberal-capitalist-internationalist ethos rested. The Radical Right includes fascism[8] but is broader, incorporating such doctrines as distributism, Social Credit and 'aristocratic anarchism'.

Property and the Undermining of the Liberal Spectrum

The origins of the Radical Right worldview lay in the late Victorian and Edwardian period when terms such as 'constructive conservatism' first made their appearance, 'construction' being understood as Gladstone understood it, 'taking into the hands of the state the business of the individual man'.[9] Through much of the nineteenth century, Left and Right polarized around the essentially political issue of liberty against authority. The Left sought greater liberty for the individual by the extension of democracy and the limitation of the power of the state and its authoritative institutions such as the Monarchy, the Church and the territorial aristocracy; the Right urged the need for authority and restraint. At one extreme, the Far Right toppled off the edge of the liberal spectrum into reactionary 'Church and King' movements; at the other, the Left went beyond liberty into anarchy.

But behind democracy lurked the question of property. During the French Revolution, from which the left-right polarity derives, Jacques Roux pointed out that for the poor purely political liberty was not enough. 'Liberty is but a vain phantom when one class of men can starve the other with impunity.'[10] From the opposite point of view the rich were equally concerned. Lord Wemyss, later President of the Liberty and Property Defence League, believed in 1866 when parliamentary reform was again under discussion, that 'the central question' was 'one of property'.[11] It was so because, as the future Lord Salisbury put it: 'the bestowal upon any class of a voting power disproportionate to their stake in the country must infallibly give to that class a power ... of using taxation ... as an instrument of plunder ...'[12] Roux was arrested and like so many critics of the state committed suicide in prison. Wemyss and Salisbury were ignored, and the second reform act of 1867 was passed by a Conservative government.

But by the time of the third reform act of 1884, the socio-economic dimension of liberty, and with it the whole issue of the ownership and distribution of property, had become more central. Socialism, both Marxist and Fabian, gained a foothold in Britain in the 1880s, although of greater immediate impact was the publication in Britain of *Progress and Poverty* by the American land reformer, Henry George. George visited Britain in 1882 and 1884 to campaign on behalf of his scheme for the taxation of land values, and his ideas continued to have considerable influence within the left wing of the Liberal party until the First World War. Land was the most exposed form of property because of its association with the political establishment. It appeared especially challenged in the early 1880s as Gladstone reformed Irish land tenure in an attempt to end agrarian violence and break the link between rural agitation and the Irish demand for Home Rule.

Landowners, not entirely without reason, saw this as the thin end of the wedge of state interference with property throughout Britain. They were confirmed in this belief by Joseph Chamberlain's campaign on behalf of the 'Radical Programme', published in the *Fortnightly Review* between 1883 and 1885, which included controversial proposals for land, rating and taxation reform. Chamberlain demanded that property pay a 'ransom' in the form of higher taxation in return for the security it enjoyed. He spoke as a junior Liberal cabinet minister, but one regarded as the potential leader of a radicalized Liberal party in post-reform politics. The 'Radical Campaign' was the harbinger of 'new Liberalism' which, by the 1890s, had partially integrated into mainstream liberalism the argument that property owed at least some part of its value to society, and that the state had a right to such socially created value to use for social reform in the general interest.

New liberalism, however, went further in undermining the classical liberal political spectrum. It abandoned the atomistic concept of society as an aggregation of individuals in favour of organicism. Individual liberty could only exist and be extended within society under its agent, the state, rather than against the state. The common good benefited all, and took precedence over the rights of individuals, including, or perhaps especially, their property rights. Liberalism was evolving from a predominantly individualist creed into a collectivist form that its greatest contemporary theorist, L. T. Hobhouse, called 'Liberal-socialism', and its individualist critics called more bluntly 'socialism'. The usage was loose, but it meant excessive interference by the state with the rights of the individual. Individual liberty was the objective of the new liberalism as of the old, and new liberalism remained as committed to liberal internationalism. But the difference of means was crucial. The Left, even the moderate Left of 'liberal socialism' had become the advocate of the strong state.

In response, a growing section of the Right found itself questioning state authority. The trend could be traced back at least to the formation of the Liberty and Property Defence League in 1882. To the Left's contention that economic security was essential to real liberty and social reform was a proper function of the state, this libertarian Right countered that security of individual ownership was an essential attribute of individual liberty. In his pre-1914 classic, *Conservatism*, Lord Hugh Cecil defined such ownership in absolute terms, as 'the right of using property at the discretion of the owner ... it is a test of true ownership that an owner may do with his property what others think he ought not to do.'[13] On the crucial question of taxation, the most pervasive of all forms of state intervention that so interested Chamberlain and worried Salisbury, Cecil agreed that the state had the right to levy taxation. But 'taxation is distinguished from confiscation only in degree' and should never be used for the redistribution of property in the name of social reform.[14] The addition of a socio-economic dimension thus threw the classic liberal political spectrum into disarray. Once that issue was introduced, there were advocates of a strong state and a minimum state on both the Left and the Right. Liberty and authority ceased to be a meaningful means of differentiation.

Property and Purpose

For Wemyss, Cecil and much later for 'new right' libertarians like Thatcher, property had no purpose beyond itself. One of the challenges thrown down by social imperialism and the Radical Right from beyond the liberal individualist political spectrum was to question this doctrine, and argue that property had a social function which was the justification for its existence. Chamberlain's response to critics of his doctrine of 'ransom' was that in the face of the socialist challenge to the institution itself, he was putting 'the rights of property on the only firm and defensible basis'.[15] As an argument, it looked back to a far older, moral conception of property and society rather than forward to the economic sophistication of new liberalism. Chamberlain, like a great many Victorians, was an instinctive organicist before a fully developed secular theory of society as an organism had been built upon Darwinian foundations, drawing his inspiration from the Bible and that mutuality that Ruskin described as 'social affection'. It could be expressed in other ways. 'What', asked the eccentric Conservative, Sir Francis Fletcher-Vane in 1908, 'is the connection between feudalism and socialism. There is no connection because they are the same.'[16] They were the same because they both denied the absolute right of individual ownership.

From this point of view, property, if it was to exist, had duties as well as rights. The institution of private property was challenged because its owners were, or were no longer, providing a justification for their wealth through leadership. Property and wealth provided leaders with the power to lead. If they did not lead, then they had no need of the power, or the property. The Radical Right's vision of an elite was non-materialist. The elite identified itself through its personal qualities, through character; it was an aristocracy, but an aristocracy of merit, not wealth. Merit included the ability to govern, but the distinguishing feature of an aristocratic elite was less its abilities than its moral qualities, its sense of honour, its willingness to shoulder burdens and ultimately to sacrifice itself, individually or collectively, for those it led and the nation it represented.

'Ransom' was a doctrine to give legal sanction to the performance of its duties by property when the individual conscience had failed. As a result, like new liberalism, it made the state a purposive moral agent, but in enhancing the state it substituted bureaucracy for aristocracy in a way that was not to the liking of all of the Radical Right. 'Aristocracy' provided the basis for the principal anarchist strand that was implicit even in so state-centred a programme as Mosley's corporate state. Leadership through character did not require the machinery of state control and coercion; properly displayed, leadership would be recognized and followed. On this line of thinking, state bureaucracy was an indication that the elite had failed, and sought to maintain through the imposition of an artificial hierarchy the power that it could no longer sustain through the exercise of natural authority. More usually, however, the doctrine of aristocracy led to the view that the elite should rule through the state.

In such a society, there was no place for democracy, or at least not individualist democracy. The Radical Right argued not only that men were not all equal in abilities, but that they should not be equal in rights. Service and duty came first, and rights, including the right to vote, were dependent upon performance. In its most extreme form, there was no value in the individual per se, only in what he could contribute to the whole, the function he performed. This was implicit in the organic conception of society. In the human body analogy of which organicists were so fond, the elite, as the brain, gave the commands; the body, or body politic, obeyed. There was no use in a disobedient or malfunctioning member which/who might need treatment or removal if the weakness threatened the body as a whole. Function, however, offered a route to an alternative form of democracy, the occupational franchise. It was proposed on the grounds that it would produce an informed electorate. It had the additional advantage that those who performed no function had no vote, but those who performed multiple functions might have multiple votes consistent with their multiple contributions to society.

One consequence of this thinking was that there were a number of apparent tensions within the Radical Right outlook, especially when viewed from within the liberal spectrum. Both the more authoritarian and the more anarchic elements wished to retain private property, the former because of the incentive towards efficiency it was thought to provide, the latter to create economic security as the basis of individual liberty. But both saw the need for state supervision of private property in the collective interest so that the 'rights' of property were limited. Similarly, even the authoritarian section justified its attitude with reference to individual liberty.

These were, however, tensions, paradoxes rather than contradictions, reconciled by the primacy given to duties above rights, of economic liberty, or security, over purely political liberty, and of the collective, not over the individual, but as the essential matrix within which the individual realized himself. Ideally, such priorities would be internalized with the evolution of the 'higher type of man'. As with Chamberlain's doctrine of 'ransom', the intervention of the state was required only when, or because, the individual neglected his duties to the collective. The aristocratic aspect of Radical Right thinking made it, in some respects, potentially a highly individualist doctrine, but based on the identification of the values and aspirations of the individual with those of the community, race or nation.

The State, the Nation, the Race and Purpose

'Nation' is a complex concept and becomes more so when applied to Britain with its component Welsh, Irish, Scottish and English 'nations', and the additional complication of an independent and distinct southern Irish 'nation'. The concept contains elements of territoriality, language, culture, religion and race but is not exclusively territorial, linguistic, cultural, religious or racial. The Radical Right's idea of nation included all of these elements, except perhaps religion, but the most important was race, whether defined culturally or biologically. Its 'nation' was the 'race-nation', either domiciled in Great Britain and Northern Ireland or as an imperial diaspora, in which case it was the 'British nation'. Alternatively, and particularly after 1945, in defiance of conventional terminology, the nation might be 'Europe – A Nation', or the 'Aryan Nation', both of which had indeterminate territorial boundaries, especially in the east.

Racial stereotyping tended to be in terms of distinctive abilities or purposes. In such stereotypes, the Germans were, by the start of the twentieth century, regarded as more efficient and disciplined, but lacking initiative and imagination. The Jews were characterized as the epitome of economic man, excelling all other races at making and handling money. But the hierarchy that evolved from stereotyping did not rest primarily on power, technological supremacy or wealth. It helped that 'we have got the Gatling (or Maxim) gun and they have not', because conquest was a visible affirmation of superiority, but it was not sufficient in itself. German ruthlessness in the suppression of colonial revolts was an indication that their efficiency and power were self-serving, morally debased. The exploitation of the Congo by Belgium could be regarded in the same light.

The desire to become rich was similarly selfish, the product of low moral standards. Jews stood condemned by their very success; the richer they became the more their moral inferiority was confirmed, the greater was the danger of corruption by their presence because they were seen as seeking wealth for its own sake, not for the good uses to which it might be put. There was, then, a hierarchy of racial hierarchies differentiated on ethical grounds, rather than a simplistic all-embracing hierarchy. Self-sacrifice was the highest of virtues; selfishness the worst of sins. Sacrifice was the moral code that made the British the elite among imperial races, the 'greatest governing race that the world has ever seen'.[17] From it stemmed their ability to govern themselves and govern others; because of it they were to fulfil their imperial mission. For much of the twentieth century, race itself was purposive.

Catastrophe and Action

The Radical Right had its roots in the late nineteenth and early twentieth century because of particular changes in the prevailing worldview. Liberalism, despite Gladstone, despite the judgmental nature of the Victorians' God and the all-pervasive gloom of Victorian architecture, was generally optimistic. It did believe in achievable progress towards greater liberty and greater harmony; it was very much an ideology of concord. In the later nineteenth century it was challenged by ideologies of conflict, the Freudian idea of the individual in conflict with himself, the Marxist dialectic of class conflict and the social-Darwinist doctrine of natural selection through the constant struggle for scarce resources. Between them they shattered the assumption of human rationality on which liberalism was based, and not only the prospect of social and international peace but also, for some, that peace was desirable. Moreover each ideology was, in its own way, determinist. Freud's analysis of the human condition, Marx's dialectic of history and the Darwinian struggle in nature reduced man to the victim of forces he could not control.

Within this pessimistic worldview, organicism decreed for societies, states and empires the same fate as all living organisms, to live through their life cycle and die. History was full of once great empires now vanished. By the late nineteenth century there were fears that Britain was about to join them. Social Darwinism and the cyclical theory of history reinforced each other. The Radical Right in Britain was very much bound up with empire and what might be called the white legend of empire, the civilizing mission of imperialism. It coexisted with, and progressively lost ground to, the black legend of brutality and exploitation, to the point that the current chairman of the British National Party (BNP), Nick Griffin, has declared: 'We are not imperialists. We don't want to conquer and exploit anyone else.'[18] The end of empire created many difficulties for the British Radical Right. It left an 'imperial race' without an imperial justification for its continued existence. It resulted in a sophisticated reassessment during the course of the 1980s that reconstructed the ideology of the Radical Right from a combination of old and new, third world, materials while maintaining the fundamental antagonism between nationalism and liberal capitalist internationalism.

The collapse of Soviet communism rather than, or perhaps before, the anticipated collapse of liberal capitalism had far less impact since the Radical Right had long regarded capitalism and communism as two sides of the same coin. What set both the Radical Right and the Communist Left outside the liberal mainstream was their belief both in evolutionary, historical determinism and in the efficacy of human action to alter it. For communism this amounted only to an acceleration of the dialectic; for the Radical Right there existed the possibility that evolutionary determinism might be thwarted, and a purified world restored. It was a central tension in the many tensions of the Radical Right outlook, but both it and communism were revolutionary in the liberal context, and competitors for the succession.

Chapter 1: Social Imperialism and Race Regeneration

In the last three decades of the nineteenth century, Britain's sense of security as the world's leading industrial, naval and imperial power gave way to increasing unease. Prussia's easy victory over France in 1870 and the subsequent unification of Germany was seen as an early demonstration of German efficiency and ambition. The first invasion novel, G. T. Chesney's *Battle of Dorking* appeared as early as 1871. Between then and 1914 a succession of others followed in which the enemy, usually Germany but occasionally France, surprised a complacent and unprepared Britain. Germany's decision to build a navy that could challenge Britain's maritime supremacy aggravated these alarms and gave rise to the best known of the genre, Erskine Childers' *Riddle of the Sands*.[1]

Home defence was part of a wider imperial problem. In acquiring an empire, Britain had acquired land frontiers. Wherever they looked, late Victorians could see challengers: Russia on the North-West frontier of India and in China; France in Egypt, the Sudan and Asia; Germany in southern Africa, China and the Pacific; the United States in the Caribbean and South America. From the mid-1890s too many problems appeared to flare up at once, tension with the United States, an uprising on the North-West frontier, confrontation with France at Fashoda in 1898, the Boxer rebellion in China in 1900 and above all the confrontation with the Boer Republics in South Africa that became the South African war of 1899–1902. Sending troops to South Africa denuded British home defences and reinforced the view that Britain was overstretched and overexposed both at home and abroad. 'The weary Titan', as Chamberlain observed at the Colonial Conference of 1902, 'staggers under the too vast orb of its fate'.[2]

11

Trade, Depression and 'Socialism'

Foreign competition was economic as well as naval and military. During the 1880s, sizeable sections of British industry and agriculture lent their support to the Fair Trade League and its campaign for protective tariffs.[3] E. N. Williams' *Made in Germany*, published in 1896, gave the economic invasion the coverage given to the threat of military invasion by novelists. The onset of the late Victorian 'Great Depression', which lasted well into the 1890s, virtually coincided with the emergence of overtly socialist movements and serious industrial unrest. The Marxist Social Democratic Federation was involved in the unemployed riots of 1886 and in the organization of unskilled labour unions in the late 1880s and early 1890s. The fruits of its activity were seen in the outbreak of strikes amongst previously unorganized workers, the gas fitters and dockers between 1889 and 1891. The engineers' strike/lockout of 1898 showed that traditionally moderate skilled workers were also becoming militant. Employers, squeezed by the depression in world trade, blamed union militancy for lack of competitiveness and responded in kind with the use of blacklegs and the law. A series of legal decisions culminating in the Taff Vale judgement by the House of Lords in 1901 rendered the trade union movement virtually impotent by the turn of the century. It turned the unions towards politics to amend the law.

In 1900, the socialist Independent Labour Party (ILP), formed in 1893 to secure working-class representation in parliament, achieved cooperation with a section of the trade union movement to create the Labour Representation Committee (LRC). In the 1906 general election, the LRC won 29 seats and became the Labour party.[4] Even moderate contemporaries responded with alarm. 'What is going on here', noted the Conservative party leader, Arthur Balfour, 'is a faint echo of the same movement which has produced massacres in St. Petersburg, riots in Vienna, and Socialist processions in Berlin.'[5] Less moderate men like Balfour's friend, George Wyndham, saw the election result in more apocalyptic terms that encapsulated the dramatic tension of the Radical Right frame of mind:

'Now, to-day in England we are fighting to a finish ... Two ideals and only two emerge from the vortex:-

1. Imperialism which demands Unity at Home between classes, and Unity throughout the Empire ...

2. Insular Socialism and Class Antagonism ... Between these two ideals a great battle will be fought ... If Imperialism wins, we shall go on and be a great Empire. If Socialism wins we shall cease to be. The rich will be plundered. The poor will suffer. We shall perish with Babylon, Rome and Constantinople.'[6]

Poverty, Luxury and the Race

By the start of the twentieth century, the poor were very much the focus of attention from imperialists as well as socialists. 'An Empire such as ours', declared the Liberal Imperialist, Lord Rosebery, 'requires as its first condition an imperial race – a race vigorous and industrious and intrepid ... in the rookeries and slums which still survive, an imperial race cannot be reared.'[7] But that was simply a statement about living conditions. C. F. G. Masterman expressed the greater fear that degeneration had gone beyond environment to biology, the evolution of 'a new race ... the "City type" ... the "street-bred people"' emerging from the urban sprawl that was industrial Britain,[8] 'a race of men, small, ill-formed, disease-stricken, hard to kill.'[9]

That 'new race' appeared to be Britain's unhappy future. Whilst the birth rate overall was declining, the decline was most marked amongst the upper and upper middle classes. As the eugenicist, Dr Tredgold, commented, 'there is not the slightest doubt that the decline is chiefly incident in ... the best and most fit elements of the community, whilst the loafers, the incompetents, the insane and feeble-minded, continue to breed with unabated and unrestrained vigour.'[10] Alarmists feared that the upper classes were becoming infertile because excessive luxury and ease had sapped their vigour in marital as well as martial affairs. The suffragette movement was one indication of moral decay, the unwillingness of women to endure the rigours of childbearing in the performance of their national and imperial duty.

Investigations, including that of an Interdepartmental Committee on Physical Deterioration appointed in the aftermath of the South African War, found that the differential was mostly due to the voluntary limitation of family by the wealthier elements of society. But eugenicists provided fuel for alarmists with their research and although the Eugenics Society was small, the general principle that man as a rational being could improve on Darwinian natural selection by deliberate action was widely accepted. So, too, was the view that real progress was racial and could be achieved by breeding from the best stocks and eliminating the worst. But eugenicists admitted that thus far they had little understanding of the workings of human heredity, which largely ruled out 'positive eugenics', the deliberate selective breeding of higher racial types.

There was, in any case, the problem of deciding which were the best stocks from which to breed, although Tredgold's view that class expressed fitness was the prevailing opinion. The decadence of the elite constituted the main difficulty. There was some faith left in the territorial aristocracy and landed gentry where they remained on their estates and had not been corrupted by city luxury or marriage into the selfish plutocracy. The acid test was service, usually inadequately rewarded service, which was to be found in the professional classes, the civil service and servants of the empire where a 'natural' aristocracy of merit might be found. Apart from the Fabian proposal for 'the endowment of motherhood' which would need to be selective to assist the fit rather than the already over-prolific unfit, encouragement of the fit was confined to promoting the idea of 'hygienic marriage' between partners of sound stock, and lowering their tax burdens. Eugenics provided a critique of state welfare reform and charity both because of the burden placed on the fit, and because they kept the unfit alive and able to breed through 'false humanitarianism.'[11] Britain was thus engaged in 'race suicide'.[12] The focus of attention was less the working poor than those who were unable to work, and increasingly on those with mental defects which the Royal Commission into the Care and Control of the Feeble-Minded concluded in 1908 was a hereditary condition.[13]

But the solution in 'negative eugenics' was as elusive as that in 'positive eugenics'. Although the idea of a 'lethal chamber'[14] was familiar, extermination appealed only to an extreme fringe.[15] On that fringe there were some, like the Nietzschean, Anthony Ludovici, who wrote in praise of Nazi racial policies in the 1930s, and who advocated 'controlled and legalized infanticide',[16] and the French author, H. P. Lichtenberger, whose translator J. M. Kennedy was an associate of Ludovici. Compulsory sterilization found more support, but the majority got no further than the segregation of the feeble-minded from the community and from the opposite sex, with the possibility that in return for their release, inmates might agree to voluntary sterilization. The issue was favourably considered by Churchill who thought the 'multiplication of the unfit ... a very terrible danger to the race' and urged that the feeble-minded be 'segregated under proper conditions so that their curse dies with them ...'[17] The eventual Mental Deficiency Act of 1913 did provide for compulsory segregation but was defended by the new Home Secretary, McKenna, on the grounds of care, not racial improvement.

National Efficiency

The South African War brought the various late Victorian/Edwardian crises together. Contrary to expectations, it took nearly 3 years for the world's mightiest imperial power to overcome the force of two small republics with an army of farmer-soldiers. The war exposed the inadequacies of the army in the field and inefficiencies in government and administration. The depletion of Britain's home defences led to the formation of the National Service League in 1901 to campaign for conscription. It followed in the footsteps of the Navy League formed in 1894 to campaign for the strengthening of Britain's first line of defence. By the Edwardian era those who found it insufficiently dynamic had split away to form the Imperial Maritime League.

Most importantly, the war made the connection between poverty and power. In the larger cities, over 60 per cent of army volunteers had to be rejected as physically unfit for military service. In the words of the Inspector-General of Recruiting in 1902, 'the one subject which causes anxiety in the future as regards recruiting, is the gradual deterioration in the physique of the working classes...'[18] It was the collectivist link between the welfare and the warfare state. For social imperialists, although they used the language of eugenics and constantly referred to race degeneration, eugenic recommendations of race breeding were not politically viable and too slow in their effects. Only welfare expenditure sufficient to transform the condition of the poor would provide the country with the fit working and fighting men to defend itself, its trade and its empire, all besieged by foreign rivals.

The war provoked Rosebery to launch an all-pervasive campaign for national efficiency, 'a condition of national fitness equal to the demands of our Empire – administrative, parliamentary, commercial, educational, physical, moral, naval and military fitness.'[19] 'The true policy of imperialism' he declared in 1902 was one that related 'not to territory alone, but to race as well.' He mentioned as areas for reform, education, housing and temperance but he was noticeably short on details. The Fabian socialist, Sidney Webb, one of several Fabian supporters of Liberal Imperialism, attempted to unite imperialism and social reform as the foreign and domestic sides of the same collectivism, and hoped, in typically Fabian fashion, to provide those details. Amongst other proposals, he advocated a 'National Minimum' standard of living, 'the minimum necessary for breeding an even moderately imperial race', housing reform since an 'efficient army' could not be created 'out of the stunted, anaemic, demoralized citizens of the slum tenements of our great cities', educational reform and 'virility in government'.[20] Webb dreamed of 'a dozen planning committees', but the only planning body to emerge was an informal cross-party dining club, the Coefficients, which met from 1902–08 but was never influential.

The problem the Liberal Imperialists faced was that the Liberal party at the turn of the century, including the Liberal Imperialist faction, was as divided upon social reform as it was on imperialism. Collectivist imperialists like Webb were opposed by wealthy individualist Liberals like the veteran Methodist, Sir Robert Perks, and the wealthy industrialist, Weetman Pearson. For these individualists, imperialism was a means of ridding the Liberal party not only of its anti-imperialist but also its state interventionist elements in order to reclaim the propertied middle classes for the party. The Liberal Imperialists failed their first serious test, opposing, with two exceptions, the Conservative government's education bill in 1902 despite its object of bringing efficiency into educational administration. As the first clear party of social imperialism, the Liberal Imperialists were rapidly overwhelmed by the campaign for imperial preference that Joseph Chamberlain launched upon a startled political world in May 1903.

Chamberlain and Tariff Reform

Having left the Liberal party in 1886 over Home Rule, Joseph Chamberlain was, by 1895, Colonial Secretary in a coalition government dominated by Conservatives. Chamberlain, however, had lost none the dynamism that had characterized his career as a constructive radical before 1886; it had been redirected into constructive, or radical, imperialism. For Chamberlain, imperialism was a matter of developing Britain's imperial estates both as an economic and a moral imperative. His analogy with British landed estates indicated not only his approach to empire, but also his justification of property. Chamberlain was a paternalist industrialist, a paternalist imperialist and an advocate of the paternalist state when private paternalism failed.

The South African War offered one ray of hope for the future. Dominion forces had participated in the struggle; the empire had acted as a unit. Since taking office, Chamberlain had been seeking to unite the empire more closely, but had hitherto failed to find the means. The imposition of import duties, which Chamberlain proposed in 1903 to give preferential treatment to imperial produce, was his response to Dominion proposals for reciprocal preference at the Colonial Conference of 1902, but it rapidly became an intellectual conviction. 'Commercial union', Chamberlain argued, 'in some shape or another, must precede or accompany closer political relations.' Without it 'as all history shows, no permanent cooperation is possible.'[21] Preference inevitably involved duties, however moderate, on food imports. To counteract the outcry against this, Chamberlain was forced to concede reductions in existing duties on tea, sugar, coffee and tobacco so that there would be no overall rise in the working-class cost of living, to make up the lost revenue by a 10 per cent revenue tariff on manufactured imports, and to abandon his original linkage of tariff reform with old age pensions. In this process, despite Chamberlain's initial intentions and explicit denials, tariff reform became protectionist.

In his campaigns in the country Chamberlain used distinctly protectionist arguments. Britain's problem was not, as the Liberal Imperialists maintained, her own inefficiency, but unfair foreign competition from protectionist countries. Britain under free trade was a 'defenceless village' and it was the working-class which suffered most. Chamberlain made a direct bid for working class support, and after his policy was rejected by the Trades Union Congress (TUC) set up the alternative, but totally ineffective, Trade Union Tariff Reform Association (TUTRA). In the manner of Sidney Webb, he also presented tariffs and welfare legislation as two sides of the same collectivist approach. Industrial legislation protecting working conditions 'raised the costs of production ... If these foreign goods come in cheaper ... either you will take lower wages or you will lose your work ... You cannot have free trade in goods and at the same time have protection of labour'.

Chamberlain thus identified the enemy of British workers as foreign workers, not British employers. Those who tried to persuade the workers otherwise, that 'the whole thing was a struggle between themselves and the capitalists and that if only they can squeeze the capitalist a little more they will get more wages' knew nothing of trade and industry. Real economic conflict took place at the national level between competing states, not within nations between competing classes. British workers thus had a common interest with British employers, and both had a common enemy, 'the foreigner'. Domestically, whilst improving conditions by insulating the economy from world conditions, the social objective of tariff reform was vertical integration.

But tariff reform was not primarily an economic policy designed 'to make this country, already rich, a little richer'. The 'economic side of the question', Chamberlain noted in 1904, was 'secondary'.[22] 'The character of a nation is more important than its opulence. What I care for is that this people shall rise to the height of its great mission.' In Chamberlain's usage, the term 'character' had a double meaning, 'the character of the individual' and the socio-economic composition of the nation. The former depended 'upon the greatness of the ideals upon which he rests', and these ideals derived from the empire. The empire 'made us what we are – it has taught us the virtue of national sacrifice.'

Sacrifice lay at the core of Chamberlain's vision of the British and the British empire, not profit. But without drastic and rapid change

> we shall lose not only our commerce, but the whole character of the country will be changed; and, in the course of another generation, this will be much less an industrial country inhabited by skilful artisans than a distributive country with a smaller population consisting of rich consumers on the one hand and people engaged in the work of distribution on the other.

Britain would be 'richer than ever, and yet weaker. We may have more millionaires and fewer working men and that is the direction in which we are tending.'

The outlook amounted to a redefinition of national wealth in non-monetary terms. Wealth was not a question of tax receipts, interest on foreign investments or cheques cleared but the 'product in men and the number and proportion of its population which it can keep in comfort and happiness, and for which it can find remunerative employment'. Some forms of monetary wealth, such as interest on foreign investments were, indeed, counterproductive, representing employment given to foreign competitors through the export of British capital. The importance of imperial preference lay not just in securing imperial markets before foreign penetration led the various component parts of the empire to drift away from Britain, but in providing employment to British workers.

In the tariff reform scheme of things, the economies of Britain and the empire were complementary. The empire supplied raw materials and food to Britain's industrial centres, Britain exported manufactured goods to the empire. Chamberlain foresaw an empire 'which with decent organisation and consolidation might be absolutely self-sustaining'. 'We conceive a system', wrote J. L. Garvin, editor of the *Observer*, 'under which our imports ... shall consist of food and raw materials, the products of British [i.e. imperial] soil, raised by the hands of British subjects ... carried over British railways to British ports, shipped by British vessels to British people.'[23] Thus secured in men, markets, raw materials, manufactured goods and food, Britain and her empire could ignore the rest of the world. 'We shall be isolated ... but our isolation will be a splendid one ... '

Tariff Reformers saw international relations as a social Darwinist struggle, 'a race for existence that has been going on ever since the world began'. 'I want to prepare you, now', Chamberlain told his audiences, 'while there is still time, for a struggle ... from which, if we emerge defeated, this country will lose its place, will no longer count among the great nations of the world.' It was a struggle in which the future belonged to large states, not small islands. Just as it allowed Britain to cheat the cyclical theory of history because the empire was, as Chamberlain asserted, 'a new state', so the empire allowed Britain to cheat geography, to become, as J. L. Garvin described it, a 'Super Sea-State', 'Oceania', rivalling the great land powers of the United States, Russia and Germany. But the sea empire needed what the land powers already enjoyed, secure lines of communication. The existence of the empire, according to Garvin 'depends upon the control of all the sea-communications of the world, and the possession of naval superiority ... which is nothing less than the dream of universal monarchy realized on one element'.[24]

But time was running out. Imperial cooperation in South Africa and the offer of reciprocal preference at the Colonial Conference of 1902 was an opportunity, but 'this is the parting of the ways ... If you do not take this opportunity, it will not recur ... We must either draw closer together, or we shall drift apart'. There were two alternative futures, the 'creation of an empire such as the world has never seen ... an Empire which may be, which ought to be, greater, more united, more fruitful for good than any Empire in human history', or failing to meet the challenge, in which case, 'this England of ours would sink from the comparative position which it has enjoyed throughout the centuries ... It would be a fifth rate nation, existing on the sufferance of its more powerful neighbours'. Chamberlain estimated the time left as less than 20 years. As the Conservative moderate, Lord Salisbury, observed without irony, Chamberlain adhered to 'the catastrophical theory of politics'.[25]

Social Imperialism

In 1906, Chamberlain suffered a stroke which removed him from active politics and the effective leadership of the Tariff Reform movement. Leadership passed to men who never understood party as the route to political power or despised the party system altogether. With each passing year they felt more intensely the need to seize the fading opportunity, a tension increased by the presence after 1906 of a Liberal government that seemed increasingly anti-national, infiltrated by aliens and bent on dismantling the empire.

In December 1906 Milner, whom Salisbury thought also adhered to 'the catastrophical theory of politics', restated and developed the basic principles of tariff reform. For Milner, imperialism and social reform were 'inseparable ideals, absolutely interdependent and complementary'.[26] The British people needed to be prosperous and fit to sustain the burden of empire; the empire was essential to Britain to maintain the power upon which her prosperity depended. Milner had no objection to being called 'socialist' for his advocacy of state intervention. He denounced that 'odious form of socialism ... which ... lives on the cultivation of class hatred' but proclaimed:

> a nobler socialism which ... realized the fact that we are not so many millions of individuals each struggling for himself with the State to act as policeman, but literally one body-politic; that the different classes and sections of the community are members of that body, and that when one member suffers all the members suffer.[27]

Unlike Chamberlain, Milner never considered tariff reform as sufficient in itself, but 'an element ... in a larger policy ... Stunted, overcrowded town populations, irregular employment, sweated industries, these things are as detestable to true imperialism as they are to philanthropy'.[28] In the autumn of 1907 he delivered a series of speeches to put flesh on these bones, juxtaposing, as Wyndham had done, 'true imperialism' and 'socialism'. Socialism arose because of 'the abuse of private property, the cruelty and failure of the scramble for gain ... let us be more, and not less, strenuous in removing the causes of it ...' Milner was perfectly prepared to take 'some forms of property' into the public domain, and elaborated an extensive programme of interventionist reform: 'the multiplication of small landholders and ... landowners, the resuscitation of agriculture ... better housing in our crowded centres; town planning;

sanitary conditions of labour; the extinction of sweating; the physical training of the people; continuation schools ...' But these were illustrations of areas for state action. Milner set no limits, and specifically added: 'and all other measures necessary to preserve the stamina of the race and develop its productive power'.[29]

Milner voiced not solely his own ideas, but those of a think tank that was a roll call of tariff reform radicalism, including Austen Chamberlain, Bonar Law, Garvin and Fabian Ware, editor of the radical imperialist *Morning Post*, Richard Jebb, L. S. Amery and J. W. Hills. The result of their deliberations appeared a year later in the *Morning Post*, and amounted to a new programme of 'unionism'. 'The basis of all Unionist policy is Union. All national questions, whether domestic or Imperial, should be treated in relation to this fundamental principle, implying the union of classes within the State, national union of Great Britain and Ireland, Imperial union of the self-governing nations and dependencies under the Crown.' Tariff Reform was a prerequisite: 'essential to the union of classes ... essential to the national union of Great Britain and Ireland ... essential to the union of the Empire'. On defence, the programme advocated the two-power standard for the navy and a 'citizen army' based on 'universal service'; 'some positive constructive policy' for Ireland; reform of the House of Lords 'to increase its fitness to perform the onerous duties now devolving upon it', and old age pensions 'the most important question now before the country ... in the field of social reform'.

Old age pensions achieved such prominence because the Liberal government had just passed its own non-contributory scheme. These social imperialists preferred a contributory scheme, but really wanted pensions to be considered as 'part of the bigger question of State insurance against incapacity to work, from whatever cause the incapacity may arise' and dealt with 'in relation to other questions of national organisation ... Such a system would carry with it the incidental advantage of effecting the registration of our industrial population which is a condition essential to the solution of unemployment and other pressing social problems'. Amongst those problems ready for treatment was sweating, where the principle of Wages Boards and a state imposed minimum wage was accepted; the extension of smallholdings, agricultural cooperation schemes and a 'thoroughgoing reform of local taxation'.[30] Social imperialism had come a long way since 1903.

In October 1910, these ideas were developed still further by the Reveille movement, a group of 'wealthy and active' MPs led by Henry

Page Croft and Lord Willoughby de Broke. It proclaimed a 'National Policy' in which tariff reform was 'an essential element but... far from the whole of it'. In particular it linked protection to national insurance by arguing that protection would create 'a rising market for labour' which was necessary to make insurance 'and other measures of social reform' practicable. 'By insurance, and by the increase of... small owners of land, the ends which the Socialists have in view will be attained by practical instead of fatal methods. Destitution will gradually be abolished but without a loss of industrial initiative...' It was a theme which was to be repeated by the Radical Right for much of the century.

But domestic reform was not enough. 'Only by gathering together the several nations of the Empire can we cope in the international balance of power with the newly organized continental states.' The manifesto rested, according to the *Morning Post*, on

> the statement that it is the business of the State to foster the dynamic energies of the people. This end can only be attained by a conjoined and inter-related scheme which embraces the whole field of national life from foreign policy to the Navy and Army, from the military forces to the defensive development of national industries on which the support of armaments depends, and from the industrial security behind the Tariff to social advance and prosperity within the area the Tariff protects...[31]

Thus would the nation be equipped for the eternal social-Darwinist struggle of nations.

Parliament and Parties

The formation of the Reveille group was the response of frustrated social imperialists to the Constitutional Conference of 1910. The rejection of the 1909 budget, with its proposed new land taxes and increased licensing duties precipitated a constitutional crisis over the powers of the House of Lords. The ensuing general election of January 1910 greatly reduced the Liberal majority and left the government dependent upon the Irish Parliamentary Party to stay in office. It secured Irish support for the budget despite Irish opposition to the licensing duties only by promising to deal with the veto powers of the House of Lords and thus ensure the passage of a Home Rule Bill. For imperialists this presaged the dismemberment of the empire, and the end of British power and prosperity. On the death of Edward VII in May 1910, the leading figures of the Conservative and Liberal parties agreed to a conference to avoid, if possible, confronting George V with a major crisis at the very start of his reign.

The members of Reveille were not, however, the only ones concerned by the conference. Hilaire Belloc, whose suspicion of the influence of plutocrats in politics predated his election as a Liberal MP in 1906, found his suspicions confirmed by his parliamentary experience. His critique, *The Party System*, written with Cecil Chesterton, was published in 1911. Much of *The Party System* dealt with an issue of which most in politics were already aware, the increased power of the respective front benches and their control over their party members. Beyond that, Belloc saw collusion as the norm. The apparently rival front benches were united by extensive family ties, but above all they were both indebted to, and in the power of, a small group of the very rich, the plutocracy, which subscribed to party funds. The reality was that 'the two Front benches are not two but one'.[32]

He alleged that the parties not only sold honours in return for funding, but also changed their policies. Hence the Liberal government reversed its policy on 'Chinese Slavery' after the general election of 1906 because 'the leaders of the two Front Benches consulted with the South African Jews as to what would best suit their convenience'. The Jews gave their orders 'and the politicians had nothing to do but to obey'.[33] The same principle applied to the doomed licensing bill of 1908, which Belloc saw as designed to fail. The front benches agreed to appeal to different sections of the plutocracy, but 'the two political parties need the money of rich men to conduct the sham fight on which their own prestige and salaries depend'.[34]

Parliament was an institution in an advanced state of decay, if not actually dead, as a result of the excessive power of, and excessive respect for, wealth. The aristocracy and its traditions had become submerged in 'a united plutocracy, a homogeneous mass of the rich, commercial and territorial, into whose hands practically all power, political as well as economic, has now passed'.[35] Belloc shared the common view of the Radical Right that Britain was passing through a crisis, and concluded in a similar vein: 'something is very ill with England today', and 'something must be done'.[36] But he had little to propose beyond publicity. 'Light on the nasty thing and an exposure of it are all that is necessary. It stinks only because it has been so carefully masked and covered and its natural dissolution thereby checked.'[37] By the early 1930s, he had given up on parliament altogether. 'Public life now stinks with the stench of a mortal disease; it can no longer be cured.'[38]

Plutocracy, Decadence and Aristocratic Revival

The Reveille movement went nowhere near as far as Belloc. Reveille was a wake-up call to the radical element within the Conservative party based on fears of collusion between the two front benches. Balfour had always been lukewarm on tariff reform, regarding it, quite rightly, as beyond 'practical politics'. But social imperialists had little to fear from their own leadership beyond vacillation. The Liberal government was another matter. After another general election in December 1910 which left the Liberals still in power and still dependent upon their Irish allies, the powers of the House of Lords were curtailed to a suspensive veto of 2 years. It removed the last constitutional impediment to Home Rule that restrained an 'anti-national' government. In public, the Conservative party's language verged on incitement to insurrection. Bonar Law, who became Conservative party leader in November 1911 when Balfour resigned, declared there were things stronger than parliamentary majorities, a scarcely veiled reference to extra-parliamentary force.

In private Law was more conciliatory, promising the Prime Minister, Asquith, that his party would abide by the result of an election on Home Rule. But Willoughby de Broke for one would only accept the result of an election if the Conservatives won and Home Rule lapsed.[39] He volunteered to fight with the Ulstermen to resist the imposition of Home Rule, and took part in attempts in England to raise 'commandos' for service in Ireland.[40] From his point of view, as a result of the parliament act, 'the Constitution has been abolished with the natural result that Parliamentary government has been superceded by appeal to the force of arms'.[41] At this point, Willoughby de Broke moved with ease into active, violent counter-revolution.

Willoughby de Broke refreshingly reduced things to their basics. As early as 1910 he had noted that 'physical force...still remains the ultimate sanction of parliamentary government'.[42] Nor was the possible confrontation necessarily bad. 'It may be well' he observed of Ulster resistance, 'that we should see for ourselves that men are still ready to fight, and women are still ready to load for them, when everything they love is at stake'.[43] The potential armed struggle over Home Rule was thus a means to revitalize fading patriotism. In this he reflected a deepening anxiety on the Right in the previous decade that found expression in the changing focus of alarmist fiction. Saki's *When William Came*, published in 1911, was not an invasion novel but an occupation novel about Britain after defeat, a Britain in which the ruling elite collaborated with the German occupiers, untroubled by a patriotic conscience. The focus was no longer complacency, but decadence. Thus, for Willoughby de Broke, 'the real value of the Home Rule struggle will be to stiffen the sinews, summon the blood and show the enemies of England at home and abroad that they still have to reckon with the old spirit'.[44] Similarly, 'if there was ever a pure Socialist majority in the House of Commons ... the appeal to physical force between the "Haves" and the "Have-nots" would be the only arbiter'.[45]

As he wrote to Bonar Law shortly after Law became leader, 'I am convinced in my own mind that we ... ought to found a school of thought that will stand by us in future hours of need ... the Unionist party wants a doctrine, and a reaffirmation of nationalist principles. To get people to think rightly will do much. The revival of the right spirit is now of supreme importance.'[46] Ultimately Willoughby de Broke had little faith in either institutions or legislation. The solution to decades of poor leadership lay in the race and its regeneration, not the institutions of government:

> The whole field is open to Eugenics and education, in fact the whole vast problem of heredity and Environment have to be faced if we would keep our place among the Nations. Let us rely on the National character, and aim at preserving it by breeding from the best stocks and bringing to maturity the greatest possible number of mentally and physically sound men and women, reared among healthy surroundings in the ideals of Religion and Patriotism, equipped with a trade education, protected by a Tariff from unfair foreign competition, trained to bear arms ... admitted to all the privileges and alive to all the duties of membership of the British empire ... the fine old sentiment of each for all and all for each ... no-one who is concerned for the welfare of England need be afraid of stating the case for race regeneration at its very highest.[47]

In this analysis, 'the tariff is part of the economics of a true policy for the regeneration of the race'. Like the eugenicists, Willoughby de Broke condemned 'the present policy of taxing the fit for the benefit of the unfit' because it led the fit to limit the size of their families.

'We must aim at breeding from sound stock and discourage breeding from unsound stock. The best possible environment should then be afforded to give the race thus bred an opportunity of thriving ... But the environment should be spiritual and intellectual as well as material ... Given that a boy or girl is free from hereditary disease, the state can afford him or her an opportunity of becoming a happy and reliable citizen ... Justice as well as humanity and patriotism demands that everyone who is willing to work bravely and honestly shall have a living wage and a healthy home and the enjoyment of the elementary rights of citizenship.[48]

Extensive measures of interventionist social reform might have been expected to follow from such a statement which was only reiterating in eugenicist terms what advanced social imperialists had been saying for years. Since 1907, those most associated with Milner had been proposing some sort of 'living wage',[49] and technical training was a commonplace of those concerned with national efficiency. Willoughby de Broke was a member of the Unionist Social Reform Committee (USRC), established in 1910, which attempted to flesh out social reform aspirations and produced detailed reports on housing, education and poor law reform before 1914.

But Willoughby de Broke's radicalism was strictly limited by his conception of personal freedom, his belief in the 'inalienable rights of private property' and his distrust of state power.[50] Like Belloc, Willoughby de Broke condemned the Liberal government's national insurance act,[51] and even his own government's education act of 1902 which provided only 'instruction ... of a kind calculated to discourage children from remaining on the land'.[52] All state education involved 'some curtailment of freedom', depriving poor parents of their children's services. Despite the rhetoric of technical training, his model worker was an illiterate labourer who, at the age of 69, still rose at 5.30, walked two miles to work and was always 'the first to arrive and the last to leave'.[53]

His primary concern was decadence, not poverty. 'Idleness both among rich and poor is a more difficult matter to cope with than poverty[54] ... We do not contemplate a spoon-fed and rapacious generation reared in cupidity and extravagance ... We desire to put everyone is a position of self-respect that will develop the qualities of self-reliance and responsibility ... the proper atmosphere will have to precede legislative acts.'[55] His 'higher conception of citizenship' meant the restoration of the service ideals of a mythical feudalism: 'that the rich man should serve the poor man in order that both might serve the state is the main doctrine of Feudalism based on responsibility'.[56] His Territorial Forces Amendment

Bill, known as the 'noblesse oblige bill', sought to enforce the view 'that certain comfortable and privileged people should lead the way in matters of military training'. It proposed that public schoolboys, university graduates, those entering the professions and anyone with an income of over £400 a year should be conscripted into military service. 'Those who cannot serve will have to pay. Those who will not serve will be put in prison, or lose their votes, or both.'[57] Not surprisingly, the bill failed.

The Bill identified the source of contemporary decadence as plutocracy in place of aristocracy. Social imperialism and the Radical Right looked to an imagined countryside for their values. They were anti-urban rather than anti-industrial, but wished to apply the values of an idealized country estate to industrial society. Plutocrats placed self before service and failed to acknowledge the responsibilities of property, serving as JPs, contributing to local charities and the local foxhounds, providing hospitality and advice, and if necessary ruining themselves and their estates in the performance of that multitude of local activities conventionally expected of the squire in rural society:

> Class hostility... should really be directed against the plutocrats. The most natural and strongest alliance for all purposes is that between master and man. No one understands the spirit and traditions of the alliance better than those who live in the English counties. Many industrial concerns in the towns are animated by the same spirit... It will defeat any other combination: and will break the agitator, the alien, the money-grubber, the demagogue and the politician on the make.[58]

Willoughby de Broke could state the ideal, the imagined national community, 'to breed and... rear a sound race of men and women... preserve the essence and quality of our institutions... strengthen our national defences... teach all classes to work together for the common good... make the politics of the future the regeneration of the race'.[59] But for him, race regeneration became a substitute for state action in an outlook that was at root anti-etatist, in contrast to the social imperialism of Milner and his circle.

Aristocrats and Anarchists

Participants in the discussion of race, environment and heredity made indiscriminate use of the ideas of Nietzsche, Darwin and Lamarck.

Darwin was held to have provided the scientific basis for Nietzsche's philosophy and a-morality, Nietzsche to have drawn the philosophical and moral lessons of Darwinian natural selection. Nature was 'red in tooth and claw', and had no pity for the weak or unfortunate. But whilst some, like J. M. Kennedy, were prepared to advocate a Nietzschean aristocracy that existed for itself and would 'accept with a good conscience the sacrifice of a legion of individuals who, *for its sake*, must be suppressed and reduced to imperfect men, to slaves and instruments',[60] there was a significant difference between the usual vision of the English aristocrat and the Nietzschean superman. Aristocratic leadership might be an alternative to the bureaucracy of the state, and function anarchically, but it did not function a-morally. It was based, as Willoughby de Broke argued, on the idea of *noblesse oblige*, the duties and responsibilities of property and ability. Aristocratic leadership, and the property which provided the power to lead effectively, were justified solely by the morality of service and sacrifice.

By the Edwardian period, *noblesse oblige* had gained a long pedigree. The early Victorian interest in mediaeval chivalry created a myth that was popularized by Sir Walter Scott and transmitted through an expanding public school system to successive generations of young Englishmen as an ideal.[61] Its early manifestations in Dr Arnold's Rugby, popularized by the classic public school novel, *Tom Brown's Schooldays*, mutated into muscular Christianity and the cult of athleticism and team sports. By the end of the century this in turn had developed militarist overtones, and expanded beyond the public schools into various youth movements aimed at working-class youth, of which the Boy Scouts, the Boys Brigade and the Church Lads Brigade were the best known.[62] 'Play up and play the game' was an ethic that could be applied equally to a game of cricket or to the embattled regiment in the desert, a facile transition made, for example, in Newbolt's 'Vitai Lampada'. When Willoughby de Broke proclaimed the need for a revival of aristocracy, he had in mind 'an aristocracy not of birth, or of brains, but of instinct and character ...'[63]

In his various capacities, as a leader of the Reveille movement, a member of the USRC and a prominent tariff reformer but one who instinctively distrusted state intervention, Willoughby de Broke was a maze of contradictions. This was in part at least due to the number of influences acting upon him. One of these was the exigency of parliamentary politics where he cooperated largely with the most active tariff reform social imperialists and was drawn into their vision of future policies. But in his pursuit of 'a new school of thought', he consulted well beyond the parliamentary mainstream. He corresponded with the eugenicist, C. W. Saleeby, whose influence is evident in Willoughby de Broke's language, and was in contact with the eccentric barrister, W. J. Sanderson and his circle.

A leading member of the Battersea branch of the Tariff Reform League, in 1908 Sanderson was instrumental in forming the Workers Defence Union (WDU) to defend patriotic workers against socialist pressure.[64] It became part of a wider attempt to recruit workers to the tariff reform cause as L. S. Amery and J. W. Hills revived the moribund TUTRA, and Viscount Wolmer attempted to create new anti-Labour party trade unions, taking advantage of the dispute between William Osborne and his union over payment of the political levy. These endeavours failed, and the WDU itself was never a large organization. But in Sanderson and his fellow barristers, A. T. Crawford-Cree and H. N. Dickinson, it contained radicals who developed their own brand of Darwinian-Nietzschean aristocratic anarchism, centred on race regeneration. The WDU itself disintegrated over the compulsory insurance payments required by the national insurance bill and on the attitude to be taken to the upsurge of labour unrest between 1911 and 1914. The radical wing sympathized with the Labour opposition to the insurance bill led by Philip Snowden and George Lansbury in the *Daily Herald*, sharing their view that compulsory payments were an attack on the trade union movement.

Contemporaries found the upsurge of labour militancy immediately before the First World War hard to explain. The material explanation lay in the fall in unemployment after 1910 which gave organized labour an opportunity to recover some of the losses sustained when real wages fell during the preceding decade. But within the unrest was a strong minority syndicalist strand based on the ideas of George Sorel, of which Tom Mann was the principal exponent. Syndicalism drew strength from the disappointment of the trade union movement at the ineffectiveness of the parliamentary Labour party after 1906. It proposed the concentration of both workers and managers into single industry unions which would seize control, violently if need be, from the owners, restoring control of the means of production to the workers. These syndicates, or corporations, would elect representatives to a 'parliament of industry' which would have a specialized knowledge of industrial matters and the needs of workers which a propertied, territorially elected parliament lacked.

The 'parliament of industry' could function alone, virtually as a federal society of producers, or alongside the existing parliament, its remit restricted primarily to foreign affairs and defence, depending on the degree of anarchism incorporated in the brand of syndicalism. The overall effect would be a workers takeover of industry run directly by those working in specific concerns, avoiding state socialism and inaugurating a more pluralist political system.[65] Guild Socialism, which developed from the Arts and Crafts movement shortly before the First World War, was similarly pluralist in its objectives, but left the ownership of industry in the hands of the state, with management in the hands of single industry guilds.

Sanderson and the radicals within the WDU viewed working-class militancy not as an industrial or class revolt, but a race reawakening, the revolt of English workers in defence of their living standards and thus of the race itself against exploitation by a plutocracy corrupted by alien influences. Sanderson formed the Order of the Red Rose from the wreckage of the WDU.[66] The Order deprecated the poor leadership of the trade unions and their reformist tendency to demand legislation to protect their interests but supported the institution. Properly led by men of aristocratic calibre and operating at a local rather than a national level, the unions could become the basis of a self-regulating industrial sphere, free of state intervention. After the manner of mediaeval guilds then so much in vogue, the unions could guarantee the quality of workmanship by operating a closed shop, expelling poor workers in return for the guarantee of good pay and working conditions. Like Willoughby de Broke, the Order of the Red Rose took its values from an idealized feudalism based on service. It proposed 'modernized feudalism' adapting feudalism to industry and making employers subordinate their personal interests to those of the race. If employers were unable to make a profit while providing safe working conditions and good wages for their workers, then they should abandon industrial management. Implicitly they would be persuaded to go should they not go willingly.

The Red Rose saw the anticipated civil war not as centred on Ulster and Ireland, but as one between exploiters and exploited, between patriots and parasites, a race war of which labour unrest was the beginning, but it welcomed this, both because it would purge Britain of the parasites and because war was the principal instrument of progress. War galvanized the race and was the one check on decadence, teaching again the values of service, sacrifice and patriotism. Through war, advanced races subdued backward races. The Order happily justified the enslavement of races whose qualities rendered them useful; it equally happily justified their elimination if their survival impeded the goals of their conquerors and the upward progress of humanity. It agreed also with the eugenicist argument that welfare was counterproductive, keeping alive unfit specimens of humanity to the detriment of the fit.

The Red Rose took voluntarism, self-regulation by individuals and groups such as employers' associations, professional organizations and trade unions, to the edge of anarchy in keeping with their concept of aristocratic leadership as an attribute of character which needed no external support. In theory, as Willoughby de Broke argued, aristocracy of character was classless. In practice, just as defects were hereditary, so were the qualities of leadership. The Red Rose located those nominally aristocratic virtues of duty, honour and self-sacrifice in the actuality of the landowning elite, born to rule, accustomed to leadership on their estates, honed by their training in the great public schools. All that was required was the extension of these virtues to other leading sections of society, in particular the 'captains of industry'.

Aliens

Industry was a particular problem for aristocratic revivalists. Whatever Willoughby de Broke might say about the aristocratic spirit of sacrifice permeating the 'captains of industry', industry was more associated with exploitation, and its 'captains' with plutocracy. The core of the problem was competition and acquired characteristics. Competition from exploitative foreign industries in low-wage economies forced British industrialists, as Chamberlain pointed out, to cut their own costs to survive. But in the process, the 'English' character of English employers was itself corrupted as they acquired the characteristics of their competitors, and selfishly pursued profit at the expense of their fellow Englishmen, the workers.

Corruption of character through competition returned the argument to the centrality of protective tariffs in race regeneration. But tariffs could not prevent corruption from the enemy within, most obviously alien immigrants. Hostility to alien immigrants was nothing new. Anti-Irish feeling had diminished since the riots of the mid-nineteenth century, but there was persistent low-level antipathy to immigrant groups that broke out in sporadic rioting.[67] Until the 1950s, however, hostility to aliens meant primarily hostility to Jews. In one respect, this antipathy was similar to all anti-immigrant feeling. Like other immigrants, Jews settled close to their co-religionists, often in depressed areas, creating even greater pressure locally on jobs and housing, and arousing fears in surrounding areas of cultural swamping. The increase in immigration into the east end of London from the late 1880s following pogroms in eastern Europe, thus led to the formation of the British Brothers League and the anti-alien agitation which culminated in the passage of the aliens act in 1905.[68]

The issue dovetailed neatly with tariff reform propaganda where immigration could be presented as a similar evil to the import of foreign goods. Anti-alien feeling of this kind provided a base in some localities for populist racism directed at a variety of immigrant groups throughout the twentieth century. The Jews were nevertheless a special case, because of their talent, and their internationalism. 'Much has been said, much has been written', wrote Leo Maxse, editor of the *National Review*, 'about the pauper alien and in many cases he is a curse and a pest, but he is nothing like so dangerous to national well-being or to our national security as plutocratic aliens...'[69] The Jews were equated not merely with financial acumen, which made them successful bankers, but with sharp and dubious practices, their Shylock image. They were also a race without a country, suspected of being loyal only to their internationally dispersed race, not to their host nation. Their close association with international finance only aggravated both suspicions.

The liberalization of British attitudes during the nineteenth century and the admission of Jews to Parliament provided access to positions of power and status commensurate with their wealth and aroused corresponding alarms. Even Disraeli, although an Anglican and a Conservative, was thought to be tainted by his origins. In the Edwardian era, Jews were more prominent both in society and in the government where Rufus Isaacs and Herbert Samuel were in the Liberal Cabinet. The involvement of Isaacs and Samuel together with Lloyd George and the Master of Elibank, the Liberal Chief Whip, in the Marconi scandal, and that of Edwin Montagu, the Under-secretary at the India Office, and the firm of Samuel Montagu and Co. in the Indian silver scandal appeared to bring the predicted corruption into British political life. The result was an outcry against Jews in high office by Leo Maxse in the *National Review*, and Hilaire Belloc, G. K. Chesterton and F. H. O'Donnell in the *Eye Witness*, later the *New Witness*.[70]

The international and financial connections of the Jews merged in a common conspiracy thesis with strong anti-capitalist, or anti-finance-capitalist, overtones. Capital, like the Jews, was international, and the only protection for labour was nationalism. For the Radical Right, and indeed significant sections of the Right in general, the struggle inherent in Social Darwinism had to be carried on at home as well as abroad, against an anti-national government and against internal subversives, whether socialist agitators in the unions or plutocratic and alien infiltrators in high places. The struggle had to be waged also for the hearts and minds of the working classes, and indeed for a large section of the middle and upper classes, already sinking into plutocracy.

By 1914, a significant section of the Right was preaching rebellion against the government in support of Ulster, considering the amendment of the army annual act to prevent the use of the army in Ireland and raising 'commandos' to fight in the anticipated conflict. Another was preaching and predicting civil war between patriotic workers and corrupted capitalist exploiters as labour unrest reached unprecedented heights. It was a desperate response to what was perceived as a desperate crisis in which, even without the actions of the Liberal government, time was running out. Challenged abroad, rotting at home, Britain was an imperial power in almost terminal decline to be rescued only by immediate and radical action.

Chapter 2: Patriotic Labour and International Conspiracies

The outbreak of war brought a reassertion of national unity. Forces gathered in Ulster to resist Home Rule volunteered, like so many others, to defend the empire. The implementation of controversial legislation, including Irish Home Rule, was postponed until the end of the war. Party conflict was abandoned, and a coalition government of Liberals, Conservatives and Labour formed in 1915. The much vaunted flexibility of the British constitution swung into action as the government armed itself with the draconian powers of the Defence of the Realm Act, postponed the election due in 1915, and in 1916 introduced conscription which all parties had considered electorally disastrous before the war, despite the agitation of the National Service League. The government had no mandate, asked for none, and needed none. The Right regarded the issues of the war without illusions: it was simply a struggle for supremacy between two rival imperial races upon which hung the fate of civilization.

Mainstream politics focused largely on the conduct of the war, a debate to which the Right brought its own preconceptions of a basically 'sound' people misled by incompetent or corrupt politicians, or deceived by subversive agitators. As the National Party's (NP) manifesto put it in 1917, there was a feeling that 'something in our present social and political system is at work to prevent men from obeying their natural instinct of cooperation and comradeship.'[1] Two contrasting factors gave strength to these views: the patriotic response to the war of the working classes whom some on the Right had feared would refuse to fight, and the Bolshevik revolution which appeared particularly dangerous in its early stages as the German and Austro–Hungarian empires followed the Russian into extinction. Coinciding with serious labour unrest in Britain both during the later stages of the war and after it, the spread of Bolshevism raised fears about how far its poison might reach. The patriotism of the majority of the Labour movement and the experiences of war itself seemed to offer both an antidote and a new beginning. The 'home front' gained little respect, but the 'spirit of the trenches' became a symbol of future possibilities. To Milner the war offered the opportunity he had sought before it to combine imperialism and sane socialism to build an integrated society in which, through the intervention of the state, class conflict might be stilled. 'It would be a deplorable national calamity if peace should bring with it a relapse into the class bitterness, mutual suspicion, and stereotyped habits and traditions of mind, which the shock of conflict has so largely dispelled.'[2] From such hopes sprang the two most significant political movements of the war on the Radical Right, the British Workers League/National Democratic Party and the National Party.

The National Democratic Party

The war divided the Labour movement, with the bulk of the Labour party and the trade unions patriotically supporting the war and a small socialist section largely from the ILP and the British Socialist Party (BSP) opposing it. To counter this pacifist element, the Socialist National Defence Committee (SNDC) was formed in April 1915, led by Victor Fisher and including a few Labour MPs and Alexander Thompson and Robert Blatchford of the *Clarion* newspaper. The *Clarion*, founded in 1891, was the most popular and populist of the various labour and socialist newspapers, and Blatchford's books sold in thousands, or, in the case of *Merrie England*, over 2 million. Blatchford spent 7 years in the army, and his patriotic socialism was always imbued with the regiment as an ideal form of social organization. Disciplined and purposeful, 'it has that which a mob never has: a collective mind, a collective soul ... it is an organism; all of its units are parts of a whole ... '[3]

Blatchford was close to the Milnerite outlook in his concern both for defence, for which he advocated a 'citizen army',[4] and the revival of agriculture which stemmed from his fear that in a war Britain could be starved into submission because of its dependence on imported food. This was combined with a nostalgic, romantic view of the countryside and a Blakean horror of industrial towns and their dark satanic mills.[5] Like the Radical Right, his objections went beyond material squalor to their morality. 'The factory system...is evil. It is evil in its origin, in its progress, in its methods. No nation can be sound whose motive power is greed...'[6] Unlike Milner, Blatchford was a socialist. 'Britain for the British', despite its later use, was an anti-capitalist not a racist statement, 'Britain ... owned intact by the whole people ... governed and worked by the whole people, for the benefit of the whole people.'[7] The working man deserved more than 'continually toiling and suffering in order to live'[8] simply because work created wealth. But it was still an imperialist socialism. 'The masses must be better educated, better governed, better trained and better treated or the Empire will go to pieces ... when the poor rot, the Empire is rotten...If the Empire is to stand we must have a healthy and an educated and a united people.'[9]

The SNDC came to the attention of Milner through their common interest in conscription. The Committee and its successor organizations had close links with the National Service League of which Milner became chairman in June 1915. The Merthyr Tydfil by-election late in 1915 in which the patriotic labour candidate, C. B. Stanton, with assistance from the SNDC and covert finance from the Conservative party, defeated the official Labour candidate, James Winstone,[10] provided an impetus for more extensive political ambitions. As Christopher Turnor, one of Milner's pre-war agricultural advisors, wrote following an early meeting between Milner and his associates and leading members of the SNDC, 'The only gleam of hope of saving the Empire and the Nation is in the possibility of forming a national party...'[11] Willoughby de Broke was also sufficiently involved at this point for Milner to report on this meeting. The aim, 'a Labour movement established on sane, national and Imperial lines', became reality once Milner had found financial support for a larger organization. In January 1916 he secured backing from Waldorf Astor on terms which Fisher found acceptable, and in March the SNDC transformed itself into the British Workers' National League (BWNL), open, according to a Scotland Yard report, to British subjects only.[12] It held its inaugural public meeting in May.

It was, however, intended to be not just a league, but the embryo of a new national party, something Milner had long wanted so that problems could be dealt with 'in a more or less rational and scientific way', another government of experts. This was impossible under the 'present party system which is more or less in abeyance, but will revive again, I fear, when the war is over...A National Party may still give the war a better turn.

It certainly will make for a less disastrous aftermath of war'.[13] The Manifesto of the League demanded new policies for 'the new world which the war is bringing forth', including such socialist, syndicalist or corporate nostrums as 'national control of vital industries under the joint management of administrative and industrial workers in the interests of the whole Nation', and the duty of all 'to guarantee the citizen's right to live – that is the right to work, at a full living wage'. Its Vice-Presidents, with the exception of H. G. Wells, were Labour MPs from the trade union wing of the party. In August, the League launched its own paper, the *British Citizen and Empire Worker*, which enjoyed an early circulation of 50,000 before settling at around 25,000–30,000.

Apart from aims specifically associated with the war, adequate pensions for disabled servicemen and the expropriation of enemy interests within the empire, the paper's summary of the League programme reiterated the demand for 'a standard living wage...the revival and development of national agriculture...national or municipal control of national monopolies and vital industries', and the exploitation of imperial natural resources 'in the interest of the whole people'. 'Higher industrial organisation', the editorial explained, 'will probably entail public control, in some cases combined with public ownership, of certain vital industries.' The ultimate purpose, as before the war, remained Britain's imperial mission since 'the British Commonwealth still remains the highest and finest embodiment of social life which men had yet developed...'[14]

As an embryonic political party the BWNL faced the rigours of the electoral system, which it sought to mitigate by seeking an accommodation on seats with the Conservative party. This, however, depended upon finding a common basis for a patriotic national policy, which in view of the socialist origins of the League might be difficult. Nevertheless, with the overthrow of Asquith and the formation of the Lloyd George coalition in December 1916, there were grounds for optimism. Milner became a member of the War Cabinet, John Hodge, the BWNL president, was minister of labour, and other leading members took minor offices. Moreover, Steel-Maitland, chairman of the Conservative party until the change of government, who had been handling negotiations from the Conservative side, claimed to have £20,000 to fund the new 'patriotic labour' movement. By 1917, there was an outline agreement on the allocation of seats, and by its first annual conference in March 1917 the BWNL claimed 77 branches.

The Conference changed the League's name to the British Workers League, but retained the basic programme, including the demand for a 'standard living wage'. The outbreak of the Russian Revolution, which the League welcomed in its early phase, added momentum to the League's progress. It coincided with considerable labour unrest in Britain, and Milner at least feared, as Balfour had done in 1906, that there were cracks even in England's social structure. Revolution was in the air. Russian invitations to fellow-socialists to discuss the continuation of the war, the proposal of a conference of all socialist parties at Stockholm, and the decision of the ILP and the BSP to hold a conference of British socialists in Leeds 'to do for this country what the Russian Revolution has accomplished in Russia' caused alarm on the Right at the prospect of a British revolution. Fisher saw a conspiracy whose 'immediate object has been to bring about a strike followed by rioting of such a nature that troops would be obliged to fire, and from this they hope to evolve a general strike which would bring the whole War up with a jerk here, in much the same manner as the Revolution has stopped military proceedings in Russia', and saw 'a master brain' behind the whole enterprise.[15] The BWL, with its trade union roots and according to the *Times* 'the authentic voice of the working class' appeared to be the obvious counter.

By September 1917 the BWL claimed 154 branches, and discussions continued with the Conservative party on policy and electoral arrangements. The agreed programme had elements from across the Radical Right, for example discriminatory taxation upon single men and women, and reform of public houses to make them respectable family centres, the former to penalize individuals who did not play their part in breeding the imperial race, the latter to provide a decent forum for the working classes whose only social outlet was the pub. Canals and railways were to be nationalized, a pre-war demand of the Left, although the latter only for 5 years after the war; there was to be compulsory military training for boys in cadet corps and grants to children who stayed on at school, both of which Milner had proposed before the war, and the housing programme of the USRC was adopted. The old tariff reform plan for imperial self-sufficiency was retained, as were its proposals for protecting British industry against unfair competition from foreign subsidized or sweated industries, and dumping. The state would control vital commodities and services, establish minimum wage levels and regulate profits, enforce collective bargaining through joint councils of individual trades and enforce the result when two-thirds of employers and workers in that trade agreed.[16]

Even if the programme had been acceptable to the mass of the Conservative party, rather than, as before the war, driven by its radical wing, the allocation of seats would still have been difficult because of resistance from local constituency organizations. Moreover, the BWL itself was cautious, lest in securing an agreement with the Conservative party it appeared to have sold out to former opponents, thereby losing whatever influence it had with labour. Having begun as a patriotic group within a divided labour movement, by becoming a distinct political party in coop-eration with the Conservatives the BWL now challenged the Labour party. It was accordingly ever more difficult to be a member of both organ-izations. Pressurized at the Labour party conference in January 1918, some of the Vice-Presidents of the BWL resigned from the League.

From the other side, the best the BWL could hope for was Conservative agreement not to oppose its candidates in seats the Conservatives could not hope to win. Nevertheless, the BWL, now claiming 221 branches, reconstituted itself in May 1918 as the National Democratic and Labour Party with 8 candidates selected and 18 seats under consideration. But it was less independent that it appeared. Financially, it relied on Milner's ability to secure support from wealthy sympathizers, and somewhat more dubiously in view of its purported labour and even socialist pretensions, it received considerable support from Patrick Hannon's British Commonwealth Union, which was an employers' organization linked to the Federation of British Industries.[17]

At the general election of 1918, the NDP fought 26 seats and won 9, but in only one was there Conservative opposition. It gained only 1.5 per cent of the popular vote. There was in reality, virtually no popular support for 'patriotic labour'. Nor was there any room for it in parliamen-tary politics as a separate party. As early as April 1920 the NDP itself recognized that it was 'regarded as the Labour wing of the Coalition government...' The *British Citizen* ceased publication in March 1921, and none of the NDP's MPs were re-elected in 1922. One of its historians has described the BWL/NDP outlook 'in so far as it had what could be called a philosophical position, this position was where Chamberlainite conservatism meets with socialism... The term "National Socialist", if it had not acquired a special meaning in Germany, would be a fair summary...'[18]

The National Party

The National Party that Henry Page Croft formed in August 1917 arose from concerns similar to those of the NDP: problems with the enforce-ment of conscription, labour unrest, and the apparent link between unrest, pacifism, subversion and revolution that the Right saw in the socialist conference at Leeds in June. But it approached those troubles from the other end of the political spectrum, a group of frustrated right-wingers from within the parliamentary Conservative party. Of the 7 MPs and 17 Peers who were its founding members, 2 of the 7 MPs were themselves sons of peers, and the whole tone was of landowning aristocratic wealth, heavily tinged with military connections. Unlike the BWL/NDP, the NP never seems to have had financial difficulties.

Nor, however, did it have an automatic entry into working-class politics. The NP shared the Radical Right's assumption that the working classes were patriotic but misled by politicians or subverted by agitators. There were no such problems in the trenches, experience of which moved Croft to write of the 'ennobling influence' of war.[19] Convinced by his war experience that 'nothing could divide the classes of this country if only they were agreed on national issues', he felt, like Willoughby de Broke before the war, that 'the imperative need of the hour was a faith, a positive policy, essentially national...'[20] It was this that the party manifesto, written by Milner's close associate, F. S. Oliver, set out to provide.

Justifying a new party, Oliver reiterated the familiar condemnation of party politics in which the national interest was sacrificed to the pursuit of votes and office, 'what was popular rather than what was right'. In familiar Milnerite terms he noted: 'The war opened our eyes to the weakness of a country run by political parties. There is little to choose between them... There is no politics in the fighting services... Our Parliamentary system is at fault.' In sentiments which echoed Rosebery and National Efficiency at the turn of the century, and foreshadowed Oswald Mosley and the BUF in the 1930s, the NP argued that the state must be run 'on business lines', which required 'qualified men trained for their work...' In view of these statements and its claim to a monopoly of the national interest, it would appear that the NP's ultimate aim was to become the only party in an ideal single party state.

Despite its social origins, the NP accepted the Radical Right view that the working classes had legitimate fears of unemployment and poverty, and legitimate grievances against excessive profits, lack of control over working conditions and that monotony resulted in a lack of interest and pride in work. It could all be summed up as the fault of 'the system of employment by which the worker feels he is a commodity instead of... an interested party in industry.'[21] Regeneration depended on changing this situation. 'The great hope of recovery after the war lies in working together, in the union of classes... an alliance of labour and capital...'[22]

The NP appeared in some respects radical. Many of its leading figures had been enthusiastic tariff reformers before the war. Like the BWL/NDP, but on a self-regulatory rather than state controlled basis, the party proposed that industries should create a trade association with a council representing both employers and workers whose decisions would be binding on the industry overall. Workers were to be paid a 'standard comfort wage', and others in that industry would penalize backsliding employers. In a similar self-regulatory vein, national unemployment insurance would cease, each industry providing its own scheme. Unemployment itself would be reduced, as all tariff reformers believed, by the impetus to productivity provided by imperial preference and the wider home market created by better wages, profit sharing and cooperation.

For a party that wanted government by trained experts, there was a strong anti-etatist theme to all this. Whilst the state should be run 'on business lines', it did not, according to Croft 'possess a trading mind'. Business depended on a flexibility that was inconsistent with government regulation.[23] There was no parallel to Milner's concept, expressed in a speech in Leeds in January 1916 and taken up by the BWL/NDP, that the state was 'a third partner...a controlling and harmonizing influence in the relations between capital and labour'. For Milner, the state had a right 'to share in exceptional profits' and to 'exercise a certain amount of control' over the investment of capital.[24] It was a hybrid concept, with shades of the pre-war new Liberal theory of socially created value, and of Mosley's arguments in the 1930s on directed investment. But it was enough, despite Milner's contact with individuals and his obvious influence on certain aspects of its policy, to set Milner apart from the NP, intellectually and politically.

The NP objected to state intervention in the economy, and was strongly opposed to nationalization and to any redistribution of wealth beyond that implied in its self-regulatory industrial proposals. It even objected to the excess profit tax and, perhaps less surprisingly for a group of wealthy landowners, to increased death duties. Property it argued 'must be inviolable'. As William D. Rubinstein commented, the party seemed to be 'afflicted with intellectual schizophrenia'.[25] It proposed radical policies, no doubt sincerely, but it was too hamstrung by its fundamental conservatism to achieve any coherence in its social and economic proposals.

Social reform to remove the legitimate grievances 'on which agitators prey' was, however, but one aspect of a two-pronged attack on working-class discontent; the other was 'to go for the agitators'. This, too, was the Milnerite prescription, which Milner had spelled out to Oliver in June 1917 in the aftermath of the engineers' strike. 'I do not believe they would be nearly so dangerous without the grievances', Milner had then written, 'but I do not think the removal of the grievances alone will ever disarm them. They are out for mischief...'[26] The NP was strongly anti-socialist, far more so than Milner, who did not join it, and particularly anti-Bolshevik. The Bolsheviks were, not unreasonably, regarded as active in exporting their revolution, but because of their peace treaty with Germany that removed Russia from the war, 'the Bolsheviks were instruments of Germany...Russia will become the hinterland of our enemies, and German economic expansion will have won back what German militarism has lost'.

Worse still, according to Croft, the 'oligarchy' of 32 people which governed Bolshevik Russia 'consists almost entirely of Jews, and many of them are in fact German Jews who have assumed Russian names... Bolshevik German Jews who have come to Russia with German passports, established themselves as a government'.[27] Now they were coming to England. Lord Ampthill, the party's leader in the Lords, drew attention in 1919 to 'a dangerously revolutionary movement in this country' led by Bolshevik agents.[28] The anti-alien campaign of the NP, whilst obviously directed against Germans, to the extent that Croft proposed in 1920 that 'for ten years no German should be allowed to live in this country', was also directly anti-semitic. Croft not only suggested that no-one 'not born a British subject and son of a British father' should be permitted to enter parliament or hold government office, thereby excluding women as well as aliens, but defended his position on the grounds that there should not be MPs 'who could only speak the English language through a guttural translation. Their instincts could not be wholly British.'[29]

In effect, the two campaigns, against Bolshevism and against Jews, merged into a single conspiracy thesis. Describing the strikes in Glasgow and Belfast in 1919, the *Morning Post*, reporting a speech by Croft, discovered the hidden hand of international Judaism. 'At Glasgow the chief agitator was a Jewish tailor named Shinwell and at Belfast it was a Jew of Russian descent named Simon Greenspun...Bolshevism was a loathsome and dangerous disease...He wanted to warn them against the carriers of these germs. Who were they? Jews who had no nationality and whose one object was to destroy the existing order. Bolshevism originated in German propaganda, and was being carried out by international Jewry.'[30]

Apart from its success in drawing attention to the sale of honours to raise party funds, which embarrassed both major Parties but particularly Lloyd George, the NP made no greater impact on politics than the NDP. By 1918, pressure from the Conservative party and one death had reduced its number of MPs to 2. These 2, Croft and Cooper were the only candidates of the 25 who stood in the general election of 1918 to be allowed a clear run, and the only 2 to be elected. It had some 35 branches by mid-1919, but the number declined thereafter. During 1920 it lost heavily in the 3 by-elections it contested and in January 1921 decided not to contest any more elections. *National Opinion*, the party's monthly journal set up in October 1917 ceased publication in November 1922. The 2 surviving MPs, although they described themselves as 'Independent Conservatives' found their way back into the far right of the Conservative fold.

This, despite their programmatic radicalism, was their more natural habitat. With unrest continuing after the war, the NP moved into class warrior mode, and Croft's speeches at least 'contained a thinly disguised appeal to violence.'[31] As early as February 1919 it was calling for volunteers from 'the Great Middle Classes – Discharged Service Men – Patriotic Labour... to fight the great Bolshevik menace' in what looks uncomfortably like an effort to create a British *Freikorps*. In 1919 following the strike on the Clyde in January, Croft formed the People's Defence League, a strikebreaking organization that approximated to an attempt to create a private army.[32] It was one reason why, despite the earnest wish of some contemporaries for at least 'cordial cooperation', cooperation between the two 'National' parties never occurred. There was an overlap in personnel and especially of behind the scenes advisors. But their origins differed, and their programmes, etatiste on the part of the BWL/NDP, self-regulatory from the NP, reflected those differences. Above all, the BWL/NDP could not risk losing any more of its fading credibility with the Labour movement by becoming too closely associated with an organization that sprang from, and reverted to, the far right of the Conservative party.

Moreover, the two 'National' parties never overcame the fundamental dilemma of how to be both radical and 'Right', combining both social reform and nationalism, or imperialism. The tension between state control and self-regulation that runs through the history of the Radical Right, and the even greater tension between the emphasis given to capital in the industrial process and the need to ensure adequate working conditions for British workers and eliminate class conflict proved too much. National unity might to a degree be achieved under the pressure of war, although there was little class harmony on the home front. In peacetime the conflict of interests was a stronger influence in practical politics than a sense of common nationality; it was also, whatever the respective 'National' parties might claim, a stronger influence in framing their programmes. Their ideological position might well be described as the meeting point of Chamberlainite conservatism and socialism, but that meeting point was simply the hole through which both fell.

Conspiracies

In the post-war circumstances of industrial unrest, frustrated hopes and imperial disruption from nationalist movements, particularly in India, Egypt and Ireland, conspiracy theories thrived. The NP illustrated the general evolution from hostility to Germany and a Germanic-Jewish conspiracy against Britain which originated before the war, to a Germanic-Jewish-Bolshevik conspiracy after 1917. Two publications in 1920, *The Jewish Peril*, an English version of *The Protocols of the Elders of Zion*, and *The Causes of World Unrest*, a reprint of articles from the *Morning Post*, thus fell on fertile soil. The former alleged an international Jewish conspiracy towards world domination, the latter examined the disturbed state of the post-war world in the light of that conspiracy.

Suspicion was sufficiently extensive for the *Spectator*, which dismissed the *Protocols* as 'malignant lunacy', to call for a Royal Commission to investigate the possibility of a Jewish revolutionary conspiracy.[33] Although the *Times* in 1921 proved that the Protocols were a fake, the product of pre-war Russian anti-semites probably with secret police connections, there were those who still believed, and saw in the *Times*' evidence no more than another indication of the Jewish stranglehold on the British press. In the 1930s the BUF, by far the largest and most significant organization of the British Radical Right, sometimes sold the *Protocols* at street corner meetings, and advertised the book in their press. It was, according to *Action* in 1937 'The Most Astounding Book Ever Published . . . Every Fascist should read "the Protocols".'[34]

Originally published in 1920 by Eyre and Spottiswode, publication of the *Protocols* was soon taken over by the Britons. Formed in 1919, the Britons were one-dimensionally anti-semitic, seeing in the removal of Jewish influences the solution to all Britain's ills. They neither had, nor needed, a political programme. Indeed, from the point of view of the Britons the *Protocols* said nothing new. Their solution to the Jewish problem was segregation, which might be achieved by deportation, the favourite destination being Madagascar which could be easily isolated, or extermination, although the Britons did have doubts about the humanity of this. Always in financial difficulties, its journal, successively called *Jewry Ueber Alles*, the *Hidden Hand* and the *British Guardian*, ceased publication in 1925. In 1932 the Britons and the Britons Publishing Company were separated. The publishing company continued publishing anti-semitic propaganda, including 85 editions of the *Protocols*, until the 1970s.[35]

More influential than the pamphlets of political organizations were popular histories incorporating the same message. Nesta Webster's conviction that the French Revolution was a disaster for western Christian civilization led her to attribute its outbreak to conspiracy. The Russian Revolution led her further to the conclusion that behind this conspiracy, and all threats to the social and imperial order, lay the Jews, operating in and through secret societies by occult means. It was not a unique view. H. A. Gwynne, editor of the *Morning Post* wrote in the introduction to *The Causes of World Unrest* that there had been 'for centuries a hidden conspiracy, chiefly Jewish, whose objects have been and are to produce revolution, communism and anarchy, by means of which they hope to arrive at the hegemony of the world by establishing some sort of despotic rule'.[36] Webster's *Secret Societies and Subversive Movements* went through eight editions by 1964.

Sundered Fascisti

None of the extreme Right groups in the immediate post-war era were large or particularly radical. The British Fascisti (BF), formed in 1923 by Rotha Lintorn-Orman, despite the implicit radicalism of its title, fell into this category. Thus Lintorn-Orman proposed reducing taxes 'on gentlefolk so they could employ more servants and thus ease unemployment.'[37] The name was simply borrowed because of the founder's admiration for Mussolini. In 1924 it was anglicized to become the British Fascists Ltd. Like the NP, its members came heavily from the services and gentry. It was, once again, strongly anti-Bolshevik, anti-socialist, anti-labour and anti-trade union in defense of constitutional government, law and order and the security of property. On paper it possessed an elaborate hierarchical and paramilitary organization,[38] headed by a Fascist Grand Council served by an Executive Council, and subordinate sections for intelligence, transport, propaganda, publicity and infantry sections of seven members for street conflict. In times of general unrest these would merge into larger units, controlled by district commanders for each county. In practice, it lacked the numbers to fill these various boxes. Even more than usual amongst the notably fissiparous Right, the BF had a marked tendency to split. In 1924, activists frustrated by the group's conservatism left to form the National Fascisti; in 1926 it split again when the government insisted that it drop 'Fascist' from its title and affirm its commitment to parliamentary democracy before the government would accept its offer of help during the general strike. It split again in 1931 when some of its members accepted Mosley's invitation to join his New Party, the precursor of the BUF. The short-lived British Empire Fascists and the Fascist Movement were also splinter groups from the BF.[39]

The failure of the general strike and the further taming of industrial labour in the trade union act of 1927 meant that the BF was organized to oppose a manifestly non-existent threat. Its 1927 manifesto nevertheless reaffirmed its hostility to labour, urging the outlawing of strikes, the replacement of the card vote by a secret ballot, compulsory arbitration and the disfranchisement of those in receipt of poor relief. Yet it still sought class cooperation! By 1931 the BF had caught up with emerging corporatism in proposing the establishment of Fascist corporations and guilds; by 1933 it was advocating the creation of the Corporate State. It had become more radically etatist, aiming to 'capture the political power of the state' as a body transcending class conflict by creating a meritocracy. It had also become overtly anti-semitic, wanting Jews excluded from public office and the destruction of the power of international finance. Much of this sudden radical lurch may have been in response to the far more clearly programmatic and radical BUF formed by Sir Oswald Mosley in October 1932. Mosley's wealthier, larger organization led by a nationally known figure resulted in defections from the BF that ultimately proved fatal to it. It perished in September 1935, deeply in debt, 6 months after the premature death at 40 of its founder.

By the time the BF had begun to discover the more radical aspects of fascism, the National Fascisti had risen and collapsed. Its pursuit of greater dynamism entailed condemning democracy and constitutionalism in favour of government by an 'aristocracy' of character and brains, elected by those 'qualified' to do so; the abolition of the right to strike; firm treatment of subversives as part of its wider hostility to socialism, and opposition to aliens and 'the Bolshevik-Judaeic menace'. In the absence of satisfactory government action, the National Fascisti adopted a policy of systematic street violence. It engaged in street brawls, broke up political meetings, raided premises that were 'centres of internationalism', and four of its men armed with revolvers hijacked a *Daily Herald* delivery van. It was the first party to adopt the Fascist black shirt in Britain. It also provided stewards for Conservative party meetings. But it had few members, and was chronically short of funds. It was disbanded in 1927 after a violent split at the centre when its president, Lieutenant-Colonel Henry Rippon-Seymour had been accused of misappropriating party funds and confronted his accusers with a revolver and drawn sword.

The Imperial Fascist League

The Right was slow to realize that the failure of the general strike in 1926 removed the threat of serious labour unrest in Britain. In November 1928, Brigadier-General D. Erskine Tulloch formed yet another imperialist, anti-socialist organization, the Imperial Fascist League (IFL).[40] Initially controlled by a triumvirate of Major J. Baillie, Leslie H. Shepherd and Arnold Leese, the League had an elaborate hierarchical organization. A Lictors (or Graduates) Association was to form the basis of the future fascist elite; ordinary members were grouped into Fascist Legions with a full uniform of black shirts, union jack armbands, khaki breeches and puttees with black boots and cap, suggestive of its paramilitary intent; three confederations of employers, employees and professionals were to publicize the League's corporatist social and economic policies.[41] But with a membership estimated at only 'a few hundred'[42] and perennially short of money, it was another largely a paper organization.

In the first issue of its monthly journal, the *Fascist*, in March 1929, its aims were stated as: '1. Recognition of the failure of political democracy. 2. Formation of a new governing caste of character and service. 3. Organisation of all industrial and economic interests into a Corporate State.'[43] In theory, the 'Corporate State', offered the prospect of an innovative policy to address the problems of industrial decline rather than the suppression of its symptoms. The Upper House was to be composed of men chosen for their distinguished record of public service, whilst the lower served as an 'Industrial Parliament' to which corporations nominated representatives according to their industry's importance in the national economy. It replaced democracy and the alleged evils of weak parliamentary government and party rivalry by an elite, the 'governing caste of character and service', and by industrial specialists. Its role was primarily advisory, but it did have the power to reject proposed legislation, and to approve the budget.[44] Incorporating trade unions subordinated what the IFL, in common with most 'patriots', regarded as their excessive pursuit of sectional interests, to the national interest. For the IFL, 'All should be within the state, none must be against the state.'[45]

In the early stages, the focus of the IFL was primarily anti-socialist. Aliens were a 'menace...which must be met by an unsentimental policy of sane national foresight, from which Hate must be divorced at all costs; let us keep that for Reds, alien or native.'[46] 'Sane foresight' meant restricted citizenship in which aliens could not vote, serve on juries or join the army, would only be employed if no British worker could be found, and would pay higher taxes.[47] But as Arnold Leese emerged as its sole leader, a position finally confirmed by the resignations of Baillie and Shepherd in 1932, so the League increasingly took on Leese's anti-semitic obsessions.

Leese, who had spent much of his adult life in the colonies as a specialist in camel diseases, settled in Stamford on his return to England, and joined the BF in 1924. In Stamford he became acquainted with Arthur Kitson, H. H. Beamish and the Britons, and absorbed the conspiratorial anti-semitism of the *Protocols of the Elders of Zion*. The conspiracy thesis provided Leese with an explanation for the British race's decline from its past glories, but it was not until 1930 that such views began to be expressed by the IFL.[48] Leese was squarely in the tradition of nineteenth-century 'scientific racism'. The IFL claim that 'race is the basis of all true politics'[49] echoed Knox nearly a hundred years earlier.[50] He borrowed from mid-nineteenth century anthropologists and anthropometrists the system of classifying racial types according to physical appearance, skin colour, skull shape and facial features. These, it was argued, reflected the moral and mental characteristics of the 'race' to which they belonged, and determined that race's position in the hierarchy of races.

Biology was the determining factor. Such qualities were hereditary and immutable,[51] the gulf between higher and lower races permanent. Leese approved of war as a natural outlet for a conquering elite race,[52] and imperial rule by Aryans was both a racial imperative and a historical inevitability: 'We are Imperialists to our Aryan backbone.'[53] Colonial self-government would only result in the retardation of civilization, so that 'sooner or later, the white man will have to climb back into the saddle and regain control of the Jew and his allies the Niggers.'[54] Against the

'Aryan' or 'Nordic' races on which civilization depended[55] stood the Jews. Jews, according to the IFL, were not a 'true racial type',[56] but a 'mongrel' race with a strong dose of 'Hither Asiatic' blood, which accounted for their supposedly sadistic, cruel, vengeful and treacherous nature.[57]

The struggle between Aryans and Jews was a struggle of civilization against barbarism, light against darkness, 'a duel with the Devil'.[58] The ultimate aim of the Jews was, following the Protocols, 'World Domination'; their influence was everywhere. Control of the world's gold supply and banking system gave them 'control over the Gentile by sheer weight of money power', control over the press and the media meant that 'hardly anything unfavourable to the Jewish interest is allowed to appear in a journal'. These were, of course, familiar assertions. Jews were also held responsible for all those aspects of modern life that the League rejected as symbols of decadence, from modern art and psychology to female emancipation and the decline of family life. Given the significance attached to elite leadership, aristocratic decadence was of particular concern.[59]

There was, apparently, no limit to Jewish deviousness. As well as corrupting the Aryan race by intermarriage, particularly with the aristocracy, Jews disguised the real extent of their infiltration by paying gentile families to raise illegitimate Jewish children as their own. The deception was only revealed by the physical characteristics of the offspring, and the sudden accession of wealth to formerly poor gentile families. On this basis, Leese was able to assert that the real number of Jews in Britain, usually estimated at about 370,000, was closer to 2.5 million.[60] Everywhere, Aryan civilization had been penetrated and undermined by a group 'inevitably antagonistic to the character and ideals of Nordic civilization'.[61] The IFL made the customary link with Bolshevism, which was not communism but 'state capitalism run by Jews in the Jewish interests'.[62] It had been facilitated by the inferior racial qualities of the Russian people, but despite the superior qualities of their Aryan origins, the British had exposed themselves to similar dangers by the adoption of democracy. 'Democracy', according to Leese, 'works out as the Dictatorship of Organised Money Power and that is a Dictatorship of the Jew.'[63]

The primary role of the Corporate State was thus racial rather than economic, to 'care for the best blood.'[64] In terms already made familiar by eugenicists, the IFL condemned 'humanitarian' democracy[65] and its attendant welfare reforms. The solutions were again simplistic: the removal of the 'unfit', either by letting nature run its course unimpeded by humanitarianism, or by more direct action, the 'sterilization of con-veyors of hereditary diseases.' The state should also supplement natural selection by encouraging breeding by the fit, who were, as usual, 'the more highly cultured elements of the population'.[66] But such measures would be useless without 'removing the bestial influence of the Jews from every branch of our culture', whether by prohibiting intermarriage,[67] segregation or extermination. 'Civilisation is Aryanisation, and Aryanisation is Civilisation...The absolute subjection of the Jew to the Aryan is the first necessity for the preservation of civilization, and it is the first object of Racial Fascism to accomplish it, because all other reforms are useless until it is done.'[68]

The IFL was more ruthless than most, but had no new proposals to deal with the alleged 'Jewish menace'. Assimilation 'no decent Nordic man or woman could consider seriously',[69] and sterilisation was adminis-tratively too complex.[70] Extermination, 'the most certain and permanent way of disposing of the Jews...by some humane method such as the lethal chamber', was 'quite practicable' but unlikely to be acceptable.[71] The League thus fell back on segregation, the Madagascar solution already proposed by the Britons, with whom the League maintained a close relationship. Several leading Britons, Blakeney, Lt-Col A. H. Lane,[72] Kitson and the Britons secretary, Anthony Gittens,[73] were also members of the IFL, whilst H. H. Beamish was the League's Vice-President.[74]

In 1936 Leese's anti-semitism led him to revive the old charge of ritual murder against the Jews as evidence of their penchant for sadism. Found not guilty of seditious libel, he was convicted of conspiring to cause a public mischief and spent 6 months in prison after refusing to pay the fine.[75] His anti-semitism remained unaffected by the Second World War. He denounced the Nuremberg trials as 'an act of Revenge' against those who had tried 'to free their country from the twin plagues, Jewry and Freemasonry', and offered to give evidence on behalf of the defen-dants.[76] In 1947 he was again imprisoned for attempting to help two Dutch nazis escape to Argentina. In 1953 he still maintained that 'the Jewish Extermination Policy...as long as the destruction was done in a humane manner...was to the advantage of everyone.'[77] The money left to him by H. H. Beamish in 1948 was used, as Beamish intended, to fur-ther anti-semitism,[78] and when Leese himself died in 1956, the legacy was passed to Colin Jordan.[79]

The IFL was closer to Nazism, to which it switched its allegiance from Italian fascism in the early 1930s, than any other movement of the Right in interwar Britain. As early as 1932 it was asserting that 'Hitlerism at its base is the true Fascism of the Northern European, and true guide to our own politics in the years ahead'. It offered 'something more far-reaching for the White Man than there is even in the Italian movement', and in 1933 the League superimposed the swastika on its union jack armband to symbolize 'the White Man's Good Faith against the Jewish pollution of his civilisation'.[80] But this recognition of a parallel racial fascism never supplanted the more conservative, patriotic elements in the IFL's ideology. Leese might denounce the Versailles treaty as a 'Kosher Conference' with 'Kosher results' such as the League of Nations,[81] but he was not prepared to revise it to restore Germany's former colonies,[82] only to compensate Germany for her lost colonies with territory in Central and South America.[83] Irrespective of racial logic, he would not compromise on the British empire, a 'heritage to be guarded and passed on to those who follow us as a sacred birthright.'[84]

For all the virtues he ascribed to it, Leese showed little confidence in the Aryan race. The British population was so easily deceived that democracy allowed Jews to subvert the political system. The aristocracy had suffered 'racial degeneration' and fallen prey to the selfish, materialist vices of plutocracy.[85] Even Fascist groups were not immune from Jewish corruption or exploitation. Leese accused Mosley's BUF of being 'pro-Jewish' and considered the 'British Jewnion of Fascists',[86] a deliberate attempt by Jews to draw people away from the IFL.[87] Despite his imperialism, his outlook was essentially defensive. Imperial consolidation and self-sufficiency would give the empire the strength to secure the racial purity of those within it, but it was the strength of isolation, removing the risk of contamination to which the Aryan British were apparently so prone.[88] After the fall of Nazi Germany and the expansion of Soviet Russia, Leese took isolationism a stage further, proposing Britain retreat behind the Channel to build up its Aryan stocks.[89] It hardly justified the title of the pamphlet in which the proposal appeared – 'Mightier Yet'.

The Question of Radicalism

Apart from the extremism of its racial views there was little new in the IFL outlook, or radical in the attitudes of any of the minor post-war groups that sprang up in response to the perceived threat from the international 'Left' and international Jewry. The fascist 'aristocracy of service' repeated the views of Willoughby de Broke; the concern that the race was deteriorating because the upper and middle classes were having smaller families reiterated pre-war fears that were similarly snobbish; the IFL's condemnation of Christianity as a Judaicised religion preaching internationalism and universal brotherhood set it apart from the Christian Britons and the Militant Christian Patriots, but had been anticipated by pre-war Nietzscheans; the self-sufficient defensive empire dated back at least to Chamberlain's tariff reform campaign, and the necessity of a strong agricultural sector was maintained by most elements of the Right. Even the belief that this was necessary not only for economic reasons, but because the 'preservation of the mental balance of our people is threatened by want of contact with nature'[90] was an Edwardian theme.

The BF, as the first group on the scene, acted as a hub around which the leading figures of these mutual admiration societies of malcontents revolved. Its president, Brigadier-General Sir Robert R. D. Blakeney, was also a member of the Britons. He left the BF in 1926 and subsequently joined the IFL and the BUF; also members were the conspiracy theorist, Nesta Webster, most closely associated with the Duke of Northumberland's journal, the *Patriot*,[91] Arnold Leese, founder and driving force of the IFL, and William Joyce, E. G. Mandeville Roe and Neil Francis-Hawkins, all future prominent figures in the BUF. Basil Peto and the Reverend Gough, once of the NP, became members of the BF, as did Patrick Hannon and T.D. Pilcher of the British Constitutional Union and Maxwell Knight of the British Empire Union. The Assistant Director, and then Director of the Economic League, John Baker White, sat with Hannon on the Grand Council of the BF; from the National Citizens Union, Col. Sir Charles Burn, sat on the BF Executive Committee. In a similar way, the Britons acted as a training ground for the IFL with many leading figures belonging to both organizations. None of this gave these societies much influence outside their own self-reinforcing circles. If anything it may have diminished it.

The war experience and the frustrated aspirations that it created were central to the Right as it developed in the interwar period. It served as a paradigm of what might be achieved by a nation united for a common purpose, both in the enhanced role of the state disciplining and organizing all for the common good, and in the class harmony that the 'spirit of the trenches' embodied. It highlighted all that was wrong with contemporary liberal politics. The politicians who won the war not only could not win the peace, but apparently had no wish to do so. But the 1920s was not a fertile decade for innovation either within or beyond liberal politics. With the supposedly dangerous left contained by parliamentary Conservatism after 1926, there was little need for men of action or violent remedies.

Chapter 3: Sir Oswald Mosley and British Fascism

For a brief time in the early 1930s, it appeared that the crisis of liberal-capitalist Britain had finally arrived. With world trade contracting and protectionism rampant, unemployment rose to over 3 million and Britain was forced to abandon the gold standard. Trapped in economic orthodoxy, the governing elite had no response except tariffs, which were finally introduced in 1932, and the reduction of government expenditure. Radical alternatives, associated most prominently with J. M. Keynes, had been under discussion throughout the 1920s, and were an essential factor in the emergence of the highly programmatic radicalism of British fascism. For Mosley, fascism was rational, constructive revolution. Rotha Lintorn-Orman considered him almost a communist.[1]

Sir Oswald Mosley

As early as 1925, in a style reminiscent of Chamberlain at his most apocalyptic, Mosley saw

> a desperate situation. We have reached a supreme crisis in the history of humanity. We stand, indeed, at the cross-roads of destiny. For good or ill we live in an epic age. Once again the lash of great ordeal stings an historic race to action. Once more the soul of man is on the march ... We must awaken and mobilize our country to save itself by heroic measures before the sands of time and fate run out.[2]

Mosley was heavily influenced by Oswald Spengler's doom-laden, *The Decline of the West*, and its argument that civlizations were organic entities with a quasi-biological life cycle of birth, growth, decline and death. But he rejected Spengler's inevitability; science provided the modern age with the means to regenerate western civilization if it had the will. In reaching this conclusion, Mosley drew upon Shaw's concepts of 'Creative Evolution' and the 'Life Force', which Shaw regarded as identical to Bergson's '*élan vital*'.[3] According to Shaw, 'Life itself is a tireless power which is continually driving onward and upward...growing from within by its inexplicable energy into ever higher and higher forms of organization...continually superceding the institutions which were made to fit our former requirements...we must, like Prometheus, set to work to make new men.'[4]

The 'Life Force' was inseparable from life itself, but only realized by, and assisted by, an elite, the highest type of man, which Shaw variously termed the 'realist', 'hero' or 'superman', 'men selected by nature to carry on the work of building up an intellectual consciousness of her own instinctive purpose.'[5] Such men were characterized by the strength of the 'Life Force' within them, their 'joyous vitality', fearlessness in facing reality,[6] and their will to overcome it. 'The true joy of life' as Shaw expressed it, is 'being used for a purpose recognized by yourself as a mighty one...being a force of nature.'[7] Both Shaw and Mosley exploited Hegel's theories of the dialectical dynamic of evolution; each success generated a new problem for civilization, a new challenge to the hero. Mosley drew upon Nietzsche as well as Shaw for the supreme importance of the 'Will', which he termed 'the will to achievement'.[8] The assertion of will over circumstance opened the prospect of spiritual renewal and escape from the predestined degeneration of materialist determinism. Men were not impotent in the face of Darwinian natural selection, Marxist economic determinism, liberal market forces, Freudian sexual determinism or biological racism. Circumstances provided the challenge; men, Fascist men, found the solutions. It was another doctrine of aristocracy.

The First World War was a watershed for Mosley. From it he derived his intense abhorrence of war that in part lay behind his peace campaigns of the 1930s. He was constantly aware of being part of the war generation and of a sacrifice to be atoned.[9] His scathing attacks on the 'old gang' of politicians were an expression of the frustration and betrayal he felt when it became apparent that not only did they lack both the will and the ability to make good the promised post-war reconstruction, but were willing to preside over mass unemployment and poverty, and within 20 years lead the country into another war for which it was poorly prepared. But the war was also the watershed in his ideology of decline and rebirth. 'For this age is dynamic and the pre-war age was static...The types which have emerged from the pre-war and post-war periods are so different that they can scarcely understand each other's language...'[10] The language of modernity condemned 'the spirit of lethargy and surrender...This is not an age of dreams and fancies; it is an age of iron, in which an iron spirit and iron will are needed by men to cut their path through to victory...'[11]

Mosley's belief in the disintegration of the old forms of western civilization, and in both the necessity and the possibility of creating a higher civilization from its ashes, promised in theory to move the Radical Right to a new degree of radicalism. Hitherto, whilst the changes proposed had been considerable, they had only partial. The anti-capitalist implications of the social programme of radical tariff reformers led only to the confusions and 'intellectual schizophrenia' of the NP; the anti-semitic, anti-Bolshevik stance of the post-war groups only to the excision of allegedly anti-national elements, specifically the Jews.

Mosley was elected Conservative MP for Harrow in the general election of November 1918, supporting Lloyd George's Coalition government. He became secretary of the centre party group, seeking either to fuse the Conservatives and Lloyd George Liberals into a new 'national party', or to prolong the coalition itself.[12] His admiration for Lloyd George's capacity to get things done was an early indication of his executive approach to politics. By November 1920, he had abandoned the Conservative party in opposition to repression in Ireland, but retained his seat as an independent Conservative both in 1922 and 1923. By then the post-war boom had collapsed, unemployment had passed 1 million, and the promise of post-war reconstruction and a land fit for heroes had been abandoned.

By the end of 1923, Mosley had begun to question economic orthodoxy, criticizing deflationary policies in a recession, and advocating public works to combat unemployment. In April 1924, regarding Ramsay MacDonald as 'the leader of the forces of progress'[13] he joined the Labour party, but narrowly failed in his attempt to unseat Neville Chamberlain as the MP for Ladywood, Birmingham. In 1926, he re-entered parliament having won Smethwick at a by-election. In the interlude, he laid the foundations for the economic ideas which were later to form the basis for British fascism. Keynes, with whom Mosley communicated, had already written his

Tract on Monetary Reform (1923), and proposed government investment to restart the economy. In particular, Keynes had pointed out that particular policies favoured particular interest groups, and that deflation, as prescribed by classical economics, favoured non-productive bankers and rentiers, finance capitalists, against producers, whether employers or workers, a view which Mosley took on board. Like Keynes, Mosley regarded economics as a political issue in which governments made choices, not a determinist law of nature against which men were impotent. Like Keynes, too, but also like most of the Radical Right, Mosley also assumed a natural alliance of producers, workers and employers, against finance capitalism, nationalism against internationalism.

Revolution by Reason

Mosley's Birmingham Proposals of 1925, later embodied in *Revolution by Reason*, started from the premise that economic depression and unemployment were the major problems of the day, and that it was the function of government to act swiftly and decisively to deal with them. In the modern age, science and technology had provided the means to eliminate unemployment, and its consequence, poverty, if the idle resources of men and machines were put to work. To achieve this, Mosley proposed the nationalization of the banks and issuing consumers' and producers' credits to stimulate consumer demand and the cycle of increased production, employment and further demand.

Since capitalism depended ultimately on credit, the proposals, almost incidentally, would give the government control of the capitalist system. By directing both consumer and producer credit, it could determine both what was consumed, and what was produced. The key was planning, for which Mosley proposed an Economic Planning Council to ensure that demand met supply, but did not exceed it, to avoid inflation. This emphasis on a planned economy made Mosley an economic nationalist from the first. The British economy should be controlled by the British government, and not subject to 'the gold jugglery of foreign statesmen and international financiers.'[14]

From the same standpoint he also questioned the importance attached to the export trade. Acknowledging the need to import food and raw materials, he proposed producing at home manufactured articles currently imported. Inspection of the mass production techniques pioneered by Ford at Detroit during a visit to America in 1926 reaffirmed his conviction that modern technology could replace the age of poverty by an age of plenty, and provided the basis for his subsequent argument that costs of production were determined by the scale of production rather than by the level of wages. But it also forced upon his attention that such techniques allowing the use of cheap unskilled labour meant that the loss of Britain's traditional export markets would be permanent as those countries progressively industrialized.

Unorthodox economic ideas, whether from Mosley or any other element of the party, failed to make any headway with the Labour party leadership. It led Mosley to question further the inadequacy of the existing political system not only to act with the urgency required, but even to realize that the situation required urgent action.[15] It was again a basic theme of his fascism in the 1930s, but it took the experience of serving in the Labour government elected in 1929 and the failure of the New Party experiment of 1931–32 to convince him finally that new institutions were needed as much as new men to make new ideas work.

In the new government, Mosley was given the minor office of Chancellor of the Duchy of Lancaster, outside the Cabinet but assigned to assist the Lord Privy Seal, J. H. Thomas, in considering unemployment. Months of frustration followed as it became increasingly apparent that the government was wedded to economic orthodoxy which entailed the revival of the export trade and continuing deflation. In January 1930, Mosley's frustration boiled over. The 'Mosley Memorandum' was a direct challenge to both political inertia and the economic crisis. It proposed an executive committee of the prime minister and his leading colleagues working with full-time expert advisers.[16] Policy would deal with long-term solutions to Britain's industrial malaise, 'a great transition of our industrial life from a pre-War to a post-War basis...by scientific thought and the scientific method'. Mosley explicitly rejected the export solution in favour of an enlarged home market achieved through state provision of long-term industrial credit and planned development which would create employment and permit the change from a 'low wage basis of production to a higher wage basis of production, the greater rate of which in response to a larger demand more than offsets the increase in labour costs. Once that awkward transition is achieved our future employment can rest increasingly on the growing Home Market.'[17]

Unorthodox and expansionist, the proposals proved unacceptable to ministers and civil servants alike. Mosley resigned from the government on 20 May. On 22 May, the parliamentary Labour party overwhelmingly backed the government. Mosley's resignation speech on 28 May reiterated the policies he had outlined in his memorandum, and his demand for strong executive government. In typical Radical Right fashion he predicted that if nothing was done, 'we may soon come to crisis, to a real crisis', or even worse 'a long, slow, crumbling through the years until we sink to the level of a Spain, a gradual paralysis, beneath which all the vigour and energy of this country will succumb'.[18] It was a parliamentary triumph, but no action followed.

The obvious difficulty, if not impossibility, of insulating Britain alone from world economic conditions drove Mosley towards imperial autarky. In June 1930, he advocated directly what Chamberlain and Milner had inferred, 'conscious control and direction of the united economic resources of our Commonwealth' and came close to Garvin's 1903 argument that with secure markets and the economies of scale that followed, the Dominions would be able to maintain, or even reduce, prices. Extending the 'area of insulation to embrace the whole commonwealth of nations within whose borders can be found nearly every resource, human and material, which industry requires', he admitted on 16 July 'would be a better policy with far greater prospects of success' than mere domestic insulation.[19]

Mosley made one last attempt to convert the Labour Party at the annual party conference in Llandudno in October. There he reiterated his demand for public works, his criticism of leaving rationalization to the banks, the importance of the insulated home market and the need for planning and control. If its proposals were rejected in parliament, the party should appeal directly to the electorate. The 'great national crisis', was not a difficulty, 'it was their supreme opportunity...with courage, vigour, decision and a policy they could use the situation to remodel the whole structure of the country'. It was better, Mosley argued, to 'go down fighting for the things they believed in. They would not die like an old woman in bed; they would die like a man on the field'. This was the heroic appeal, born of wartime experience and ideology alike.

With imperial autarky added to his programme, Mosley sounded increasingly like a pre-war tariff reformer, emphasizing foreign industrialization, sweated labour and dumping as reasons for the permanent loss of foreign export markets, the consequent need for an expansion of the domestic and imperial markets, and imperial organization to facilitate planning on the imperial scale.[20] Economic nationalism was 'the alternative both to international finance and international socialism.'[21] It also shared the same assumption of the identity of interest of producers, whether worker or employer, against finance-capitalism, and implied class cooperation, or the transcendence of class identities altogether. As Stanley Baldwin commented Mosley was 'now producing ideas which I remember giving voice to in 1903'.[22]

The New Party

Mosley almost, but not quite, won in Llandudno. Failure meant he had to find a new constituency outside regular party politics. The manifesto of 13 December 1930, drafted by Mosley, Aneurin Bevan, John Strachey and W. J. Brown, temporarily dropped the imperial schemes which were interesting Conservatives, even those hitherto as unsympathetic as Neville Chamberlain, in an attempt to woo Labour supporters. That apart, the manifesto reiterated Mosley's programme, the planned expansion of the home market, the regulation of imports and protective tariffs imposed by a Commodity Board of both producers and consumers if it was satisfied by the efficiency, pricing and wages of the industry concerned. The war provided the precedent for the proposed cabinet of 5 ministers freed from specific ministerial responsibility, with 'power to carry through the emergency policy' subject only to the 'general control' of parliament.[23] Only 17 Labour MPS signed the manifesto, to constitute themselves the New Labour Group. The Manifesto, however, together with Mosley's dynamism, did impress Sir William Morris, the car manufacturer who, in January 1931, provided Mosley with £50,000 to form a new party.

The New Party was announced on 28 February 1931, with the promise of running 400 candidates at the next election. But although there were sympathizers in all parties and in the Press, the party, like Mosley's earlier efforts, made little effective impact. It gained 16 per cent of the vote at the Ashton-under-Lyne by-election in April 1931. The poor performance could be explained away on the grounds that the party had had no time to prepare, had no organization and faced determined opposition from the Labour party. But it also revealed that Mosley had not only carried few of the working classes with him, but had incurred the intense hostility of many.

Despite the hopes of winning support from all classes as an industrial party uniting employers and workers in a recognition of their common interest, the New Party was forced increasingly into an anti-labour stance. There was a dialectical process at work. The Left saw in the New Party the potentially Fascist party that was the predicted response of beleaguered capitalism to crush the working classes. Mosley's connections with his young Conservative sympathizers aggravated this impression. Disruption of New Party meetings led Mosley to counter violence with violence, the organization of trained and supposedly disciplined young members to act both as stewards at meetings, and in the longer term to preserve order against anarchy and communism in the expected revolutionary crisis to come, 'an iron core... around which every element for the preservation of England will rally'; less respectfully the 'Biff Boys'.[24] By September, after further violence at a meeting in Glasgow, he concluded 'this forces us to be fascist and we need no longer hesitate to create our trained and disciplined force'.[25]

Characteristic of the Radical Right in trying to combine the orthodox opposites of Left and Right, the New Party was characteristic also in its failure to hold them together. It began to collapse only a few months after its formation. In July, the leading figures of the Left, Mosley's long-term associates John Strachey and Allan Young, resigned against what they saw as Mosley's drift towards fascism, and the party decided to fight only 50 seats at the next election. Subsequently this was reduced to 25. Politics remained divided, ideologically if not electorally, on those class lines that Mosley's principles and party existed to transcend. Moreover, when the National Government was finally obliged to take Britain off the gold standard on 21 September, Mosley's criticisms of deflation became peripheral. Mosley nevertheless refused to align himself with the National Government, and thus gain a possible influence over policy. He remained locked in the abstractions of Spengler and Shaw, still anticipating the final crisis, chaos and rebirth, rather than reconstruction.

Divided and disorganized, the New Party fared disastrously in the general election of 1931. Most of its candidates lost their deposits, and overall the party did far less well than even the Communists. After this, the New Party was all but shut down. Three paid officials were retained, but the central offices and regional organizations were closed. Its journal, *Action*, intended 'to imbue the nation with a new idea and a new faith' ceased publication in December.[26] Only the youth organization, NUPA, was retained, and with it the aspect of violence.

Having closed down the New Party, Mosley went to Rome. 'Tom cannot keep his mind off shock troops, the arrest of MacDonald and J. H. Thomas, their internment in the Isle of Wight and the roll of drums around Westminster', Harold Nicolson recorded in his diary, 'he is a Romantic'. Mosley found Mussolini suitably dynamic, and thus inspired finally announced the end of the New Party in April 1932. His plan, as recorded by Nicolson was 'to coordinate all the fascist groups with NUPA and thus form a central fascist body under his leadership.'[27]

The BUF, formed in October 1932 with the *fasces*, borrowed from Italy, as its emblem, and black shirts as its basic uniform, was what its name suggested, an attempt at Fascist unity. It was to be 'a great and hazardous adventure' for its members, 'a movement which aims at the creation of a classless brotherhood marked only by functional differences.'[28] Mosley sought to retain private enterprise, and thus the initiative and drive of capitalism, but combine that with social and economic collaboration. His classless society was not to be egalitarian, but a meritocracy in which power and reward were earned.[29] Here Mosley grasped the nettle which had bedeviled the Radical Right since it had become involved with the minimum or 'comfort' wage while retaining the absolute rights of private property. In the new Fascist state there was to be no automatic inheritance of private property; prospective heirs would justify their right by demonstrating their ability. In theory it would be a willing renunciation. BUF members were 'to be prepared to sacrifice all...to dedicate their lives to building in this country a movement of the modern age...fighting that a great land may live'.[30] In practice, the state would have ample power to enforce obedience.

The Greater Britain

The BUF began with a clear, detailed programme worked out by Mosley over most of the previous decade and expounded in *The Greater Britain*, which he wrote during the summer of 1932. The book reiterated Mosley's belief in 'the necessity for fundamental change' because 'economic life has outgrown our political institutions'. A 'constructive policy' was required 'to reconcile the revolutionary change of science with our system of government and to harmonize individual initiative with the wider interests of the nation.'[31] Hence 'The main aim of a modern and Fascist movement is to establish the Corporate State.'[32] The crisis was the familiar one. Science had revolutionized the capacity to produce without any corresponding increase in purchasing power, resulting in unemployment which, in turn, reduced purchasing power further, and so on in a vicious cycle of depression. 'Today we have passed from the economics of poverty to the economics of plenty. Our problem is no longer how to produce enough to live; our problem is how to consume what is produced.'[33]

Since government had failed to respond to what was a permanent problem in the modern age, it followed that the system of government had also to change. Parliament was a time-wasting 'talking-shop'[34] and the party system merely hindered dynamic action. In contrast, the Corporate State would have both the power and the expertise to ensure the planned expansion of the home market that would solve the problem of over-production. 'It means a nation organized as the human body with each organ performing its individual function, but working in harmony with the whole and co-related with the general purpose by a directive and controlling intelligence.'[35] This was a blunt repetition of Edwardian organicism, but it neatly avoided the problem of personal liberty within the corporate state, since the individual realized himself and his liberty as part of the whole. True liberty, Mosley maintained, was economic liberty, a freedom-plus-security package in which the individual would be able to realize liberty in the private sphere, while yielding individual and sectional interests to the common good as determined by the state in the public arena. In the same manner, the press would be free to print the 'truth', but not to contradict the national interest. Liberty of any kind remained subordinate to that overriding priority: 'there will be no room in Britain for those who do not accept the principle "All for the State and the State for all".'[36]

The corporate state would be made up of 20 corporations with representatives of workers, employers and consumers, the last appointed by the government. These would set the levels of production, wages and prices for their respective industries, raising 'wages and salaries over the whole field of industry as science, rationalization and industrial technique increase the power to produce. Consumption will be adjusted to production, and a Home Market will be provided by the higher purchasing power of our own people'.[37] Although described as 'wholly self-governing',[38] they would effectively be subordinate to a National Corporation, planning and controlling the economy 'under the guidance of the Minister'.[39] Its functions included settling disputes between corporations, but for all practical purposes, the Minister of Corporations, and thus the government, would be in real control. The crucial issue of credit would be the responsibility of a National Investment Board, 'working in conjunction with the National Corporation of Industry', and thus also effectively controlled by the government.[40]

To enable this planning to succeed and a high wage economy to survive, the British economy was, as before, to be 'insulated', by 'scientific protection' which would exclude all goods that could be produced at home, and exclude British employers who continued to pay low wages. Mosley repeated his argument that high wages would not adversely affect exports because the costs of production were determined by the rate of production not the rate of wages, and Britain's rate of production would be increased as economies of scale followed greater production as a result of the expanded home market. Moreover, through the corporate state controlling foreign trade, Britain could negotiate better terms. Ultimately, these measures and the expansion of British agriculture would result in 'a Britain as nearly as possible self-contained and an Empire entirely self-contained'. Insulation from the world economy would be complete; there would be no more foreign trade, only inter-imperial trade, regulated by 'a permanently functioning machinery of economic consultation and planning'.[41]

Dynamic action was to be ensured by placing executive government with either a small group, the former cabinet of five, or an individual Leader, with 'complete power of action by order'. Parliament was reduced to a supervisory body, although it could censure and dismiss the government, but its structure and the electoral system were both to be radically changed. Functionalism was the central principle of the corporate state, and elections were to be based on an occupational franchise. This, it was argued, would create a more informed electorate since they would understand the issues that arose from their occupations, and a more informed parliament of 'experts' since members would be elected for their understanding of industrial issues. Insofar as this was a dictatorship, whether of one or a few, it was a plebiscitary dictatorship, the government being 'dependent upon a direct vote of the whole people held at regular intervals' of not more than 5 years. 'Party warfare will come to an end in a technical and non-political Parliament which will be concerned not with the Party game of obstruction, but with the national interest of construction.' Much the same pattern applied to local government. Local councils were to continue, but in a largely advisory capacity. Power would be in the hands of executive officers, the local Fascist MPs. 'Fascism', as Joyce put it, 'in its very essence cannot conceive of the sovereignty of the people'.[42]

The BUF and Anti-Semitism

These ideas remained at the heart of BUF policy for its entire existence. Initially, it looked as if that existence might be of political significance.

By mid-1934 the BUF had an estimated membership of some 50,000.[43] But this was in the aftermath of the political and economic crisis of 1931. It was also the era of 'respectable fascism' when fascism seemed, in Baldwin's words, only 'ultramontane conservatism',[44] the January Club was formed to permeate the establishment, and Mosley enjoyed the support of elements in the right-wing press, notably Lady Houston's *Saturday Review* and, for the first 6 months of 1934, Lord Rothermere's *Daily Mail.* As Sir Thomas Moore remarked in April 1934, 'there cannot be any fundamental differences of outlook between Blackshirts and their parents, the Conservatives'.[45] The rapprochement was in marked contrast to the virtual press boycott which had hindered the New Party, and was to hinder the BUF after 1934. Respectability was nevertheless limited. In 1933 the BUF leased Whitelands Teachers Training College in Chelsea and renamed it Black House. Here, and in other centres, the new 'Biff Boys' were housed and trained for their paramilitary role. Street violence continued, as did the expectation, or fear, of a final cataclysm in which fascism, or the fascism that Rothermere called 'sound, commonsense, Conservative doctrine'[46] was all that stood between the respectable classes and anarchy leading to communism.

By mid-1934, however, it was becoming clear that the apocalypse would be at least delayed. Somewhat less visible was the creeping drift of the BUF into anti-semitism. In 1932 Mosley stated that 'anti-semitism forms no part of the policy of this organisation, and anti-semitic propaganda is forbidden', sentiments he reiterated in 1933.[47] Ted 'Kid' Lewis, the ex-boxer who trained the New Party's 'Biff Boys' was Jewish, and Jews were not excluded from the BUF until the autumn of 1933. But Mosley's outlook and policy alike drew him into conspiracy arguments and thus towards anti-semitism.[48] There was, he declared in 1932, 'within the nation a power, largely controlled by alien elements, which arrogates to itself a power above the State, and has used that influence to drive flaccid governments of all political parties along the high road to national disaster'.[49] He associated finance capitalism, which he all too often called 'international Jewish finance',[50] with the Jews, and both with international communism.[51] The criticism was of Jewish activities, not of Jews as a race or Judaism as a religion. It was a cultural or ethnocentric antisemitism, but as Christine Bolt has observed of Victorian racism, culture and race become 'dangerously linked', especially when the effects are the same.[52]

Moreover, the upper echelons of the BUF did contain committed antisemites, such as William Joyce and A. K. Chesterton, whose anti-semitism was either biologically racist or inclined in that direction. The same is true of the rank and file, with such figures as E. G. 'Mick' Clarke, 'Jock' Houston and James 'Bill' Bailey squarely in the tradition of belligerent East London anti-semitism that could be traced back to the late nineteenth century and the British Brothers League. For his part, Major-General J. F. C. Fuller took up Nesta Webster's conspiratorial theme: 'For over a thousand years, the Jews have been a world wide power, a net of conspiracy and of race interests stretched over half the globe', responsible for the overthrow of empires and civilizations from ancient Egypt to the Russian Revolution.[53] It is not, therefore, surprising that Jews responded to the emergence of fascism in Britain which drew on both a British tradition and an international ideology. With its core of committed anti-semites in high places, its anti-communist, anti-trade union programme and its similarities to continental anti-semitism, uniformed, aggressive stewards, street-corner meetings and newspaper vendors, the BUF was a potential threat. The result was a dialectic of violence with both sides acting out pre-ordained roles from entrenched positions.

The almost predictable outcome was the confrontation at Olympia on 7 June 1934. Planned communist disruption and aggressive BUF stewarding resulted in a level of violence that shocked the audience and raised a spectre that haunted the BUF for the rest of its existence. The next major meeting in London, to be held at the White City, had to be cancelled because of fears of further violent confrontation. It marked the end of respectable fascism. In July, Rothermere withdrew his support, according to Mosley because Jewish advertisers had threatened to remove their business.[54] But Rothermere and Mosley had completely different visions. For Mosley, fascism was not 'commonsense' conservatism, but inspired revolution.

Mosley incorporated significant attacks on Jews, as distinct from responding to hecklers, in his speeches from the autumn of 1934, thereby lending his backing to the more strident anti-semites in the BUF. Nevertheless, Mosley's cultural, derivative anti-semitism allowed him, in contrast to biological racists like Leese, to discriminate between 'good' and 'bad' Jews, and, indeed 'good' and 'bad' foreigners of all kinds. Although the BUF policy was deportation, those that demonstrated their allegiance to Britain and put British interests first would be allowed to remain. This included, as his 1933 article 'Shall Jews Drag Britain to War' revealed, recognizing that events in Germany, or indeed anywhere outside the empire, were not Britain's business.[55]

Membership and Finance

Like Chamberlain in his tariff reform campaign, the BUF targeted specific areas and industries which were thought to be most receptive to the new message. As well as cotton in Lancashire, where in 1938 200 meetings were held in a single week, other targets included the woollen industry in Yorkshire, shipping in Liverpool, coal mining and, of course, agriculture, on the expansion of which the BUF always placed great emphasis for both autarkic and moral reasons. For all its avowed modernism, the BUF shared the Radical Right's rural nostalgia. Such campaigns were essential after Olympia and the loss of the Rothermere press. Despite the poor publicity, Olympia produced a temporary upturn in recruitment, but by October 1935 membership had fallen dramatically as the respectable fled in droves.

Speculation on the size and nature of BUF membership is an unrewarding exercise. In the absence of verifiable membership lists, estimates by historians are founded largely on figures from official sources. These 'guesstimates' show a peak of 50,000 in mid-1934, from which membership declined to around 5000 by late 1935, after which it rose steadily to 10,000 in March 1936, 16,500 by December 1938 and 22,500 by September 1939. But Birmingham was 'moribund' after 1935; in Lancashire membership held up during 1934, but declined thereafter and there were no more than 100 active members in the north-west by 1937. In Cardiff in 1935 only 7 of the 200 members were active; in Leeds, 10 out of 66, figures which suggest a high degree of inactivity in this period.[56]

It meant that for the middle years of the decade, until east Londoners reacted against Mosley's endorsement of Munich, the movement was heavily reliant on its support in the East End which still had a tradition of anti-semitism. Nevertheless Thomas Linehan's detailed study of east London concludes that not even anti-semitism provided any unity in this key area: 'the "east London movement"...simply did not exist...what did exist was something far less coherent, far less imposing and much more erratic, a series of aberrant phenomena whose histories ebbed and flowed as part of the general drama of local political and communal life...'[57] As a peripheral movement relying on sporadic campaigns either in specific regions, or on specific issues such as the 'Mind Britain's Business' campaigns opposing sanctions against the Italian invasion of Abyssinia in 1935, and war with Germany in 1938 and 1939, the BUF was always likely to have a variable appeal and membership across regions, classes and time, and thus, like the NF later, to have large numbers passing through its ranks rather than a stable membership beyond a small committed core.

The decline in membership adversely affected the movement's finances. Income from subscriptions from the 10,000 members the BUF had in 1936 was only £8,000–10,000.[58] It was helped during the middle period of its existence, 1934–36, by secret funding from Mussolini, apparently in regular monthly instalments. The first 'Mind Britain's Business' campaign may not have been entirely unconnected with these subventions, although the campaign was also entirely consistent with Mosley's strong opposition to war and European involvement. After 1936, the gap between subscriptions and expenditure was largely filled by Mosley himself.[59] By the autumn of 1934, with the economic crisis fading into the distance, the taint of illegal violence hanging over it, without any significant support from business or the unions, the BUF bubble, such as it was, had burst, to be marginally reinflated by the approach of war in 1939.

Decline

Predicated on the inevitable collapse of the existing regime when it might be swept to power by a desperate nation, by late 1934 the movement found itself needing to work within a regime that it detested and which it hoped to replace, to become in some senses at least, a conventional political party in a liberal democratic system. Retrenchment, reorganization and tactics all became entangled with factional in-fighting from which the BUF was no more exempt than any other Radical Right grouping.[60] Between 1934 and 1937 there was constant rivalry between the more radical 'doctrinal fascists', principally Joyce, Beckett, Chesterton and Raven-Thompson, who wanted to stress the revolutionary dynamic of fascist ideology, together with anti-semitism, through platform speeches and literature, and a more moderate 'organisational', group headed by Fuller and F. M. Box, a professional political agent and BUF Director of Political Organisation, who wished to reduce the demagogy, violence and anti-semitism and concentrate on building up an electoral machine and recruiting respectable sympathizers.

The BUF began with an elaborate organization on an area basis descending through regions, branches, groups and sub-groups. In 1934–35, the Area Headquarters were abolished, administration was centralized, and the regions and branches were placed under National Headquarters inspectors. In January 1935 a new Political Organization was set up, with powers to develop constituency organizations, in theory with agents working from local constituency offices. As a further shift from a dema-gogic, populist image, the Political Organization included a new category of non-uniformed members. The remaining uniformed members were reorganized into a 'Blackshirt Command' operating locally in five man units, acting as an auxiliary to the Political Organization, helping with canvassing and street propaganda, knocking on doors rather than throw-ing bricks through windows.

During 1935–36, there was a brief and partial resurgence of the 'radi-cals'. The Political Organization lost executive authority, which was now centralized under the Blackshirt Command, although non-uniformed membership and the realignment of branch organizations to parliamen-tary constituencies continued. Box was consigned to Department of Technical Instruction, dealing only with electoral matters; he resigned in December 1935. In yet another administrative restructuring, the country was divided into southern and northern zones, with a new northern zonal headquarters in Manchester. Early in 1936, a new weekly, *Action*, was announced in *Blackshirt*, and a new uniform, the 'Action uniform' was introduced but awarded to committed members only. In June the BUF added 'National Socialist' to its title, reflecting a shift in identifica-tion from Italy to Germany. It corresponded with the increasing reliance on east London as the one area where the movement appeared to be making headway in the midst of increasing irrelevance elsewhere. Mosley's speeches laid ever-greater stress on the Jewish menace.

But the revival of the radicals was limited and extremely short-lived. Neil Francis-Hawkins, a recruit from the BF and an 'organiser', was placed in command of the Blackshirt organization as early as June 1935. In January 1936 he became Director-General of Organization, and had executive authority over the entire movement. In east London, the run-ning battle between Fascists and anti-fascists culminated in the 'Battle of Cable Street' in October 1936, when anti-fascist organizations barricaded the streets and successfully stopped a Fascist march in its tracks. Hailed as an anti-fascist victory in their private war, the ultimate victors were the police and the government, the greatest losers, despite a brief period of sympathetic meetings and improved recruiting, was the BUF. In view of the increasing difficulty in preserving public order, the government intervened with the Public Order Act of 1936, which came into force at the start of 1937.

The act banned political uniforms, paramilitary organizations, the use of force for political objectives and the possession of offensive weapons at meetings. It reasserted the role of the state and its instruments, the police and the army, as the sole authority responsible for public order, and the sole institution that could legally use force in pursuit of its objectives. The police were also given powers to regulate public demonstrations, and, with the Home Secretary's approval, to prohibit them indefinitely. The Act left the BUF with few alternatives unless it wished to confront the police, the army and the government head-on. In east London, abuse of Jews diminished; within the BUF hierarchy the power of the 'organiser' faction was enhanced, that of the 'radical fascists' reduced. In October, Francis-Hawkins gained control over all Headquarters staffing and internal affairs of the BUF. In December, the organization was demilitarized, and in March 1937 it was the Department of Organisation that oversaw the London County Council election campaign.

The failure in that campaign to win even a single seat in east London was followed by another bout of reorganization and bloodletting. Even apart from the election failure, further retrenchment was required. Mussolini's funding had virtually ended, and there had been no compensatory increase in membership, still less benefactors from the British establishment. In March the zonal system was scrapped, the Manchester office closed and the paid regional organizers dismissed. The drastic reduction of Headquarters staff from 129 to 57 included the dismissal of Joyce and Beckett and the majority of the Policy Propaganda Unit, the base of the 'radical fascists', together with the paid speakers it controlled. On 2 April 1937, Joyce and Beckett formed the pro-Nazi National Socialist League, an extreme anti-semitic body which, like the IFL, remained miniscule, with only some 50 members.

The BUF itself was almost a spent force, with no organization worthy of the name in large parts of the country. Staffing was further reduced in February 1938, and shortly afterwards A. K. Chesterton resigned. The BUF nevertheless fluttered briefly to life in the run up to the Second World War. Mosley's peace campaign rested on the arguments that he had proposed from the first, that wars had their origins in economic competition and that international trade, far from promoting interlocking economies and reducing the risk as liberal economics argued, greatly increased the chances of war. Autarky was not only the solution to Britain's economic problems, but also the way to maintain peace.

Mosley's vision, again after the pattern of Edwardian tariff reformers, was of large economic blocs, each self-sufficient and self-contained within tariff walls, having as little contact with each other as possible. 'Mind Britain's Business' had a deliberate double meaning, but in both senses Britain's business was with her empire, not Europe. The campaign in 1938–39 also included Mosley's anti-semitic, conspiratorial gloss on his logic, 'the jackals of Jewish finance are again in full cry for war'.[61] Briefly, the BUF had an audience again, of those who had had too much of war, which included Mosley above all. Eleven thousand people heard him speak against war at Earls Court in July 1939, although the shouts of 'Sieg Heil' may have disturbed many. The peace campaign continued up to, and after, the outbreak of war itself. By then, Mosley had become involved in discussions with other anti-war campaigners that, whether innocent or not, seemed dubious to the government. The government, which had remained in control all the time despite Fascist expectations and posturing, arrested Mosley and leading BUF members in May 1940, and outlawed the BUF in July.

Fascism and the Radical Right

Although larger, the BUF was as irrelevant to mainstream politics as all the other minor Radical Right groups. Mosley was already well known as a politician before his departure for the political fringe, and his aristocratic background, his life-style and his ability as a public speaker gave the new movement glamour. But in the wider context, 'Fascism next time' was an all too transparent slogan to avoid fighting the 1935 general election in which the movement faced only humiliation. Even in east London, where the movement could tap into long-standing resentments, and created a considerable stir because of the association with, and encouragement of, street violence, it failed miserably in local elections. The BUF was born of an anticipated catastrophe in liberal-capitalism when supposedly its disciplined paramilitary units would maintain order, its heroic leaders would confront the crisis and its policies would transform the political and economic system. When there was no crisis, the BUF had lost its *raison d'etre*.

Financial difficulties and retrenchment led to a series of reorganizations which were more twitchy than dynamic. For a movement that was to restructure British politics and the British economy, it displayed a remarkable incapacity to organize itself. Moreover, the programme itself had one almost certainly fatal flaw, the neglect of colonial nationalism and the obvious conflict between the self-governing colonies' desire to industrialize and the role allocated to them in the self-sufficient empire. The real significance of Mosley and the BUF to the British Radical Right lay in its attitudes, and its detailed radicalism. The Shavian doctrine of heroic vitalism gave it, superficially at least, a confidence in the potential future unseen since the Edwardian tariff reform campaign. Its programme addressed real problems directly, and in rejecting absolute property rights contained the radicalism required to overcome the contradictions that had hitherto beset the Radical Right.

The BUF embraced progress, both in the practical transformation of politics and the economy and in the transformation of individuals into new, modern men. 'Fascism', Mosley wrote in the 1934 edition of *The Greater Britain*, 'is a thing of the spirit. It is acceptance of new values and of a new morality in a higher and nobler conception of the universe.'[62] Yet 'fascist man' was not as 'new', as Mosley believed. Mosley claimed that his fascism was the synthesis of Nietzsche and Christianity, reconciling the concepts of struggle, the will and the superman of the former with the doctrine of service, duty and sacrifice of the latter. But in differentiating 'fascist man' from Nietzsche's a-moral superman, fascism's spiritual or cultural renewal turned out to be restorative, not the creation of new values, but a return to what A. K. Chesterton called 'the old heroic fidelities...courage, service and self-sacrifice',[63] beloved by Willoughby de Broke. Brought up 'in feudal fashion',[64] Mosley clung to feudal values and lamented the degeneration of an aristocracy 'ignobly lending their prestige and their abilities to the support of the predatory plutocracy' as 'flunkeys of the bourgeoisie'.[65] The supposedly new 'fascist man' was the aristocratic crusading Christian knight in modern dress; the corporate state, feudalism industrialized, fascism, the church militant secularized.

Chapter 4: Alternative Economics and Peace-Loving Patriots

Whilst Mosley's ideas developed in the direction of the all-powerful state, an anarchist strain in Radical Right thinking, vividly expressed by Hilaire Belloc and G. K. Chesterton, was increasingly concerned with the expanding powers of the existing state. Belloc's *The Servile State*, published in 1912, was the most significant critique of collectivism to emerge either before or after the First World War and set the tone for opposition to state intervention at least until the advent of the libertarian 'New Right' in the 1970s. Belloc looked back to a time when Europe was a Christian unity, a society of peasant proprietors, with craftsmen and merchants organized into guilds which regulated competition, set prices, ensured quality and provided stability for what he called the 'distributive system' or the 'Distributist State'. In that society most families owned their own means of production, a guarantee of economic independence which ensured their liberty, 'for the truth is, that to the moderately poor the home is the only place of liberty'.[1]

Distributism

According to Belloc, the mediaeval distributist state was undermined by the growth of capitalism which gradually concentrated wealth in the hands of a small minority, 'the English landlord-mercantile plutocracy', thereby creating the 'Capitalist State'. Like many others from Marx to Mosley, Belloc believed that capitalism was unstable since the working classes were permanently insecure and excluded from the system's benefits. To stabilize capitalism, the state intervened with collectivist social reforms which provided security, but provided it from above, disciplining the poor into behaving as the state wished by such means as compulsory education, health inspections and compulsory national insurance. From the capitalist state would emerge the 'servile state', to be administered partly by public officials, partly by employers. The thin end of this wedge was the national insurance act of 1911 under which employers acted on behalf of the state in collecting the compulsory insurance contributions from their workers. Insurance benefits would not be paid to workers dismissed for misconduct or on strike, and the insurance cards that recorded workers' contributions provided an employment record which employers could use to identify troublemakers.

Collectivism reinforced the ownership of the means of production by the plutocracy with the authority of the state. Permanently divorced from the means of production, the workers were constrained to accept the condition of their own servility in exchange for welfare security. Socialism, the ownership of the means of production by the state, was not an alternative to the servile state but maintained the separation of the worker from the means of production, and subjected him to an even more concentrated source of oppression. The only real alternative to servility was the wider distribution of property, the recreation of 'the peasant state', or more accurately the peasant anti-state, since the whole objective was to destroy the overweening interference of the state in everyday life. It was, as J. L. Finlay commented 'an argument directed against the state; it was in essence anarchist...'[2]

The Servile State contained the seeds of distributism which was yet another product of the Edwardian intellectual ferment. But it was not until the mid-1920s, with the foundation of G. K.'s Weekly and the formation of the Distributist League that distributism fully emerged as a 'third way' beyond capitalism and socialism. 'Our purpose', Chesterton declared, 'is revolution. We do not want to tinker with the capitalist system, we want to destroy it.'[3] Yet there was no clear, agreed outline of the future Distributist state to set against Mosley's exposition of the corporate state, nor any plan of how to achieve it. Beyond the overall desire to re-establish a system of small ownership in land, craft industries and small businesses, the Distributists found it impossible to agree. 'The Distributist movement', as Margaret Canovan observed, 'was a sorry spectacle',[4] a small group of intellectuals perpetually quarrelling about the details of a non-existent society.

The problem arose in part from the failure of some Distributists to understand Belloc's linkage of property, economic independence and freedom. Thus Arthur Penty's suggestion that service to society should justify all private property denied the essence of distributism by making property contingent. Penty, like many Distributists, floated between distributism, guild socialism and Social Credit, and eventually drifted into fascism. Similarly, Maurice Reckitt's proposal that instead of redistributing land itself the income from industry should be redistributed, simply turned distributism into a form of Social Credit.[5]

Reckitt nevertheless identified the principal and ultimately insoluble difficulty, the incorporation of large-scale industry into the Distributist state whilst ensuring workers' control of large-scale production in such a way that the worker retained his autonomy. It was an issue which Distributists shied away from, except to reject the possibilities offered by guild socialism or social credit. Their failing, from the distributist point of view, was that they accepted industry and mass production as the norm, and would fall prey to the very domination of managers, experts and bureaucrats that distributism existed to destroy. They were thus, like existing trade unions and the Labour party, reformist, not revolutionary.

Distributism was always more of a moral than an economic programme. Its core was an objection to 'bigness' itself, big industries, big trade unions and the big state, on behalf of the 'little' man, the small farmer, the small shopkeeper, the small businessman, and beneath them, the unconsulted poor. The intention was not to abandon industry, but to destroy the domination of capitalism by redistributing property to such an extent that small ownership would set the tone of society and offer a means of escape from the factory system to those who sought it. H. E. Humphries concluded: 'if a man wants to do things by machinery, or work in a factory, he will do so... those who do not want responsibility will work for a wage on the farm or in the workshop. Our conception of a civilized state is one in which men will want responsibility and the exercise of their own wills in the control of their own business... The essential is liberty...'[6] Belloc similarly argued that the very existence of peasant proprietors and craftsmen would 'be an object lesson in freedom... and... a hint to his neighbours to change their own condition... from one of wage slavery to one of independence.'[7] Before the economic revolution, there had to be a revolution in attitudes, after which the economic revolution would happen automatically as men chose liberty.

But even those who wished to become peasant proprietors required the means to do so. There were some privately financed schemes,[8] particularly Catholic land movements, but private initiatives would never transform society as a whole. Distributists were forced to look to the state for assistance in their anti-state project, proposing the abolition of primogeniture in favour of the division of inherited property, cheap state credit and differential taxation whereby the revenue from the higher taxation on large firms could be used to assist small businesses.[9] Not surprisingly since their object was revolution, they looked in vain.[10] But distributism, as Belloc recognized, also suffered from the problem common to all restorative movements, that even success would do no more than place society at an earlier point on the road to the present. To survive, the Distributist state required constant state intervention to prevent the re-evolution of capitalism.

Distributism thus either despaired, or drifted towards fascism. By 1936 Belloc had concluded that the destruction of 'bigness' by the 'restoration of property' was virtually impossible. All that could be done was to expose the vices of the system, and await the revolution in outlook. Having lost faith in parliamentary government and representative democracy, Distributists dreamed of a public-spirited monarch or a benevolent despot. Failing these, they were inclined to see virtue in aspects of fascism. Both Belloc and Chesterton construed Mussolini's regime as the use of public power to remove 'the miserable parliamentary figures of the old degraded days' and destroy the secret conspiracy of plutocrats who hid behind liberalism.[11]

The *American Review*, founded in 1933 and edited by Seward Collins, drew explicitly on the ideas of Chesterton and Belloc in expressing the views of what it called 'Radicals of the Right', or 'Revolutionary Conservatives'. Fascism, according to Collins, was a movement that would restore 'monarchy, property, the guilds, the security of family and the peasantry, and the ancient ways of European life'. It was a fascism far removed from Mosley's technocracy, but in it Collins saw, as Chesterton and Belloc saw in Mussolini, the means 'of setting the power of the people through its government above the power of the plutocratic regime which has brought us to chaos and to the threat of the orderly but servile refuge of collectivism'.[12]

This was to emphasize the negative, but perhaps most important, side of distributism, the desire to destroy a corrupted liberalism that could not reform itself. The problem, as Chesterton pointed out, was

> not the rich, but the Very Rich ... certain powers and privileges have grown so world-wide that they are ... out of the power of everybody except a few millionaires ... The things that change modern history, the big national and international loans, the big educational and

philanthropic foundations, the purchase of numberless newspapers, the big price paid for peerages, the big expenses often incurred in elections – these are getting too big...'[13]

Chesterton condemned 'cosmopolitan finance', Belloc Britain's excessive dependence on America 'the *pied a terre* of the wandering international financier'. Both expressions were conventional euphemisms for international Jewish finance.

Distributism was heavily tinged with anti-semitism, founded on a cultural form of racism, hostility to international finance and the secret plutocratic conspiracy that was enslaving Britain. Jews could not be Englishmen because of their cultural differences. As Chesterton wrote, 'Jews are Jews; and as a logical consequence... they are not Russians or Roumanians or Italians or Frenchmen or Englishmen.' Jews not only exercised 'colossal cosmopolitan financial power... the modern societies they live in also grant them vital forms of national political power', which they acquired and used in secret. For Chesterton, a Jew might 'occupy any political or social position which he can gain in open competition... but ... let there be one simple and sweeping law about Jews... that every Jew must be dressed like an Arab.'[14] As with Mosley and Social Credit, it was difficult to see where anti-capitalism ended and anti-semitism began.

Mussolini's invasion of Abyssinia split the Distributist movement into those who denounced Fascist imperialism and those who considered that Mussolini had been forced into aggression to escape the sinister machinations of international finance. Chesterton, as so often, sympathized with both sides, condemning both Italian imperialism and those 'capitalists who could afford to work behind the backs of their victims by substituting dollars for bullets'. Above all he feared 'the rehabilitation of Capitalism, in spite of the slump...'[15] With his death in 1936, the movement began to disintegrate. *G. K.'s Weekly* was renamed the *Weekly Review* in 1938, and became increasingly sympathetic to fascism as it became more alarmed by Bolshevism. As early as 1936, Gregory Macdonald, who wrote on foreign affairs for the *Weekly*, had argued that 'Russia, with its explicit atheism, has been associated with the implicit atheism of money.'[16] Belloc similarly saw an impending confrontation between Christianity and Bolshevism, the latter inspired by a 'group of men... Cosmopolitan and largely Jewish, with the Jewish intensity of purpose... the Jewish indifference to property and national ideals... there has been much exaggeration of the Jewish element in Bolshevism, but... it colours the whole affair'.[17]

The Spanish Civil War, regarded as a prologue to the war of European Christianity against atheistic Bolshevism-Capitalism, pushed distributism further towards both the right-wing dictatorships of Salazar and Franco, fascism, and even Nazism. In 1937, the *Weekly* proposed an alliance with Hitler.[18] In 1938 it supported the Alien Restriction Bill proposed by Archibald Maule Ramsay, an obsessive pro-Nazi anti-semite and founder of the Right Club, and after his resignation from the BUF A. K. Chesterton became a regular contributor. Obsessed by Bolshevism, distributism became just another small voice amongst the many small voices calling for Fascist reform in Britain and accommodation with fascism abroad. When the Distributist League was closed down in 1940, distributism, as Maurice Reckitt put it, 'sputtered out as a damp squib mid the showy and mechanical fireworks of fascism'.[19]

Social Credit

Social Credit was discovered by Major Clifford Hugh Douglas, a retired army engineer, almost accidentally, during the First World War.[20] The theory shared many features in common with distributism, an outlook that bordered on anarchism, the objective of redistributing wealth, combined with conspiracy theories, hostility to plutocracy and anti-semitism. Social Credit seemed to several perplexed Distributists to overcome the central problem of distributism, the redistribution of actual property, and the overlap in the leading personnel of both movements was extensive. Social Credit, however, had very different origins, and centred around the potential of technology rather than its dangers. Like Mosley, Douglas was struck by the coexistence of immense productive power and widespread poverty and concluded, again like Mosley, that the problem arose from a lack of purchasing power.

Douglas explained his discovery as the 'A + B theorem', in which 'A' represented all payments made to consumers as wages, salaries and dividends, and 'B' other payments such as raw materials, taxes and interest on loans. Whereas the total cost of production was thus 'A + B', the money available to purchase the goods produced remained only 'A'. As Colin Holmes summarized the doctrine, Social Credit 'hinged on the belief that there was a permanent deficiency in consumers' aggregate income compared with the aggregate price of productive output...In the established economic system where there was a constant deficiency between aggregate income and aggregate prices, Douglas argued that the continuance of economic activity depended upon the supply of credit which gave considerable power to financiers', from which Douglas concluded that there was 'a power-seeking conspiracy...a very deeply laid and well considered plot of enslaving the industrial world to German-American-Jewish financiers.'[21]

This was not quite the whole story. Douglas recognized that increasing mechanization meant that more and more time and money was spent producing the machines that would ultimately manufacture the final product. During the period before the product hit the market 'A' payments would still be paid, but because of the time delay there would be a deficiency in the aggregate products available for purchase, a case of 'too much money chasing too few goods'. By the time the final product did appear on the market, much of the money that had gone into the final cost had already been paid as 'A' payments and spent again, so that there would be insufficient money or too many goods. This was the prevailing condition during the interwar depression. Continued consumption depended upon credit to make up the deficiency and irregularity of the money supply, enabling the financiers to tighten their stranglehold on society, industry and government. Yet this arose in the first instance from wrongly attributing to money a real value that it did not possess. According to Douglas, 'money has no reality in itself'. It reflected real wealth but only as a medium of exchange. It could be 'gold, silver, copper, paper, cowrie shells or broken tea cups. The thing which makes it money, no matter of what it is made, is purely psychological...'[22]

By attributing real value to money, finance capitalists thus not only stole 'purchasing power from the individual', they also robbed the people of their birthright, their 'Cultural Heritage', the skills and productive powers developed and handed down by previous generations that enabled modern industry to be as productive as it was.[23] The 'A + B' theorem also implied that since the final selling price 'A + B' included all the costs of production, the consumer had in reality purchased not only the product, but also the means of production considered as part of the 'Cultural Heritage'. Douglas was opposed to nationalization involving compensation, since that merely provided a state guarantee for private economic power. Confiscation on the other hand, was justifiable since society had 'already bought and paid for many times over, the whole of the plant used for manufacturing processes'.[24]

The key to liberation, as Mosley also stressed, was to recover control of credit, either by nationalizing it or neutralizing it. Mosley took the former course, placing credit under the control of the Corporate State through the mechanism of the National Investment Board. The Douglas solution was to neutralize it by distributing it as producers' credits to cover the gap between the initiation of a project and the appearance of the marketable product, and as a 'National Dividend' equivalent to the gap between the aggregate price of goods in the market and the aggregate purchasing power needed to clear them. The National Dividend would be provided as a right of citizenship irrespective of work. In a manner similar to the redistribution of property advocated by the distributists, the National Dividend transcended the existing economic system, offering the prospect of economic independence and an escape from the wage slavery of the capitalist 'servile state', without falling into the alternative trap of monolithic state socialism. Such a distribution of purchasing power was legitimized by the idea of the Cultural Heritage.

To guard against the potentially inflationary impact of thus increasing the money supply, Douglas introduced the concept of the Just Price. The purpose of the Just Price was to ensure that price and purchasing power balanced and the market was cleared. The determination of that price was assumed to be a simple technical problem, and Social Credit in its economic application a simple technical doctrine that had no political allegiance.[25] All that was required was a body of statistical experts, acting as a National Credit Office, to determine the Just Price and thus the National Dividend. The alternative was continued reliance on private credit, ever-increasing indebtedness and enslavement to the banks, and ever-increasing technological unemployment. Although it was not inherent in the 'A + B theorem',[26] Social Credit assumed, like Mosley, that the existing system would eventually collapse.[27] Douglas, in a phrase to achieve far more political notoriety in a later context, mentioned the 'rivers of blood' that would follow if the system remained unaltered.[28]

Social Credit, Distributism and British Fascism

Economic ideas were one of several points of contact between Social Credit and Mosley's fascism, something that was not lost on the critics of both.[29] It was, as one social credit sympathizer in the British Union maintained, 'quite possible to believe in Social Credit and to belong to the British Union'.[30] By the time that Mosley came to formulate his Birmingham resolutions in 1925, the ILP had been considering Social Credit for 4 years, and debating it at the national level for two. Mosley's associate, John Strachey, was, according to Finlay, virtually a Social Crediter[31], and the credit proposals of the Birmingham Resolutions as detailed in Strachey's own *Revolution by Reason* were very similar to the ideas of Social Credit.[32]

More generally, both Mosley's analysis and that of Douglas rejected orthodox liberal capitalist economics in favour of underconsumptionist arguments, drawing attention to the productive potential of modern industry and the paradox of poverty amongst plenty. Distributism, Social Credit and fascism all stressed that true liberty depended upon economic security, which was impossible as long as the economy remained dominated by the power of finance-capitalism. All also slid into anti-semitism from this attack on finance-capitalism through a similar process of guilt by association, stereotyping and the conspiracy theory. In Social Credit thinking, however, the Jews were more the dupes of the financial conspiracy than its main instigators.[33] Both Social Credit and fascism emphasized economic nationalism, which was built into Social Credit theory as the necessary matrix for the expert management of credit, and aggravated by the assumption of an international financial/Jewish conspiracy. But perhaps most significant was the realignment of the fissures in society from the horizontal conflict of classes that characterized the radical left to the vertical antagonism between society and bankers that characterized the Radical Right from social imperialism onwards.

Allowing for internal tensions, there were also significant similarities in the ideal societies envisaged by all three movements, or elements within them. Fascism, no less than distributism or Social Credit, had its Utopian dreams. These were modern, even futuristic, as befitted 'the modern movement' in their architectural vision, their 'motorways' and 'streets in the sky'. But within the BUF as a whole, nostalgia played an important part. The novelist-farmer, Henry Williamson, rejected the city entirely, for from it came only 'big business, fornication and death'. In the nostalgic future, the 'yeoman or small working farmer' was restored, 'the yeoman and peasant and craftsman will again enjoy their ancient status...', and 'thousands have gone back to the land...Farming districts all have their own big schools and nurseries, cinemas and theatres'. Despite the production line technology of Mosley's economic thinking, the schoolteacher, Louise Irvine, still saw in the doctrine of the BUF the message 'small is beautiful'.[34] In nostalgic mode, Fascists echoed the Distributists. After 1945, even Mosley became concerned by the ecological implications of what he called 'surplus growth'.

Ruralism of this kind linked not only the movements of the interwar years to each other, but connected them backwards to the Edwardians, and forward to the National Front and the British National Party. It was a very English and very constant fantasy, an 'imagined community'[35] that achieved 'the subordination of economic to non-economic motives...greater social integration and cultural unity', with or without the vexed aspect of 'more planning and central control'.[36] Within this community, fascism, like Social Credit, envisaged leisure for individual self-development. The Fascist message was nonetheless ascetic and strenuous, at least for its elite figure, 'Fascist Man', stressing 'the spiritual instinct of self-sacrifice', and dedication to a cause 'that transcends self' in a manner similar to the 'political soldiers' of the NF in the 1980s, but was alien to the more relaxed politics of distributism and Social Credit.

Thus, whilst Fascists were to be prepared to 'build up their corporate life with sweat and the agony of labour'[37], Social Credit looked askance at the whole idea of work. Douglas criticized the existing 'world financial system' as a system of constraint, 'a Government based on the theory that men should be made to work...intermixed with the even stronger contention that the end of man is work'. For Social Credit, economic activity was 'simply a functional activity of men and women...therefore economic organisation is most efficient when it most easily and rapidly supplies economic wants without encroaching on other functional activities.'[38] Work, insofar as it was necessary, was a necessary evil, and its necessity was steadily diminishing with the advance of technology. Unemployment in turn became not a problem but an opportunity.

Fascism never escaped either the necessity or the desirability of work, reflecting perhaps Mosley's Labour party credentials. Within the ILP, social crediters confronted the rival, but considerably more conventional, demand of the 'Living Wage' which was similarly underconsumptionist, but solved the problem of the lack of purchasing power by a statutory minimum wage. But it presupposed the need to work. In 1929, the ILP finally came down on the side of the living wage as the means to expand purchasing power.[39] The BUF took the same line in the 1930s. Despite the potential of 'plenty for all', Mosley continued to consider the main social problem to be lack of work, and Raven Thompson in *Blackshirt* demanded 'Work not Maintenance'.[40] In contrast to such statements, Douglas stated bluntly 'that the distribution of cash credits to individuals shall be progressively less dependent upon employment. That is to say that the dividend shall progressively displace the wage and salary'.[41]

Social Credit as Anarchism

Social Credit was at its most radical in its attitude to work. It contradicted not only over a century of internalized industrial discipline, but a central tenet of puritan Christianity. With economic liberty secured by the National Dividend, the Age of Plenty became the Leisure Society,[42] in which the individual could freely realize his potential. 'Systems were made for men, and not men for systems, and the interest of man, which is self-development, is above all systems...we must build up from the individual, not down from the State.'[43] The effect was to make Social Credit wary of all systems and large organizations because of their potential for coercion. Some, at least, of Social Credit's anti-semitism derived from this. Douglas found Disraeli's description of his people as ' "a splendidly organized race"...significant. Organisation has much of the tragedy of life to its debt; and organisation is a Jewish speciality.'[44]

A similar wariness was apparent in Social Credit's attitude to democracy. Representative democracy through regular elections was condemned as 'quinquennial abdications of responsibility'.[45] Democracy, according to Douglas, meant 'the will of the people...not rule by majority.' Because 'the people' did not think, he concluded that whatever mechanism of representation was used, 'we can represent only a desire, not a technique.'[46] Douglas conceded that there was 'the rough machinery of democracy', but had little faith in it.[47] Nor could democracy ever comprehend the technical application of Social Credit. 'A satisfactory modern cooperative State may be broadly expressed as consisting of a functionally aristocratic hierarchy of producers accredited by and serving a democracy of consumers.'

To safeguard the individual, Social Credit took functionalism to its logical limits, dispersing authority as it dispersed credit. 'Any policy which aims at the establishment of a complete sovereignty, whether it be a Kaiser, a State, a Trust or a Trade Union, is a policy of Domination, irrespective of the fine words with which it may be accompanied.'[48] Individuals possessed authority in respect of their function but no more. It reflected once again the emphasis that Social Credit put on technical expertise. The ideology was not simply a-political, for much the same could be said of fascism once it had achieved power, but anti-political. Just as the socialization of credit would secure economic freedom for the individual, so the dispersal of political authority combined with devolved power or direct democracy and small-scale organization would free the individual politically.

The difficulty with what began as a technical, non-political, or anti-political monetary reform, lay precisely in that it was the expression of a philosophical outlook, effectively a life-style philosophy, which, like most 'life-style' philosophies, fell foul of problems of definition. 'Leisure' was the absence of work or of the compulsion to work, the availability of time, but Social Credit did not specify how this time might, or should, be used, except in the extremely vague idea of self-development. Insofar as the question was faced, it revealed the aristocratic association of its anarchism. Social Credit sought to 're-establish man in recognition and enjoyment of his common value, and thereby free his particular value – the aristocratic in him – for unrestrained and healthy expression.'[49] Social Credit resolved the contradiction that lay at the heart of the Fascist combination of the technological state expertly managed and the constancy of struggle by removing the need to struggle.

The Social Credit Movement

Distrust of organization did not prevent attempts to organize the Social Credit movement, but rendered them ineffective. Pressure for organization came in two principal bursts, in 1923 and 1932–35. At the Stanwick Conference, the rejection of its demands for greater organization led the activist Sheffield group to found its own Economic Freedom League (EFL), which produced the paper the *Age of Plenty*. It included Kitson, and a Coventry printer, H. E. B. Ludlam, who took Social Credit into local politics in 1928 by becoming a candidate in the Coventry municipal elections.

By then, Social Credit had attracted the attention of the charismatic leader of the Kibbo Kift, John Hargrave.[50] The Kibbo Kift was an anti-war woodcraft movement founded in 1920. Shortly afterwards Hargrave was expelled from the Scouts, having denounced its militarism too publicly. Baden-Powell in return considered Hargrave 'communistic', and the Kibbo Kift a political organization with 'Bolshevist tendencies... promoting socialist ideas.'[51] Despite this judgement, with its Anglo-Saxon nostalgia, a uniform of Saxon cowls and an idiosyncratic language in which its annual council became the 'Althing' and London HQ the 'Big Smoke Middle Thing',[52] the Kibbo Kift was a 'folkish' movement with some distinctly right-wing tendencies. It rejected the party system and parliamentary democracy, towns and industrialism in favour of a return to the countryside and nature, 'the Green Revolution'. It sought, as the Radical

Right usually sought, 'national' or 'social' regeneration by being 'faithful for the truth, for honour, for the upright life against greed, gain, sordid commercialism and industrial slavery.' Regeneration would come through the leadership of an elite and its individual leader, 'a New Race of Scout Men...a new offshoot of evolution.'[53] In the creation of this elite there was a eugenic strand, at least to the extent that members would not be allowed to marry until they were 'trained'.[54] With a membership around 500,[55] the Kibbo Kift was a very small elite.

Early in 1924, with the Kibbo Kift losing its supporters from the London cooperative movement and no longer expanding, Hargrave discovered economics, possibly under the influence of his fellow folkist, Rolf Gardiner, who had founded the Cambridge Social Credit circle in 1921. Equally, however, he may have been influenced by his connection with John Strachey. During 1924 and 1925, at the cost of some resignations, Hargrave gradually brought his woodcraft movement round to Social Credit ideas and political activism, albeit one operating 'outside the House of Commons'.[56]

In 1926, Hargrave attended the annual conference of the EFL, and in 1928 secured a personal triumph as its principal speaker. His contribution to the otherwise intellectually orientated Social Credit movement was his stress on the need of links with the masses, especially the unemployed, and of discipline. His theory of 'Unarmed Mass Pressure'[57] required a mass movement built up around a disciplined elite corps of perhaps a 1000. In 1929, as Douglas and the quietist section, some 14 groups and 1000 members, sat back to await the coming collapse which would prove their arguments and inaugurate Social Credit policies, Hargrave lost patience, and established the Economic Party from the EFL. The party's principles, according to the Age of Plenty, were that credit power belonged to the country, cash credits should equal the aggregate price of goods on the market, and that the sole function of finance was to facilitate consumption, so that the aggregate production of goods and services would be consumed.[58]

The EFL/Economic party soon disintegrated, with Kitson leaving to found the Monetary Reform Association, and Ludlam gradually drifting towards the BUF. In April 1932, This Prosperity, the journal of the newly formed activist group, The Social Credit Association of Producers, Distributors and Consumers, made its appearance urging the formation of another new political party and direct action through withholding that proportion of taxation that went towards the maintenance of the national debt. It launched the 'Prosperity Campaign' to raise awareness

of Social Credit amongst the electorate. At the same time, the Marquess
of Tavistock formed the National Credit Association (NCA), which in
turn attracted the attention of the West Riding Social Credit Association,
with its ironically named journal, *The Leadswinger*. Douglas, however, still
suspicious of organization and action, reacted against these developments and established the Social Credit Secretariat, a purely advisory
body, as the orthodox, quietist alternative. It nevertheless cooperated
closely with the 'Prosperity Campaign'.[59]

Meanwhile, in militant Coventry, George Hickling set about following
Hargrave's precepts by organizing the unemployed into the 'Crusader
legion' with an elite corps, the Iron Guard, which, at Hargrave's insistence, adopted the Green Shirt uniform in 1931. As a result of reorganization in 1931, the Kibbo Kift and the Greenshirted Legion became
effectively a single entity. The latter lost its arcane language, the
'Althing' became no more than an annual Assembly, the 'Tallykeeper' a
General Treasurer, and the 'Bok-hords' the library. The combined unit,
with its new London HQ was re-titled the Green Shirts Movement for
Social Credit. It was, according to Hargrave in 1932 'the only organized
bulwark against Bolshevism on the one hand and Fascism on the
other.'[60]

In the maelstrom of extremist politics in the interwar years, the
Greenshirts, like other movements, held their marches with banners and
drums, spoke at street corners and sold their newspapers. Hargrave gave
specific instructions that members should not become involved in disor-
der, nor obstruct the police. It was, as Mark Drakeford has observed, a
'curious duality... a self-avowed revolutionary movement, dedicated to
the overthrow of parliamentary democracy by mass pressure on the
streets, while yet determined to maintain its respectability',[61] but it was a
duality not uncommon on the Radical Right. The Greenshirts nevertheless fought both Communists and Fascists, not least because the
Communists regarded the movement as Fascist and attacked accordingly.

Yet the movement also welcomed the marches of the unemployed into
London, supported their rallies, and cooperated with the Communists in
the anti-fascist struggle in east London.[62] In common with similar movements, the Greenshirts demanded complete commitment. In Bradford,
Greenshirt activities took up six nights a week, which included two of drill
and two of street patrols. Its newspaper, *Attack*, claimed 7000 members at
the movement's peak, but again like similar movements, the membership
was unstable, with branches going from claims of 2000–3000 members to
complete collapse in a matter of weeks.[63] It always suffered from financial

problems, and *Attack* often made a loss because the branches retained the proceeds from sales to pay their own expenses.

The movement grew rapidly between 1933 and 1935, and in 1935 became the Social Credit party of Great Britain, participated in the wider electoral campaign, and ran one candidate, Wilford Townend, in South Leeds, where he gained 11 per cent of the votes.[64] The decision to take part in the political activity of a general election was not limited to the Greenshirt militants, but reflected a more general shift towards action within Social Credit, inspired in part by the electoral success of the Social Credit party in Alberta. Some reunification took place amongst the various organizations between 1933 and 1935. In 1933, the NCA and the 'Prosperity Campaign' merged in support of 'a nationwide coordinated policy of action' and in 1935 the NCA merged with the Secretariat.

The electoral strategy was to threaten to withhold votes from candidates who refused to pledge themselves to support the National Dividend. The two candidates, H. G. Bell at Erdington and Reginald Kenny at North Bradford who stood in addition to the Social Credit party's candidate in South Leeds, ran simply as National Dividend candidates. Beyond the Greenshirts, however, hesitancy characterized the entire operation. Placing the campaign in the hands of the Secretariat provoked a revolt against centralization and the formation of the League to Abolish Poverty in April 1934, with Tavistock as president and the almost identical aim of creating an organization in each constituency to enrol voters pledged to vote for the National Dividend.

After the election, the Social Credit movement disintegrated rapidly. The Greenshirts were hit hard by the Public Order Act of 1936 and turned to stunts such as painting green slogans on the Bank of England in pursuit of publicity. Relations between the various wings of the movement deteriorated to the point where, in 1937, the Greenshirts broke up a Social Credit meeting.[65] The action aggravated growing doubts about Hargrave's authoritarian leadership. In 1936, a Conference at York to which Douglas was hostile split from both the Secretariat and the Social Credit party. It led in 1938 to the establishment of a Social Credit Coordinating Committee, but its aim was limited to providing a focus for the surviving local groups. In the same year, the Secretariat itself quarrelled with Douglas who then established his own rival secretariat and journal. In the spring of 1939, the original Secretariat collapsed and the Coordinating Committee bought up its assets. Hargrave finally closed down the Greenshirts in 1951; the Social Credit movement continues to campaign for its cause.

Peace-Loving Patriots

1936 was not quite the end of Social Credit as an influence within the Radical Right. In May 1939, Tavistock formed the British People's Party (BPP) and became its president, with John Beckett, formerly of the BUF, as secretary, and Ben Greene as Treasurer. Tavistock himself had written in support of autarky for Orage's *New English Weekly* (NEW) in the early 1930s when the paper was briefly impressed by Hitler's new beginning in Germany. By April 1933 the NEW had revised its views, concluding that 'nothing distinguishes the new German dictatorship from the dictatorship of Central Banks in general'. Tavistock, who claimed to have introduced Hitler to Social Credit, remained more loyal to Hitler than to the paper.[66] In 1938 he denounced it for its anti-German stance, arguing that Hitler was 'supported with enthusiasm by large sections of the population because he gave German youth faith and hope in the future, restored their self-respect and did much to reduce unemployment', and had no expansionist ambitions against his non-German neighbours.[67]

The BPP had a reforming, if vague, domestic programme that included the 'right to security and social justice', the 'security of labour in its industrial organisation' and 'the abolition of all class differences'. There was a hint at a Social Credit implementation of these objectives by 'the abolition of a financial system based upon usury which perpetuates social and economic injustice', combined with 'safeguarding the employment and integrity of the British people against alien influence and infiltration'. But coming in the aftermath of Hitler's occupation of Czechoslovakia in March 1939, the BPP was primarily an anti-war organization. Its declared foreign policy aim, 'the abolition of all military alliances and political and economic commitments which may involve this country in wars which in no way affect the security and national independence of our peoples'[68] was, like that of the BUF, isolationist. In practice, given its background and membership, it was, as Linehan observes a 'pro-Nazi, fascist' group.[69] Its leader, Tavistock, was so concerned to avoid war that even after the war had begun, he made contact with the German embassy in Dublin and thought he had secured peace terms, but ultimately to no avail.

Until the end of 1937, Nazi Germany had appealed to a wide variety of opinion well beyond the Far Right. It offered, or appeared to offer, an example of national regeneration that was not only material, but more importantly 'spiritual', in particular the restoration of national pride. This was visible on many fronts, from the unilateral reoccupation of the

Rhineland, regarded by many as a necessary correction of the Versailles treaty, to German youth movements and the cult of fresh air and green fields to offset the ravages of urban life. In Nazi Germany the Right saw the selflessness, duty and discipline that were, it believed, so much needed in degenerate Britain. The obverse of this, the attack on the decadence and corruption of Weimar, the rejection of jazz, Negro music and American popular culture, the hounding of 'inverts' (i.e. homosexuals) in favour of the restoration of morality, clean living and family values met with similar approval.

Of greater significance than its domestic lessons, however, was the role of Nazi Germany as a bulwark against Bolshevism. The Distributists were but one example of this. Approval of Germany in this role rose as the image of France fell. The formation of the Popular Front in France and the signing of the Franco–Soviet pact in 1936 seemed to indicate that France might well drag Britain into war on behalf of, rather than against, Bolshevism. The success of the Olympics and the Nuremberg rally, to which selected British guests had been invited and given privileged treatment, and some moderation of domestic repression, gave Germany a degree of respectability. Hitler's demand for the return of the former German colonies caused some conflict within the Right between its admiration for Nazi Germany and its patriotic British imperialism, but had little influence on the general wish for rapprochement. The Anglo–German Fellowship, aimed at those thought influential in Britain, the *Anglo–German Review*, edited by C. E. Carroll, and the Link, the brainchild of Admiral Sir Barry Domvile, were all established during 1935–37.

But by the end of 1937 the tide that had been flowing towards Germany was slowly beginning to turn. The German reunification with Austria, the 'Anschluss' of March 1938, whilst it could be easily dismissed as another rectification of the Versailles settlement, also revealed Hitler's willingness to use force. Nazi Germany was emerging as a mixed blessing; a bulwark against the Communist threat it was also an increasing threat itself.[70] In November 1938, the 'Kristallnacht' pogrom against Jews also indicated that the more moderate interlude in Nazi domestic policy was at an end. Nevertheless, the Munich agreement between Chamberlain and Hitler was popular. As Bruce Lockhart put it, 'Was Europe to be plunged into war in order to keep 3,000,000 Germans in and under Czechoslovakia against their will?'[71] Hitler's occupation of the rump of Czechoslovakia in March 1939 removed most remaining illusions. Those that survived beyond March 1939, largely because of the fear of communism, were destroyed by the Nazi–Soviet pact of August 1939.[72]

After March 1939, there remained only the diehard Right and a few doctrinaire pacifists willing to pursue rapprochement. Those that did so were the obvious groups, the IFL, the BUF, the secessionists of 1937 in the NSL, the English Array and the New Pioneer Group, both centred around Lord Lymington, the Link, the BPP and the Right Club which was formed in May 1939 by Captain Archibald Maule Ramsay.[73] The motivation for continuing to seek peace with Germany was varied. There was still some sympathy with the achievements of Nazism in regenerating German society; fear of communism remained strong, as did imperial isolationism on the basis that there was no necessary conflict of interest between a Germany seeking expansion to the east and the security of the British empire, a view to which both Mosley and Domvile subscribed.[74]

Behind such attitudes lay the persistence of anti-semitism, and in particular the belief in the international Jewish conspiracy and its presumed connection with both international finance and international communism. Mosley's view in 1938 that 'Germany...has offended this world power by summary dealing with the Jewish masters of usury. So every force of the money power throughout the world has been mobilized to crush them, and that power does not stop short of payment for its vendetta in British blood'[75] was still common on the Right. Ramsay, who had only that year discovered that the much hated Bolshevism was really Jewish, described the 'main object of the Right Club' as 'to oppose and expose the activities of Organised Jewry, in the light of the evidence which came into my possession in 1938... Our hope was to avert war, which we considered to be mainly the work of Jewish intrigue centred on New York.'[76]

Contemporaries were also well aware of the potentially disastrous effects of another major war upon Europe and upon the British empire. 'War' according to the Duke of Windsor at the time of Munich, 'would have destroyed both the democracies and the dictatorships, and the victory would have gone only to communism'.[77] Lymington, then busy with his English Array, came to the same conclusion: 'War between ourselves and Germany with a final victory for ourselves can only mean Bolshevism in both countries and the loss of everything both countries stand for apart from political creeds.'[78]

With the outbreak of war, some of the extremist pro-German groups like the Nordic League and the Link closed themselves down, or changed their name. The IFL became the Angles Circle thereby avoiding an overt Fascist connection. However, the significance of this was limited. The IFL continued to meet under its new identity, whilst leading figures in the Nordic League still met privately. Moreover other groups with similar pro-Nazi, or at least pro-peace and anti-semitic, views like the BPP and the BUF continued to function and served as alternative rallying points. At its meeting of 11 September when it decided to disband, the members of the Nordic league were advised to join the BUF.[79] The relatively small size of the various right-wing organizations, and their frequently overlapping membership also facilitated re-grouping at this moment of desperation. The membership of the BPP, for example, if not a complete roll-call of those Linehan calls 'maverick fascists, fanatical anti-semites, fascist fellow-travellers and naïve pacifists',[80] nevertheless included a large number of the usual suspects. John Beckett's position thus evolved from being, like Mosley, a member of the ILP to a Labour MP[81] via the BUF and the National Socialist League to the BPP. Ben Greene also migrated from the ILP, as did John Scanlon who, like Beckett had also been a member of the BUF. Other members included Viscount Lymington, from the English Mistery, the English Array and the New Pioneer Group, Anthony Ludovici whose right-wing lineage stretched back through the English Mistery to the Order of the Red Rose and who was also associated with the New Pioneer Group, the Social Crediter Philip Mairet, and Gordon Canning from the BUF.[82]

Lymington's English Array and New Pioneer Group were linked to the NSL through the British Council against European Commitments formed at the time of the Czechoslovakian crisis,[83] and in terms of personnel through Beckett, and for a short time, Joyce. Other members of the New Pioneer Group included A. K. Chesterton from the BUF, H. T. 'Bertie' Mills of the IFL and another of Beckett's mushroom organizations, the People's Campaign Against War and Usury,[84] John Scanlon, and Major-General J. F. C. Fuller, another of the BUF recruits, as well as the eccentric anti-semite, George Lane-Fox Pitt Rivers.[85] Ramsay's Nordic League included another veteran, Brigadier-General Blakeney of the IFL and the British Fascisti, whilst the Right Club included the ubiquitous William Joyce.[86] The British Council for Christian Settlement in Europe included ex-members of the BUF, the Link and the Nordic League, as well as current members of the still active BPP.[87]

The closure or otherwise of particular organizations therefore made little difference to the cohesion of various elements of the Right, whilst the threat and then outbreak of war put pressure on them to sink their various factional differences and cooperate in the immediate cause of rapprochement with Germany. In late July 1939, before the outbreak of war and the advice to Nordic League members to join the BUF, Mosley, Ramsay and Domvile attended the same dinner.[88] By mid-September, Special Branch believed that Mosley and Ramsay had agreed a common approach to the issue of war,[89] and between October and December 1939 there were regular fortnightly meetings of leading figures from the BUF, the Link, the BPP, the New Pioneer Group, the Right Club and the Nordic League.[90]

Even under the pressure of war, however, it seems these disparate individuals could not cooperate. Relations between Mosley and Ramsay had cooled by the turn of the year, and Mosley roundly denounced the ex-Nordic League members. The number of meetings declined sharply in 1940. One early in February convened by Domvile and including Mosley and Francis-Hawkins from the BUF but apparently not Ramsay, met to decide to fight the Silvertown and North East Leeds by-elections, which provided another area of cooperation albeit with dismal results[91], and Tavistock's mission to Dublin occasioned a brief revival of activity in March. By this time, however, government pressure was beginning to tell as successive individuals were gradually interned. Even before the outbreak of war, William Joyce and Margaret Bothamley had fled to Germany, the former to launch a new career as the Nazi propagandist, 'Lord Haw Haw'. The private meetings of the officially disbanded Nordic League held in Oliver Gilbert's house, ended with his internment on 22 September.[92]

Internment was initially restrained by the government's desire not to interfere too greatly with individual liberty. This ended with the Nazi sweep across Europe in April–May 1940 that led to Churchill becoming prime minister on 10 May. Any resistance to widescale internment was removed by the discovery of a threat to national security emanating from the connection between Anna Wolkoff of the Right Club, Tyler Kent of the American embassy, and the Italian embassy. As part of this connection, Ramsay had been shown the secret and potentially damaging correspondence between Roosevelt and Churchill. Tyler Kent was arrested in possession of incriminating documents on 20 May. Initially, it was decided to arrest only 25–30 leading members of the BUF as well as the Right Club figures, but ultimately, the final count was closer to 750.[93] Leading Fascists and German sympathizers were rounded up, including Mosley, Domvile and Ramsay, though Lymington, despite being denounced by his neighbours,[94] and Tavistock were left at liberty. The Right had been expecting this for some time. Leese evaded capture from May until November 1940[95], 'Jock' Houston of the BUF for four months[96], whilst Domvile, who did not hide himself, successfully hid his all too revealing diary. The BUF itself was proscribed on 10 July 1940, effectively bringing an end to the operations and aspirations of the interwar Radical Right.

Chapter 5: The Union Movement and the National Front

Many of the leading figures of the pre-war Radical Right were released during 1943–44 with their world-view unchanged. The post-war impotence of Europe in the new world of superpowers and the westward expansion of Soviet communism appeared to confirm the pre-war Right's predictions. Domvile's belief in the international conspiracy of Jews and Freemasonry, 'Judmas', was intensified by his internment; Ramsay raised the issue of the conspiracy almost immediately upon his release; well before the end of the war, Leese was again promulgating his own brand of racial fascism; the Britons continued to publish, and popular anti-semitism erupted again in widespread rioting in 1947.[1]

Nevertheless, it was a new world into which they emerged. By 1945, Keynes's ideas had become the new orthodoxy and the Labour government was committed to state intervention. It was not the corporate state, but it undermined Mosley's criticism of an inert 'old gang', and obscured the distinctiveness of his economic policies. The greatest problem, however, for all sections of the Radical Right which could be indiscriminately, and often inaccurately, labelled 'Fascist', was the legacy of the struggle against fascism and the revelation of Nazi atrocities. Belief in heroic resistance to an evil regime in a just war for liberty against tyranny reinforced Britain's self-image as the bulwark of liberal democracy.

Throughout the second half of the twentieth century, the Radical Right faced the difficulty of either dissociating itself from, or rehabilitating, Nazism. One consequence was the denial of Nazi atrocities and in particular the 'Holocaust'. Another was the continued and aggravated isolation of the more extreme sections of the Radical Right from the mass of British opinion. For those who followed in the tradition of Arnold Leese and biological racism, Hitler became a hero-martyr. Neo-nazism became in consequence less British and more Aryan and Northern European. Purely British nationalism, although it continued to exist on the Radical Right, was progressively weakened by the loss of empire. With it went that expansive confidence that had been a feature of social imperialism. In the second half of the century, particularly as the empire came to Britain in the form of coloured immigration, the Radical Right became ever more defensive.

European Socialism

In 1945, the immediate problem was rehabilitation. Leese maintained what was, despite the formation of the National Workers Movement, virtually a one-man agitation, and the BPP continued in existence under the protective patronage of the Duke of Bedford[2], but it was the Mosleyites who had the residual supporters and organizations.[3] By 1947, the most significant of these was Jeffrey Hamm's League of Ex-Servicemen and Women which held regular meetings of 2000–3000 people in north-east London. Mosley's own cautious re-entry into politics was the publication in 1946 of *My Answer*, a reprint of *Tomorrow We Live*, with a new introduction that justified the pre-war contention that 'to fight Germany where no British interest was involved would be to create a Communist danger to threaten every British interest.'[4] During 1946–47 Mosley published a monthly newsletter which helped keep his reduced band of supporters together, and in October 1947 a major statement of his post-war philosophy, *The Alternative*. Like *The Greater Britain* in 1932, *The Alternative* was intended to provide the rationale for a new political movement suited to Britain's post-war situation. The Union Movement was formally launched in February 1948.

The major innovation in Mosley's programme was the substitution of Europe for Britain as the nation, and Europe–Africa for the empire. Europe – A Nation, by which Mosley meant 'the complete integration of the European peoples',[5] rested on the contention that a 'common culture would make possible voluntary political and economic union',[6] and that such a union would ultimately generate a 'nationalist' European state. 'No lesser degree of union than that of an integral nation can give the will and power to act on the grand scale ... No lesser space than all of Europe, and the overseas possessions of Europe, in a common pool can given the room within which to act effectively.' With unity, Europe would become 'a third force' to compete with America and Russia.[7] Mosley outlined the dream in November 1947: 'If they linked the Union of Europe with the development of Africa in a new system of two continents, they would build a civilization which surpassed, and a force which equalled any power in the world... From that union would be born a civilization of continuing creation and ever-unfolding beauty that would withstand the tests of time.'[8] Such an ideal would inspire the regeneration, as much moral as social, political or economic, that Mosley always believed was necessary.

The first step, announced by Mosley in October 1948, was the election of a European Assembly. Nominally, within the new European state, the European government could be dismissed by the European parliament, basic rights would be preserved, and opposition permitted.[9] But as in his pre-war Fascist plans, Mosley's intention was still strong government, 'armed with the power to act by the free vote of the people... within the limits so prescribed, the executive shall have a free hand to carry out the mandate conferred by the people's vote.' Opposition parties could criticize, and contest elections, 'but they will not be able by obstruction to impede the work of an elected government and thus to thwart the people's will.'[10]

Europe–Africa was a similar reworking of pre-war ideas. As an area large enough to provide its own raw materials and markets, it could be insulated from 'the chaos of world competition', and survive as a high-wage economy in a low-wage world. Within the self-sufficient insulated area the central problem was that of bringing supply and demand into balance, 'to equate production and consumption by raising the standard of life equally through comparable industries as science increases the power to produce'. But Mosley's insistence that all reward should be 'for work, skill and service and for that alone',[11] conflicted with 'the planned and regulated raising of wages over the whole field of industry' required to maintain consumption as production increased.[12] Moreover, in recognizing that technology allowed ever-increasing production with ever-decreasing manpower, he was also forced to consider the problem of 'surplus growth'. By 1970 he had become 'green' to the point of admitting that some labour should be employed in stopping pollution.[13] Despite the dynamism generated by technology and strong government, Mosley's new system veered towards the static.

In his post-war plans, Mosley also abandoned the corporate state as excessively bureaucratic, preferring government leadership to state planning. In place of the corporate state he substituted the Social Credit sounding 'wage-price mechanism', in practice a prices and incomes policy to bring production and consumption into balance. It was still government by experts, and in the hands of his projected strong government the mechanism was still a powerful weapon of economic, and potentially of political, control. Through 'definite, conscious and deliberate economic leadership', the government could 'guide the industrial state in the necessary degree and in the desired direction by fixing wages in comparable fields of industry', and thus 'shape' the economy overall. It would 'decide which industries continued and which ceased to exist... The flow of labour could be controlled as directly as the flow of water by differential levels...It is the most potent instrument for shaping the future development of industry which could be devised.'[14] 'Leadership' and 'guidance' came very close to planning in disguise.

'European Socialism', as Mosley termed his new economic system was more than 'simply...a synthesis between private enterprise and syndicalism'.[15] It involved 'devising a natural transition from one to the other...the development of new enterprise is best done by an unfettered private enterprise', but when 'the concern becomes too big for any individual management, we prefer workers' ownership to state ownership.'[16] In competition, private and syndicalized industries would prevent the latter having the power to 'hold the community up to ransom...without the continual interference of the state.'[17] The exceptions were those industries which were 'natural monopolies, for example the railways', where competition would not fix prices. There, 'the state must surely fix both the price charged and the wage paid in the industry...but over the whole field of industry, it should not normally be necessary for the state to interfere so intimately...'[18]

Mosley continually modified the details of 'European Socialism', and made a virtue of the fact that it was 'a dynamic and not a static creed'. The details were irrelevant because Mosley's ideology, pre-war and post-war, functioned within the theory of creative evolution. 'European Socialism' was an organic system, evolving in 'accord with nature which is ever evolving and developing to higher forms'.[19] The introduction of profit to induce the 'creative individual' to start new enterprises was a compromise which 'recognized the basic fact that the pure ideal of service is only for a dedicated elite'.[20] The 'creative individual' nevertheless played a crucial role in 'creative evolution'. 'The creative spirit, whether he be scientist, technician, individual pioneer or the deviser of new forms of service to the people which enrich or illumine daily life, is the key of our system because he is the key to higher forms of life.' Those higher forms, were characterized by their commitment to service, duty and sacrifice, men 'ready to step into greatness without persuasion. Those few are the leaders of mankind'.[21] The 'creative individual' was Fascist man reincarnated.

There were two complementary processes in the creation of Europe— A Nation. The first was 'a revolution of the spirit', the emergence of a 'a self-proved elite, moved by an idea and not by the present materialism… the revolution in ideas is the premise of all achievement'. The second, in which Mosley still believed, was 'the manifest breakdown of the present system which will open the way to their ideas'.[22] Mosley remained scathing in his criticism of the British ruling establishment. 'A great country does not fall so far and so fast', he wrote in 1954, 'unless a deep moral rot has first occurred.'[23] Only the pressure of events would compel 'men of the old world', men of 'small minds', to follow in the wake of the revolutionary elite. 'Ideas so great and so decisive as the union of Europe are only fully implemented with the aid of some compulsion from events.'[24] But under those circumstances, 'European Socialism' would come into its own. 'The combination of an attack which can roll up the left flank of labour by its syndicalism, with an attack which can roll up the right flank of conservatism by its support of the creative individual and the freeing of his enterprise… can capture the main position of the present system in classic fashion, as its centre collapses through an internal disintegration which is already well advanced.'[25]

The Union Movement

Mosley might claim that he offered 'a synthesis of the best elements of fascism and of the old democracy',[26] but he was remembered for his fascism and associated with treason. The Union Movement relied almost entirely on remnants of Mosley's old guard of the 1930s. The campaign for Europe–A Nation began in February 1948. It was particularly poor timing since the Fascist revival had peaked in 1947 and from mid-1948 fascism was in retreat, declining rapidly in 1949.[27] Moreover, idealism was rapidly crushed beneath the weight of the past. Race and anti-semitism were prominent issues and street violence continued between Mosley's followers and Jewish and left-wing organizations. Mosley himself descended to simple abuse, telling the movement's conference in 1949 that European investments in Africa should not be threatened by African governments of witch doctors and ju-ju men.[28]

Such comments revealed the racism underlying Europe–A Nation and Europe-Africa.[29] Africa would receive technical assistance, but not financial aid, from Europe in opening up the 'Dark Continent'. From European energy 'directed to win wealth from the richest Continent on Earth...a new civilization will be born', but that civilization would be white and European. At the base of Europe–Africa lay absolute apartheid along lines already familiar before 1914, a division of the continent on the basis of climate, effectively altitude, in which the white areas would be in the south and east. Mosley differentiated this 'real separation of the two peoples into two nations which enjoy equal opportunity and status' from 'the bogus apartheid which seeks to keep the Negro within white territory but segregated into black ghettoes which are reserves of sweated labour...'.[30] Nevertheless, it was clear who provided the direction and received the benefits. 'Our economic problems', he thus observed, 'could be solved by Negro labour under white direction in Africa.'[31]

His view of multiracialism as economic exploitation by finance capitalism was easily transferable from Africa to Britain. Coloured immigration from the late 1940s provided the Radical Right, including the Union Movement, with a new form of a traditional issue. But condemnation of the 'invasion' and allegations of dope peddling, molestation of white women and black crime added nothing to the litany of accusations traditionally levelled against aliens. Mosley's solution was to stop immigration by removing the right of free entry that commonwealth citizens enjoyed, together with investment in the West Indies and guaranteed markets to induce immigrants to return.

From 1951, when he went to live abroad, Mosley's direct involvement in British politics was intermittent. He returned in 1956 to address his first major meeting for 5 years, and in 1959 stood for election in North Kensington. This was opportunistic, taking advantage of the race rioting that had broken out in 1958 in Notting Hill. The campaign exposed the dualism that afflicted Mosley and the Radical Right in general, high ideals on the one hand, racist taunts and street violence on the other. But in focusing on immigration and linking it to jobs and housing, Mosley, the prophet of technology and the age of plenty, exploited the politics of scarcity.

Mosley gained fewer than 3,000 votes, 8 per cent of the total, and for the first time in his career lost his deposit. The Union Movement continued to campaign into the 1960s, and the campaigns continued to be marked by outbreaks of violence. It peaked in the early 1960s with some 1,500 members and 10,000–15,000 sympathizers.[32] Mosley himself stood again in Shoreditch in 1966, but gained only 1,600 votes (4.1 per cent), which led to his retirement from active politics. With his departure the Radical Right lost much of its radical dynamism, at least until the 1980s. Mosley presented a detailed programme for economic, social and political regeneration in the social imperialist tradition that went far beyond anything attempted by his contemporaries. Like social imperialism, his aspirations rested on a particular view of the British race and its leading role in western civilization, but his usually cultural conception of race avoided the determinism of biological definitions. Nevertheless, the immediate future lay with the biological racists.

Racism: the Leese Tradition

Other organizations as well as the Union Movement were active in Notting Hill and similar areas of immigrant settlement. In 1954, Mosley's former colleague in the BUF, A. K. Chesterton, formed the League of Empire Loyalists (LEL). Chesterton had not been interned, but fought with the British army in Africa, avoiding the taint that hung over former members of the BUF. His loyalty to the empire and his strong anti-communism were close to the beliefs of right-wing Conservatism, and in the consensus politics of the 1950s to mid-1970s, the LEL filled a void on the Far Right on issues such as immigration and the abandonment of empire. But there was another side to Chesterton's political outlook, an intense belief in conspiratorial anti-semitism and international finance that placed the LEL far more in the tradition of Nesta Webster, Arnold Leese and the IFL, and gave it a distinctly anti-capitalist and anti-American tinge to accompany the anti-communism. The LEL thus attracted not only the 'respectable' imperialist Right, but a range of white supremacists, anti-semitic conspiracy theorists and neo-nazis.

The LEL, which had some 3000 members at the time of the 1958 riots, but had declined to 300 by 1961,[33] served as a training ground for the next generation of the Radical Right. Its respectability and elitism were nonetheless frustrating for those who sought a mass movement. Colin Jordan, who became Arnold Leese's political heir, left the LEL in 1956 to form the White Defence League (WDL), organized from the house formerly owned by Arnold Leese. In what was a synopsis of anti-immigrant allegations, Jordan claimed 'The National Assistance Board pays children's allowances to the blacks for the coffee coloured monstrosities they father... Material rewards are given to enable semi-savages to mate with the women of one of the leading civilized nations of the world.'[34]

But behind coloured immigration lay the traditional enemy, the international Jewish conspiracy. Coloured immigration was just another ploy to dilute the British race through mixed marriages, resulting in degeneration that would make it easier to control and exploit. In 1960, the WDL merged with the National Labour Party (NLP), formed by John Tyndall and John Bean in 1957, to become the first British National Party, with Jordan as the national organizer, Andrew Fountaine, a Norfolk landowner who in 1958 had founded a short-lived NF, as president, Mrs Arnold Leese as vice-president and Bean as the editor of *Combat*, the journal inherited from the NLP. The BNP was an explicitly Nordic folk-racist organization dedicated to delivering England from 'the domination of the international Jewish-controlled money-lending system and preservation of our Northern European folk', by permitting only northern European immigration and repatriating alien immigrants.[35] Its active membership was about 350.

Early in 1962, disagreement between the more openly nazi Jordan and Tyndall and the more cautious Fountaine and Bean led to a split in the already small BNP. Fountaine and Bean retained the BNP title and its journal, *Combat*, whilst Jordan and Tyndall formed the National Socialist Movement (NSM), in which Martin Webster was leader of the London A section. In Jordan's words 'the light which Hitler lit is burning… National Socialism in coming back'.[36] The NSM lost little time in acquiring notoriety. At a rally in Trafalgar Square on 1 July 1962, Jordan declared: 'Hitler was right… our real enemies, the people we should have fought, were not Hitler and the National Socialists of Germany, but world Jewry and its associates in this country.' To this Tyndall added: 'in our democratic society the Jew is like a poisonous maggot feeding off a body in an advanced state of decay'. Both were sentenced to short prison terms for 'insulting words likely to cause a breach of the peace.'[37]

There were now two distinct elements in the racial politics of the Radical Right, an openly anti-semitic NSM, and nativist hostility to coloured immigration. The first attracted the attention of anti-Fascist and Jewish defence organizations such as Yellow Star and the 62 Group, and the police who were particularly concerned about the paramilitary activities of Tyndall's uniformed 'Spearhead' group. International connections also drew attention to what appeared to be the re-emergence of nazism. The NSM announced a summer conference to be attended by the American nazi leader, Lincoln Rockwell. From this emerged the World Union of National Socialists. It sought to unite 'all white people in a (National Socialist) world order with complete racial apartheid', to 'protect and promote the Aryan race and its Western Civilization' throughout the world irrespective of nationality, and to 'find and accomplish on a world-wide scale a just and final settlement of the Jewish problem.' Only organizations and individuals that acknowledged 'the spiritual leadership of Adolf Hitler' could become members.[38] Colin Jordan was elected world Fuhrer. In August, police raids on his home and on the NSM offices in Notting Hill found knives, pistols, uniforms, an assortment of Nazi flags and paraphernalia and five cans of weedkiller, on one of which the word 'Jewkiller' had been substituted.

By 1964, disagreement between Tyndall and Jordan over the openly nazi image of the NSM, aggravated by personal rivalry for the elegant heiress, Francoise Dior, culminated in another split, leaving Jordan with the lady, the NSM and Arnold Leese House, whilst Tyndall and Webster seceded to form the Greater Britain Movement. Its object was to protect 'British blood' by legislation against the marriage of Britons and non-Aryans and 'medical measures...to prevent procreation on the part of all who have hereditary defects, either racial, mental or physical'. In its three-year existence, the GBM had a maximum of 138 members.[39] Although its significance was less apparent at the time, the split in the NSM also revealed differences in outlook within even neo-nazi racism that were to recur in the future. Jordan's racism was 'international' in that its core was the Aryan race in northern Europe. Tyndall thought more traditionally in terms of British nationalism, the British race and the British empire, unwilling, in Jordan's view 'to recognize the call of race beyond British frontiers'.[40]

Whilst the national socialists were strutting their stuff, popular anti-immigration feeling continued to grow. Immigrants were establishing their own communities and transforming areas, to the anger of the local white residents who responded with residents associations. In 2 areas in particular, Southall and Smethwick, local protest made a rapid impact on national politics. In the 1963 local elections in Southall, 2 BNP candidates gained 27.5 per cent and 13.5 per cent of the vote, the former finishing ahead of the Conservative. As a result, Bean contested Southall in the 1964 general election, winning 9 per cent of the vote on the anti-immigrant issue. In Smethwick, the result was even more dramatic when Peter Griffiths, a hitherto unknown Tory, defeated Patrick Gordon-Walker, the prospective foreign secretary in the incoming Labour government. Griffiths denied all responsibility for the notorious leaflet, 'If you want a nigger for a neighbour, vote Labour', but it indicated the central issue just as the vote reflected local feeling.[41]

Immigration created a mushroom growth of such associations. They had varying degrees of contact with the major political parties, particularly local Conservative branches, and offered some opportunities to the Right, as in Southall and Smethwick. Many of these local groups were brought together by the Racial Preservation Society (RPS), which coordinated their activities and sought to play a wider political role. Nevertheless, the surprise results of 1964 could not be sustained. The introduction of tougher immigration controls accompanied by race relations legislation seemed to reassure public opinion. In the general election of 1966, Griffiths lost Smethwick and Bean's vote fell in Southall. Abroad, white Rhodesia's unilateral declaration of independence in 1965 produced protests, but not mass revulsion against the government's coercive reaction, or sympathy with the struggles of the British race overseas.

The Formation of the National Front

For Tyndall, the solution to the continuing failure to make a significant political breakthrough lay in unity, which he advocated in his increasingly influential paper, *Spearhead*. In March 1965, he authorized GBM members to cooperate with other groups, and a year later was urging unity even if he personally was excluded from any new grouping. The drive to unity coincided with an apparent change in Tyndall's political beliefs. In 1961, he had written *The Authoritarian State*, which included the classic Fascist formula of a corporate state elected on an occupational franchise regulating private enterprise in the national interest. It was strongly anti-democratic, blaming democracy for allowing 'droves of dark-skinned sub-racials into our country', a process exploited by Jews 'to propagate the lie of racial equality...with the ultimate result of inter-marriage and race-degeneration.' Tyndall proposed 'the honest reality of freedom, i.e. Freedom for those fit to use it and a curb on those who are not' and rule by 'a political elite'.[42]

But in 1966 in an influential booklet, *Six Principles of British Nationalism*, reissued by Aryan Unity because it 'still contains the seeds which contain the roots of our basic ideology', Tyndall proclaimed a guarded belief in democracy. Nationalists still sought strong government 'for a sufficient period of time to attend to vital tasks uninterrupted', but nevertheless a Government 'that acts within the democratic terms on which it had been elected'. He attributed the faults of the present system to poor leadership, 'archaic political institutions' and 'the madness of liberalism and internationalism'. Poor leadership had led to the loss of empire, and it was the recreation of a more equal empire of Britain and the white dominions that offered Britain the chance of recovery. Like Chamberlain and Mosley, Tyndall believed that the future lay in large states. 'In the boundless lands of Empire and Commonwealth lie all the ingredients of modern power, wanting only for a determined national policy aiming at their full coordination and development...' Britain's surplus population could be 're-settled in the great spaces of the Dominions' to create 'a civilization that could surpass in its splendour anything yet achieved by man', militarily independent and able 'to pursue an entirely British destiny'.

This white British Commonwealth would be a protected self-sufficient economic system, for the usual reasons: to avoid competition with low-wage economies, and to escape the dangers of 'international finance' with its 'sinister designs which are likely to place total world control in the hands of a few ruthless financial operators'. In a 'united Commonwealth bound together by the ethnic unity of the peoples of British stock... Industry could produce for an assured market the expansion of which would be guaranteed. Primary products would be in assured supply. The planning so much desired by Socialists would be possible', yet so too would be 'the enterprise that is the cornerstone of the Conservative faith ...The best features of both doctrines could be made to work by their synthesis in a higher doctrine, economic nationalism ...'

However, the essential unity was provided not by economics, but by race or more particularly, to distinguish it from north European 'Aryanism', 'kinship'. Tyndall's white Commonwealth both depended on, and existed to ensure the survival of, the British people and British civilization across the world. This meant not only maintaining 'racial separateness, the separate development of the different races', by stopping immigration into Britain and 'the gradual and humane resettlement of our existing coloured population in the lands of their origin,' but also the retention of British control in the regions they had colonized. 'Britons here at home should realize that the white settlers fighting to retain their position are fighting for our cause and our future, the future of British civilization the world over.' The reference was explicitly to Rhodesia and South Africa, and the 'simple principle' was that of 'white leadership'. The black population should have 'work suited to their own capacities and with progressively better rates of pay, decent houses in their own townships...social services that care for their health', but not 'power and responsibility' which it was 'ill fitted to use wisely'.

how to achieve this 'cleansing'? Violence

Domestically, the emphasis was less on social reform than moral regeneration to overcome 'decades of slow rot in the body politic'. It required 'a dynamic new faith' and 'in a crisis that is at root a crisis of leadership...not merely a new type of political party but entirely new types of men...mere material disasters alone, such as economic depression, defeat in war etc...can only do permanent damage when the product of deeper spiritual and psychological forces that have eaten into the national morale...' Society required cleansing of 'all those ideas that are systematically rotting the nation from within,' and the restoration of traditional values, 'marriage, the family, social responsibility, personal restraint, respect for the law, thrift and work'.

Tyndall sought laws against art, literature or entertainment 'by which public moral standards might be endangered,' 'the training of body and character and the instillation of real values...the basic principles of patriotism...by a full and vivid teaching of British and Imperial history'. He advocated the return of national service, not just for defence, but for its 'back-straightening influence' and the 'smartness and discipline and the values of manhood' it instilled. The residuum, 'the parasitic and the workshy' who lived on the welfare state, would find that welfare greatly reduced. Social security would be commensurate with useful effort, and 'those who prefer the life of slothful ease' would 'suffer for it by hardship, shortage and insecurity...'[43] There were elements of 'Fascist Man' in Tyndall's 'new type', and of Fascist society in his social imperialism, but Tyndall's 'Six Principles' lacked the expansive confidence of Mosley's creative evolution.

Nevertheless, the pamphlet echoed Chesterton's views on international finance, empire, race and Rhodesia, and assisted Tyndall's rehabilitation and his quest for unity. There were two impediments to this in the mid-1960s. The first arose when Dr David Brown of the RPS insisted on the formation of a new National Democratic Party under his leadership, which was sufficient to scupper talks between both the RPS and the LEL and the RPS and the BNP. But this was a short-term problem. The second, the antipathy of the 'respectable' elements of the Right to Tyndall's nazi past was more enduring. Brown insisted on excluding the GBM from any union. By the same reasoning, Colin Jordan was beyond pale, as was John Bean. In negotiations between the BNP and the LEL, Bean adopted Tyndall's tactic of self-exclusion. Tyndall's arrest with seven other GBM members early in 1966 for the possession of offensive weapons, and his 6-month sentence for the possession of a gun and ammunition only confirmed 'respectable' suspicions of the GBM and its leader.[44]

BNP, LEL, RPS = NF

There were nevertheless pressures upon the various bodies to merge. The LEL was short of money, the title was seen, even by its supporters, as outdated, and after Labour's victory in 1966 Chesterton wanted solidarity in support of Rhodesia. Like the LEL, the BNP was also short of money, and part of its interest in merger with the RPS had been the prospect of funding for publications. In its discussions with the RPS the BNP had formed 'very friendly relations' with RPS officials apart from Dr Brown, and a minority of the RPS, led by R. F. Beauclair, ultimately followed the BNP into merger with the LEL, leaving the majority with Brown in his NDP. Both the LEL and the BNP were assured that in the merger, Jordan, Tyndall and the GBM, and those 'who wanted to relive the Nazi daydream', would be barred. 'No neo-Nazi movement will be included in the NF.'[45] *then the nazis all joined*

From these negotiations the NF emerged in February 1967, still a tiny political organization, claiming 2,500 members, of whom 1,000 were nominal. With a policy that centred on ending immigration, repatriation, support for Rhodesia and opposition to communism, it was more right than radical. Moreover, neither the BNP nor the LEL had been entirely open, which was to lead to future trouble. The BNP negotiators disguised their desire to include the GBM as soon as possible, and with it, street politics and aspirations to become a mass movement. The LEL was, and wanted to remain, 'an elite' and 'to amalgamate this with numbers, but not to coarsen it'.[46] But the LEL could not resist a takeover by the BNP majority. Bean was rapidly integrated, and in April 1967 appointed to the NF Directorate. Tyndall assisted his own cause by continuing to press for unity, advising GBM members to join the NF as individuals.

Enoch Powell's Intervention

It seemed a propitious moment to launch a new movement that was hoping to capitalize on opposition to immigration. Within little over a year of its formation, Enoch Powell made his 'rivers of blood' speech at Birmingham and brought immigration into the centre of politics.[47] Powell's references to the English people who 'found themselves made strangers in their own country...found their wives unable to find hospital beds in childbirth, their children unable to obtain school places, their homes and neighbourhoods changed beyond recognition' found sympathetic echoes both amongst the wider public and within Conservative constituency associations. It was a perfect summary of those perceptions which had called into being the residents' associations earlier in the decade. In November, Powell was arguing that the real problem was no longer immigration, but that of immigrants already settled who, despite British passports, could not be truly English because of their race.[48] The NF might feel that Powell was trespassing on their territory, at least on this issue. But his intervention did assist NF recruitment, and in theory boosted their chances of entering the political mainstream at last.

If there was an opportunity, the NF failed to exploit it because of factionalism. Chesterton and Fountaine clashed almost immediately, and after Fountaine overreacted to the student riots of May 1968 Chesterton, aided by Tyndall, engineered Fountaine's resignation. Two other leading moderates followed Fountaine, Legg of the LEL and Kemp of the BNP. The dispute was largely personal, but the departure of the moderates aided the rise of the militants to control of the NF, as they had always intended. Chesterton was the next to go, but over far more fundamental issues. The elitist style of the LEL clashed with the rowdiness and scarcely veiled violence of the BNP and GBM. The BNP and GBM wanted a dynamic movement, to hold demonstrations, fight elections and capitalize on the storm that Powell had raised. Chesterton argued that the Front was not ready to fight elections.

The election results of 1970 seemed to confirm his attitude. In the municipal elections held just before the general election the NF's average vote was around 10 per cent in the constituencies fought. But in the general election, its ten candidates averaged only around 3.6 per cent.[49] For the militants, this merely demonstrated the ineffectiveness of Chesterton's elitist approach. Tyndall's public loyalty to Chesterton meant that when Chesterton finally and bitterly resigned late in 1970, there was no obvious replacement. His eventual successor, John O'Brien, was a relative newcomer, a convert from Conservatism after Powell's 'rivers of blood' speech. He founded the British Defence League, joined Dr Brown's NDP and made numerous contacts within the anti-immigration Right, including John Davis's National Independence Party. Chesterton invited O'Brien to become office manager of the NF, partly with the hope of facilitating a merger with the NDP that was then under discussion.[50] To Tyndall and Webster he seemed respectable and inexperienced enough to be malleable. He became chairman in February 1971.

But nothing enabled the NF to make the electoral breakthrough. In 1971, its 84 candidates averaged only 5.2 per cent of the vote. Nor could it overcome its divisions. O'Brien was determined to remove Tyndall and Webster whose connections with German neo-nazis and the Northern

League 'devoted to the international friendship and solidarity of all Northern European Nations'[51] kept open the festering sore of their national socialist past. It was a bitter intrigue, but it was O'Brien, equipped with copies of the NF membership lists, who decided he had to leave. Once again Tyndall outmaneuvered his opponents, and in the summer of 1972 finally secured control of the NF which initially he had not been regarded as fit to join.

National Front Expansion

As Tyndall took control, the arrival of Ugandan Asian refugees reignited the smouldering issue of immigration. In the last 4 months of 1972 the NF gained over 800 new members and several new branches and groups. In the West Bromwich by-election in May 1973 Martin Webster gained 16 per cent of the vote, and for the first time ever a NF candidate saved his deposit. The special circumstances of a low turnout and a government suffering from mid-term unpopularity could not detract from the publicity success. Further success followed in the local elections in June. In Leicester, the Front gained over 20 per cent of the votes in 3 wards, and averaged over 15 per cent. In Blackburn, every one of the 5 candidates gained over 20 per cent and the average was 23.7 per cent. There were similar, if lesser, successes in Nottingham, Bristol, Brighton, Staines, Dartford and Norwich. By January 1974, the NF had 30 branches and 54 groups, principally in South East England and Greater London.[52]

Nevertheless, in the February 1974 general election all the Front's 54 candidates lost their deposits and 19 received fewer than 1,000 votes. Only one of the five candidates who got more than 5 per cent of the vote, Mike Lobb in Newham, had Liberal opposition. In May in a by-election Lobb did even better, and gained 11.5 per cent beating the Conservative.[53] Through 1974, the NF tried to confront the problem by promoting other aspects of its policies to broaden its electoral appeal. Its campaign against the EEC had increased relevance as Edward Heath took Britain into the Common Market, but it was not a subject that aroused public interest in the NF. There was potentially more mileage in taking the immigration issue the next logical step, the impact on British society of immigrants already resident to which Powell had drawn attention, but there was a wide gulf between the specific issues of housing, jobs, education and criminality, and getting people to see these issues as part of what Martin Webster called 'the global struggle for survival between various species of humanity'.[54]

In 1973–74 the NF, or a section of it, re-emphasized the social radicalism of the Radical Right. In August 1973, Mike Lobb criticized Labour's nationalization policy as half-hearted, and proposed nationalizing foreign-owned firms and the banks, whilst in September, *Spearhead* condemned American participation in North Sea oil exploration. In December, Lobb's Newham branch joined the picket lines of striking workers at London sugar refineries, and the NF declared its support of the miners pay claim in a dispute which led to a three-day working week, electricity rationing and the general election of February 1974.[55] But one month later *Spearhead* demanded 'ruthless and drastic measures by government to get the country running', including the arrest where necessary of trade union leaders.[56] There was here the germ of an ideological difference between embryonic 'Strasserites' emphasizing the more radical aspects of the Radical Right,[57] and a more conservative approach to law and order that was to trouble the NF for the rest of the decade.

By 1974, while still desiring to gain control of the unions democratically, the NF also created an alternative, the National Front Trade Union Association, much as Joseph Chamberlain had set up the TUTRA. However, the NF's industrial policies, compulsory arbitration, secret ballots before strike action, banning the 'closed shop' and expelling any official who had ever been a member of the Communist party, were unlikely to appeal to a trade union movement which in the 1970s appeared to have the government on the run. Nor was the long-term aim of replacing the existing trade union structure by a semi-corporatist single union for each industry with legally enforceable agreements between employers and workers. The trade union movement regarded the NF as Fascist and opposed it accordingly.[58] Efforts to make headway with its policy of support for Ulster loyalism met with a similar response. Overtures led the Ulster Defence Association (UDA) to investigate its would-be friends, as a result of which Andy Tyrie of the UDA severed all links with the NF on the grounds that 'we regard the NF as a neo-Nazi movement'.[59] Old reputations died hard.

These policies were linked together by the NF's vision of the insidious workings of international finance, sometimes re-written as the multinational corporation but sharing the same vice of internationalism. The EEC was manifestly part of internationalism's ultimate design, as was immigration. 'Industrial action by Britons', whether against employers or immigrant workers was 'a racial struggle ... the struggle of a united British people fighting to preserve their freedom and identity against the forces of communism and international capitalism which seek to destroy the British nation and which use as their tool the immigrant minorities placed by them in our midst'.[60] Ulster was the victim of 'the New Papacy' which was not Roman or Christian, but which was 'today the most potent contender for a world monopoly of power. Its financial centre is New York; its forum is the United Nations; it is strangely friendly to the Soviet bloc; its enemy is the survival of national sovereignty. That is why it is attacking Ulster'.[61]

In this period of optimism, the NF foresaw 'a Nationalist government' in the 1980s, but feared that 'such a government would immediately encounter economic trading difficulties in the form of world trading sanctions instigated by international finance'.[62] It was an abiding concern throughout the decade. In January 1977 Tyndall predicted the 'possibility of an Anglo–US confrontation'. Economic pressures from 'the International Financial Elite', he then argued, would escalate to 'armed conflict at a guerilla-type level' against Britain and her interests world wide. Under these circumstances 'nuclear power would be crucial'. In February, he suggested a solution, the reconquest of Africa by Britain, France and Germany to enlarge the threatened area, and thus reduce the possibility of conflict.[63] It showed not only that the Radical Right was still committed to the international conspiracy thesis, but also that the NF had learned nothing from the Suez fiasco of 1956.

The 'Populist' Split

In the early 1970s, the NF was expanding rapidly enough for its leaders to fantasize. But expansion brought its own problems. Especially after the West Bromwich by-election, the Left took greater notice and attacked where the NF was weakest, publicizing the neo-nazi past of Tyndall and Webster. It also responded on the streets, forcing the NF to rely increasingly upon police escorts to secure their right to march and during 1974 to organize its own defence groups. It was, as it had been from the 1930s onwards, a progressive escalation of violent confrontation. This, in turn led to renewed dissension within the leadership. During 1972–73, the Monday Club disintegrated over entry to the EEC and immigration, and several leading Powellites gravitated to the NF, including Roy Painter, the Conservative candidate in Tottenham, and John Kingsley Read from Blackburn. They were from the 'respectable' right, accustomed to working within the democratic system, for whom neo-nazism and violence on the streets were both liabilities. They became known as the 'Populists'.

Signs of an impending split were visible even before the February 1974 general election. Immediately after it, Webster declared: 'the election of just one policy-trimming "Populist" would be a blow from which the NF might never recover... the mass of the people can only identify with the Nationalist cause if we maintain for our cause a separate identity far removed from the blurred images of the corrupt Old Gang parties'.[64] But the October 1974 general election confirmed the 'Populists' in their approach. The Front fielded 90 candidates, and despite contesting so many new seats, marginally increased its average share of the vote. The three most successful candidates, May in Shoreditch (9.4 per cent), Painter in Tottenham (8.3 per cent) and Squires in Wood Green (8 per cent), were all from the 'Populist' wing. On television, Kingsley Read had performed well, Tyndall and Webster badly. At the crucial Directorate meeting, Kingsley Read defeated Tyndall for the NF Chairmanship by the casting vote of the meeting's chairman. Tyndall in turn defeated Painter for the deputy-chairmanship by Read's casting vote. Determined to regain what he considered his movement, it was an olive branch in which Tyndall had no interest.[65]

During the next year the NF dissipated the mild gains of October 1974 by internal feuding. In this, Tyndall had the great advantage of being known for his diligence and commitment to the cause. He had maintained his contacts with such old comrades as John Bean, Andrew Fountaine and even Colin Jordan who, being excluded from the NF, had founded his own British Movement. In contrast, the 'Populists', recent recruits from Conservatism, were easily denounced as 'trimmers... popularity-seekers and moderates'.[66] The 'Populists' also lacked decisiveness, allowing Tyndall and his supporters to campaign within the Front against them.

Tyndall pitched his appeal to the old extremists within the movement by re-emphasizing the supreme importance of race, and Webster followed suit:

Racialism is the only scientific and logical basis for nationalism... our objections to immigration and multi-racialism spring not from the fact that 'There are too many Blacks in Britain'... we seek to preserve the identity of the British nation... if the British people are destroyed by racial inter-breeding, then the British nation will cease to exist.[67]

In *Spearhead*, too, the line was that of crude biological racism, the 'smaller brain' and 'less complex cerebral structure of the negro', and the prospect of race war in the near future in which 'the uniforms... will be

normal, has adapted, fundamentally the same
→ core of war

the colour of your skin'. In addition to colour, there remained 'the Jewish question', with Jews still portrayed as 'to the fore in promoting Communism and World Government'.[68] This was to move the argument away from the practicalities of politics to racist credentials.

Both Tyndall and Webster were elected to the Directorate in September, with Webster topping the poll. At the AGM the following month, Tyndall's proposals for constitutional reform, designed to out-flank the Directorate, were rejected, but manoeuvres to secure files and subscription lists indicated that both sides anticipated a split, not recon-ciliation. The 'Populist' plan to expel Tyndall while only suspending and subsequently re-admitting Webster, Fountaine and others was carried out amidst such confusion that an appeal to the courts led to the reinstate-ment of Tyndall and his supporters. Subsequently, the courts also restored the NF headquarters and the membership lists to the Tyndall faction. By then, the 'Populists' had already left to form the National Party, believing that they had sufficient assurances to carry the bulk of the NF membership with them. But in regaining the national headquarters, Tyndall also controlled communication with the confused branches. In the contest for the hearts and minds of the grass-roots support, the bulk of the branches and the membership stayed with the NF and better-known leaders.

Ironically, the new NP claimed to be more opposed to immigration than the NF to preserve the 'distinct racial character' of the British peo-ple. It also demanded 'the humane repatriation or resettlement abroad of all coloured and other racially incompatible immigrants, their depen-dants and descendants'.[69] To that extent, the distinction was in style and tactics, not doctrine. The 'Populists' of the NP thought in terms of organ-ization through institutions, a party with branches that could steadily accumulate support to be called upon at election time. Tyndall in con-trast emphasized the need to raise the political temperature, to generate enthusiasm by the irrational appeal of political theatre, marches 'with drums and flags and banners'.[70] It was a repeat of the clash that had arisen in the BUF in the 1930s, between the 'organizational' wing of the BUF represented by Box and Neil Francis Hawkins, and the 'radical fas-cist' wing represented by Joyce and Chesterton.

But there was also the difference of opinion on labour unrest and law and order. The more socially radical 'Strasserites' went with the 'respectable' Populists leaving Tyndall with a NF that was not only far more heavily tarred with the racist brush as a result of the conflict and the direction of Tyndall's appeal, but more authoritarian in relation to working-class aspirations. Moreover, the bitter leadership dispute had led to a decline in both membership and action. In the 1975 municipal elections there were only 60 candidates. During 1975, the NF found itself denied the use of halls, as the BUF had been before it, and still reliant on police protection for its rallies and meetings.

But in 1976 the arrival of another persecuted section of Asians from East Africa, these from Malawi, again revived the immigration issue. Amidst press scares about the 'vast queues of people all planning to surge into Britain', the NF had regained its key issue. In the 1976 local elections, it fielded 176 candidates, of whom 80 won more than 10 per cent of the vote. In Leicester, its 48 candidates averaged 18.5 per cent, with the highest achieving 31 per cent. But it still won no seats whereas in Kingsley Read's fief of Blackburn, the NP won 2. Parliamentary by-elections were even less encouraging, with not a deposit saved in 4 by-elections during a summer of mounting racial tension and violence.[71]

The municipal elections of May 1977 showed broadly similar results. Of 91 candidates in Greater London, 5 gained over 15 per cent of the vote and the Liberals were beaten in 33 seats with the best area being the traditional NF and Radical Right stronghold of the extended East End. But the average in Greater London was only 5.3 per cent. There were also the traditional problems. The NF vote fell slightly in Leicester, where the local leader, Terry Verity, resigned because of the Front's neo-nazi connections and hostility to democracy. In parliamentary by-elections, the Front beat the Liberals in Walsall North, but still gained only 7.3 per cent of the vote. In August, Tyndall predicted that the breakthrough would come in the election after next, as 'industrial anarchy . . . the ill-effects of the EEC' and increased racial tension allowed the Front to 'pick up large numbers of disillusioned Tory voters',[72] but it was an optimistic view given the Front's limited achievements thus far.

The National Front and the Crisis of the 1970s

The circumstances of the 1970s appeared superficially to favour an organization like the NF. In addition to coloured immigration, the economy faltered to such an extent that the era has been called 'the second slump'. Both Conservative and Labour governments struggled against rising inflation, rising unemployment, inner-city decay, social tensions and trade union militancy. The question of union power had been growing in importance since the mid-1960s. In 1974, the minority Labour government was forced to bow to a general strike in the Ulster and abandon its Northern Ireland policy. With Labour narrowly re-elected in October 1974, the crisis was thought sufficiently severe for two retired army officers to attempt to establish so-called private armies, the 'Unison movement' of General Sir Walter Walker, and GB 75 of Colonel David Stirling, although neither came to anything. The government itself negotiated temporary agreements with the unions to limit wage demands in return for price controls and anti-inflationary measures which removed the immediate pressure, but it failed to find a policy that would in the long term deal with either union militancy or its encroachment on the prerogatives of the state.

In effect, by involving the unions in the management of the economy, Labour, both in the 1960s and the 1970s, was invoking a mild form of corporatism, but one with which the unions would not cooperate. The Grunwick dispute in 1977, with trade union solidarity marked by 'flying pickets' and picket line confrontations, demonstrated how limited government success was in either incorporating the unions in the political process or controlling their independent militancy. For the NF, Tyndall typically urged equipping the police with 'water cannon, tear gas and rubber bullets with full authority to use those implements', and in *Spearhead* in June 1977 he called for 'far stronger measures against violent picketing and other forms of individual intimidation'.[73]

Perhaps not surprisingly in view of Tyndall's statements, the NF failed to capitalize on this economic and industrial discontent. It continued to be viewed as a one issue party and to pick up votes only in particular areas where there was local resentment of the coloured population, or in the East End and surrounding areas with a long-standing tradition of opposition to alien immigration. In this respect, as Stan Taylor argues, the NF did not become the voice of an alienated working class during the course of the 1970s, and both the alarm of anti-Fascist organizations, which provoked them into greater activity towards the end of the decade, and the optimism of the Front itself, were ill-founded.[74]

National Front optimism depended heavily on reactions to specific bouts of immigration from exiled east African Asians and on the apparent inability of the major parties to deal with the economic crisis. Tyndall observed in October 1976 that 'the great majority of the electorate can immediately recognize ... a party which has the strength and the will to govern and rule ... The image of strength is always the greatest propaganda weapon in times of chaos ...'[75] It was a lesson that the new Conservative leader, Margaret Thatcher, had no need to learn. Thatcher may have been cautious in asserting her authority over the party with the dispossessed Heath still in parliament, but incrementally under her leadership the party moved to the right and asserted its 'will to govern'.

Even before the general election of 1979, Thatcher had given an indication of her attitude on the vital immigration issue. Her reference in January 1978 to 'swamping by an alien culture', showed an instinctive affinity with the concerns of the native population. The Thatcherite 'New Right' favoured the free market, privatization, reduced public expenditure and government intervention, and a shift from direct to indirect taxation, policies which, with the partial exception of taxation, set it apart from the genuine Radical Right tradition. But it combined these objectives with the rhetoric of patriotism, the defense of British culture and firmness on immigration, law and order and militancy. Whilst the NF fought its factional battles, the Conservative party moved in to occupy its ground.

Chapter 6: *Warrior Saints and Men in Suits*

Having averaged 3 per cent in the seats it contested in both general elections in 1974, the NF could only average 1.5 per cent in 1979. It contested 303 seats compared to the 90 in 1974, but according to Taylor this poor performance was not the result of the far larger number of seats fought, but a genuine decline in support.[1] At the very least, there was nothing to sustain the belief in a breakthrough next time. Webster concluded that the NF

> won't be built on middle class foundations . . . until we have become big enough to be a serious contender for power in a situation of national economic catastrophe and a collapse of law and order, the NF will not be able to offer the middle classes anything by way of property/status that the Conservative Party cannot offer with a million times more credibility.[2]

Once again, adversity resulted in dissension. Andrew Fountaine and Richard Lawson left to form the NF Constitutional Movement, and John Tyndall resigned in January 1980 to found the New National Front which became the BNP in 1982. Andrew Brons succeeded Tyndall as Chairman of the NF, and Webster remained in the influential position of National Activities Organiser.

Amidst continued trade union militancy and rising unemployment, the NF, like Mosley before it, continued to place its hopes on an anticipated collapse of the system. With a five-year plan, 'Organizing for the Collapse', it fell back on its core street support, reasoning that

> If it is true that the NF has no hope of gaining power under conditions that are stable – economically, socially or politically – we should not be preoccupied with making ourselves more 'respectable' under present conditions. We must appreciate that the 'image' we have been given by the media and which may lose us some potential support today, will be a positive asset when the streets are beset with riots, unemployment soars, and when inflation gets even beyond the present degree of minimal control.[3]

Predictably, 'respectable' elements left to support the resurgent Conservative party. In 1983 Thatcher won a landslide general election victory, whilst the NF fought only 58 seats, and averaged only 1.1 per cent of the vote. Nick Griffin later felt that 'the skins kept the NF alive from 1980–83'.[4]

'Strasserites'

Tyndall was the last imperialist. In the early 1980s the NF rapidly reinvented itself as a new generation of leaders emerged for whom the empire, so long the basis of radical right thinking, was no longer an option. In 1980, the NF claimed that it was, for the first time in its history, 'in the hands of Revolutionary Nationalists determined to destroy the twin evils of Communism and Capitalism'.[5] Regarding the 'ruling Establishment' as irredeemable internationalist, parliament and the major parties in the grip of international finance with a Zionist programme of globalization using race-mixing to destroy nationalism, the NF objective became to build 'a revolutionary Nationalist movement dedicated to the overthrow of the ruling Establishment and the utter destruction of its parasitical system'.[6] A new journal, *Nationalism Today*, launched to replace *Spearhead*, formed the focal point for this group, supplemented by the irregular *Rising*, and from outside the NF by *Scorpion* (initially *New Democrat*), edited by the former NF central London organizer, Michael Walker, and Richard Lawson's *Heritage and Destiny*.

The evolution of the NF in the 1980s is best regarded as a combination of 'brainstorming' new ideas and the desire to provide the NF with new policies and a new organizational structure that would restore its political effectiveness. Webster was left behind in this process. Steve Brady recalled in 1992 that *Nationalism Today* had three aims, 'to radicalize members, change the direction of strategy and get rid of Webster'.[7] The coup was swift and remarkably easy. In November 1983, two of the leading radicals, Joe Pearce and Nick Griffin, condemned the NF under Webster as 'a desperately sick organisation' and criticized the policy of marches which advertized 'our weakness rather than our strength'. Since change was impossible as long as Webster continued 'with his present attitude and stranglehold on key party offices', they announced their resignations. It was a tactical move, and Webster and his close ally Michael Salt were removed from office in December.

The NF radicals were what Thurlow has called 'self-styled Strasserites',[8] deriving their name from the 'left' opposition to Hitler in the German Nazi party led by the brothers Otto and Gregor Strasser. There were several possible influences pushing NF policies in this direction. In 1980, Italian refugees from the Third Position and the NAR found safe housing in Britain. Roberto Fiore in particular developed close contacts with the radical elements in the NF, and has been credited with spreading 'Strasserite' ideas.[9] However, Martin Walker notes that in the mid-1970s Richard Lawson advocated an ideology in the NP's paper, *Britain First*, which derived from 'the "soft" National Socialism of Rohm and the SD (sic) ...'[10] When the NP folded in 1977, some members of it, including Steve Brady rejoined the NF 'to radicalize the NF from within'.[11] There is therefore some support for O'Hara's contention that 'The most important recent source of "Strasserism" in the UK far right was ex-National Party activists.'[12]

David Baker takes the source further back to A. K. Chesterton,[13] a debt which Derek Holland acknowledged in 1982.[14] After he left the BUF, Chesterton wrote for the Distributist paper, the *Weekly Review*, and the 'Strasserites' rapidly adopted distributism as their policy. But there were close similarities between their idea of 'Strasserism' and distributism.[15] Both outlooks centred on the break up of large landed estates and industrial concerns, 'back to the land', and workers' control of industry. Distributism became the 'Strasserite' third way, or third position, beyond capitalism and communism, condemning both, as Belloc had done, as paradigms of the 'servile state'.[16] 'We in Britain are lucky that with Chesterton and Belloc we have ... the roots for our own National Revolution – the ideas of Distributism.'[17]

The 'Strasserites' envisaged 'the revolutionary restructuring of British industry. Production will be split into three varying types of industrial *modus operandi*: small privately owned enterprises, nationalized concerns and workers cooperatives'. Wherever possible, large operations would be sub-divided 'into small, family and privately owned enterprises'. Where this was impossible, 'the individual concerns will be socialized and handed over to the workforce in the form of workers cooperatives', a scheme not unlike the syndicalism of Mosley's 'European Socialism'. Nationalization was a last resort where neither of the preferred distributist options was possible, 'effectively financial institutions and heavy industry'.[18]

The state would regulate the entire system through direct 'legal limits on the size of industrial concerns in private hands because ultimately wealth means power', or through taxation graduated to prevent excessive accumulation.[19] 'We believe that the State must continually intervene in the economy to preserve and, where necessary, re-establish the institution of private property.' All banks were to be nationalized, and in their place a 'state-run banking system...will issue low interest loans into the economy' to assist small enterprises.[20] At other times the proposal was for interest free loans.[21] The stock exchange was to be abolished, and the state would regulate the environment of economic nationalism in which these industries would operate,[22] imposing import controls and prohibiting the export of capital to direct investment to British industry rather than financing competitors. This mixture of state socialism, guild socialism and distributism, rested on another familiar Radical Right analysis, underconsumption.

The affirmation of the power of technology to increase production while reducing the workforce, of poverty amidst the potential of plenty, and of demand unfulfilled through lack of money was also almost Mosleyite. There was a Social Credit element in the view that interest payments to 'parasitic banks' led to 'a constant loss of purchasing power so that the population of the country can never afford to purchase all that they can produce'. The solution, that the 'credit needed to run the economy must be created interest free by the government...The people must be given the purchasing power to buy the goods which they produce' resembled the 'national dividend', just as the justification that wealth was produced by 'machines and technology developed by our race over centuries, and which are therefore part of our common inheritance', resembled the 'cultural heritage'.[23] Like Social Credit and Mosley's fascism, planning would ensure that 'increases in the money supply are proportionate to anticipated increases in the production of goods and services'.[24]

Yet industry was the lesser part of the scheme. The NF proposed to 'encourage emigration from the large industrial cities' replacing 'highly mechanized agriculture with small privately owned and labour intensive farms'. As in the 1930s, it was, together with environmental and social projects, a solution to unemployment. But it was also a reiteration of the Radical Right's condemnation of urban life. Modern man had 'been uprooted from the soil and placed in an artificial concrete world where he has become a materialist wage slave. A major return to the land is essential for the cultural, spiritual and economic health of the nation'.[25] Apart from the social benefits of restored communities, independence and 'economic freedom', Griffin also noted that labour intensive small farms were more productive per acre than large farms.[26]

The 'Strasserites', like Chesterton and Belloc, laid great stress on the freedom to be achieved by distributed ownership. 'No NF=No Freedom ... the National Front is committed totally to overthrowing the tyranny that masquerades as "democracy" in Britain to-day ... Racial Freedom ... Financial Freedom ... Economic Freedom ... National Freedom'.[27] Despite the lurking etatism of its proposals, it recognized the inherent anarchism of distributism.[28] Griffin criticized the 'the servile dependence' of the majority of the population on 'the masters and the State',[29] and like Mosley identified 'real freedom' as 'economic freedom ... dependence on others for the necessities of life is the short-cut to slavery'.[30]

Yet the 'Strasserite' priority was less individual freedom than the freedom of the nation from international control and the influence of powerful sectional interests. 'Of greatest importance', wrote Andrew Brons, 'is the break up of the biggest concentrations of wealth as a guarantee of the sovereignty of the Nation – a guarantee of its freedom from interference by sectional interests. Only a truly sovereign government can protect the whole nation.'[31] Derek Holland similarly linked agrarian distributism to national independence as well as to the diffusion of power.[32] In their concern for racial, national, financial and economic freedom, the NF 'Strasserites' tended to overlook political pluralism and the diffusion of sovereignty. Rather they argued, in true etatist fashion, that 'Parliament must have full sovereignty ... '[33]

In 1986, Michael Fishwick noted this neglect, and proposed a five-tiered structure 'giving our folk as much real freedom and control over their destinies as possible' with plural votes for individuals 'proportional to their contribution' to the nation, and indirect elections from tier to tier.[34] The issue was not fully dealt with until the NF leadership embraced the idea of Colonel Gadhafi's *Green Book*, and its system of popular government based upon the establishment of 'Popular Congresses and People's Committees. The spirit of the theory is that the masses themselves must be educated and organized into congresses for the purpose of self-government. The result is the end of the conventional definition of democracy as "*the supervision of the government by the people*", and its replacement instead as "*the supervision of the people by the people.*" ' The NF noted that 'the values cherished by Qathafi...are in every sense our own'.[35] The NF thus adopted communal political structures, building up from street councils through area, community and county councils to a National People's Council 'for each of the British Nations, with a consultative body comprising members from each',[36] and the doctrine of 'no representation without participation'.[37]

Communalism had the additional advantage of being operable within the existing system to destroy it from within.[38] By this point, the NF had become almost overly concerned with the power of the centralized state. The idea of a local militia,[39] was subsequently developed by Derek Holland, again with reference to Libya and Gadhafi, into a doctrine akin to the nation in arms. To reduce the risk that, whatever the devolution of political power and the redistribution of property, the state might seek to reassert its control by force, Holland argued that modern weapons should be made available to the people, combined with education in the responsibilities of freedom.[40] The NF programme of communalism, revocable mandates and an armed population of small property owners, intensely nationalist, hostile to banks, speculation and large-scale industry was a revolutionary solution to the central dilemma that Belloc identified in distributism, the need for, but threat from, the state. Irrespective of the Libyan example, it bore many similarities to the outlook of the French revolutionary *sansculottes*.

Violence and Terrorism

During the 1980s the NF not only failed to shed its image of street violence, but had the image of would-be terrorists thrust upon it. Griffin remarked in 1985: 'A few years ago the National Front was portrayed as a group of evil middle-aged Hitler-worshippers...We are now... "terrorists" rather than Nazis.'[41] But just as the NF saw the police, Special Branch and MI5 shading into each other, so its critics saw street violence shading into terrorism. Webster dated the beginning of the breakdown in relations with the police from the Lewisham riots of 1977, but it was not helped by the upsurge in violence at the start of the 1980s, nor by the presumption of police hostility. Noting the change 'From the "Bobby" on the Beat to the Police State', Joe Pearce claimed in 1981: 'today the British police force constitutes a State militia designed to suppress all "dissident elements"... and that, of course, includes the NF.'[42] At one point in 1985, three of the six member Executive Council were facing imprisonment.

In the Webster era the NF continued to march, demonstrate and maintain its right to defend those activities. Griffin then declared: 'the future of British Nationalism lies not with refugees from the Tory party, but with the deprived young Whites of the inner cities' and argued that violence must be met with violence: 'we must recruit members who are prepared to stand up and fight back'.[43] The creation of Instant Response Groups after Webster's removal at the end of 1983 revealed that the objective was not exclusively defensive, but also confrontational. It was still considered 'good and valuable publicity'.[44] It did, however, mean the beginning of the end of marches and demonstrations, in favour of a far more community friendly approach, and a more 'respectable' image.

The continuation of the almost private war between the militant Far Left and the militant Radical Right was a long way removed from terrorism, but in the context of bombings in Europe in 1980–81 there was concern that the British Right would follow suit because of its international connections. Rumours circulated about Steve Brady, the International Liaison Officer of the League of St George (founded 1974) before he rejoined the NF. Stories appeared of Brady's connection with Loyalist organizations in Northern Ireland and the Far Right in Europe which coincided with allegations of a plot to bomb the Notting Hill Carnival in 1981. Major Ian Souter-Clarence's 'Wessex Survival' courses were also portrayed as paramilitary training camps for the Right, including the British Movement's 'Leader Guard'.[45] In 1977, the BM did announce a paramilitary training programme, and in 1981 three Birmingham members were convicted for possessing machine guns, rifles and ammunition.[46]

The BM disintegrated in 1983. The NF itself consistently denied any intention to adopt terrorist tactics, not only because such tactics were immoral, but also because they would be counterproductive: 'Terrorism would serve no other purpose than to give the Establishment the excuse it needs to ban the National Front and lock up it members.'[47] The Front might organize for the collapse, but it was as aware as the BUF in the 1930s that it could not confront the state head on. Political rhetoric was a problem as the NF recognized. Joe Pearce's rejection of terrorism was prompted by an article in *Nationalism Today*, #16 which appeared to give the wrong impression. Numerous subsequent denials included a full-length article by Derek Holland, 'Terrorism: An Enemy of

Nationalism'.[48] The issue was nevertheless to haunt the NF for the rest of the decade.

Political Soldiers

With a disastrous electoral performance in 1983 behind it and Webster removed, 1984–85 was period of further reassessment of its position and strategy by the NF. The very limited success of the shift to revolutionary nationalism was laid bare by the miners' strike that began in March 1984. For the 'Strasserite' leadership the miners' strike was another issue to be interpreted through the lens of the 'servile state': 'The real "class war" all over the World is between the ruling class and the rest, between the bosses, East and West, Capitalist and Communist, of the Old System and those who would be free, nationally and racially as well as economically. It is a war between centralised economic slavery and individual liberty.'[49]

Officially, the NF supported 'wholeheartedly the struggle of the British miners', but not only was their offer of support rejected by the National Union of Mineworkers, it created dissension amongst the rank and file and even something of a north-south split. The revolutionaries were very far from getting across to their supporters their slightly complex message of support for the miners as white workers but condemnation of the left-wing leadership of the mineworkers' union. Too many of the rank and file took the 'reactionary' view.[50] In this they more closely resembled the position of the BNP. Tyndall urged that the government should 'arrest and charge those ringleaders responsible for organising the violence...'[51] It was consistent with his NF line in 1973–74, further revealing the ideological divide between Tyndall and the 'Strasserites'.

Rethinking proceeded on two distinct but linked lines, ideological and structural. On the former level, Joe Pearce wrote, 'it is absolutely vital that we don't restrict our fight solely to the political level. Our struggle is philosophical; our struggle is cultural; our struggle is spiritual'.[52] That spiritual aspect was set out in ascetic detail in Derek Holland's highly influential *The Political Soldier*. As summarized in the new 1994 preface,

> the essential message of *The Political Soldier* was that what is needed above all else is a fundamental shift in attitude towards struggle, towards life, towards destiny...there cannot be, and will not be, any serious change in the overall direction taken by the countries of Europe until the New Man...capable of moulding and inspiring a New

Social Order, arises and builds it...according to the objectively true principles of a creed...Some have said that *The Political Soldier* appears to be demanding the creation of Warrior Saints. And so it is.[53]

[handwritten annotation: ▷ while genocide / The Great Replacement]

The pamphlet was written 'as a spur to action', but that action was spiritual not political. Without regeneration, 'the culture of Europe is going to die within our lifetime' like the great civilizations of the past, and 'the death of Europe will signal the end of the White peoples forever... Britain will become a vague, unimportant memory...' Derek Holland states categorically that he does not consider himself to be a member of the Radical Right, but a Third Positionist and Distributist. Nevertheless, on this point at least, *The Political Soldier* reiterated the familiar Radical Right refrain of impending but avoidable catastrophe.

The 'New Type of Man' was similar in purpose, if not in nature to Mosley's 'Fascist Man'. He was inspired by 'a spiritual and religious ideal... the political Soldier must undergo a Spiritual Revolution, an inner revolution which guides, directs and pervades his life'. He could in turn inspire others, fan residual embers of their own faith 'until its flickering grows stronger and more intense, until it becomes a raging inferno engulfing our People and our Land in the quest for National Freedom, Social Justice and a truly Free Europe'. Although the language of *The Political Soldier* might superficially give the impression of a call to violence Holland explicitly rejected terrorism as 'utterly alien to nationalist tradition'.[54] Subsequently, both Joe Pearce and Steve Brady reaffirmed the spiritual and internal nature of the struggle.[55] *The Political Soldier* was the revolutionary nationalist's response 'to the materialist nightmare of this century'. Political soldiers were 'spiritual soldiers in the war against materialism' on behalf of the higher values of nations, community and family. Distributism necessitated such a statement. As Belloc had noted in the 1930s, distributism might enhance the quality of life, but it would diminish the quantity of goods.[56]

The 'Flag' Split

Strategically, the NF moved towards a more elitist structure, the cadre system, differentiating between non-voting ordinary members and voting cadres who would be chosen by the Directorate for their commitment and ability. It was done 'to turn the NF into a revolutionary cadre party – a movement run by its most dedicated and active members rather than by armchair nationalists...'[57] "Cadre" was another dubious word, although it meant only 'in simple English: highly dedicated political middle management',[58] and as before the NF was adamant that it had no terrorist intentions.[59] There were four principal arguments for the cadre system, to build a dedicated elite, political soldiers who would 'give their whole life and whole being to the...cause',[60] who would spread the revolutionary policies of the NF to the masses; to avoid attracting the wrong kind of member detrimental to the Front's image or ideological coherence; to avoid infiltration and subversion,[61] and to provide an organization sufficiently resilient to withstand the anticipated state repression as the system collapsed.[62] The cadre system was finally adopted at the AGM in November 1986.

More immediate pressures, however, came from Ireland. The Anglo–Irish Agreement at the end of 1985 provoked the NF to call for a unilateral declaration of independence by Ulster. Griffin seemed to see the situation in a way similar to Willoughby de Broke before 1914. 'The situation in Ulster is fast becoming Revolutionary. If things develop as they easily could, and if we influence them as easily as we should, then our British Revolution will start in Ulster...'[63] But Steve Brady had doubts about the effects of recent NF rhetoric, particularly in the Ulster context. In February 1986 he wrote to Joe Pearce, then in prison for race relations offences, criticizing the use of 'pseudo-revolutionary slogans' that suggested 'armies, guns, violence etc'; the image created of the NF as 'an extra-legal gang composed of skinhead thugs and Paki-bashers...and sinister terrorist conspirators linked to even more sinister foreigners', and the overemphasis on state repression.[64] Brady was suspended for his action. There was a background of other minor disagreements, in particular over the political soldier doctrine. Holland's inspiration was clearly Christian, and while commending the spiritual element, Brady rejected the 'religiosity' of a recent *Rising* editorial.[65] On 3 May disciplinary charges were also brought against Ian Anderson who had been brusquely removed from the chairmanship the previous December.

During May, the 'political soldiers' outmanoeuvred their critics, secured control of the Directorate and suspended those who opposed them. The purge was accompanied by the usual contest for control of the membership lists and equipment, and the usual litigation, both of which the 'political soldiers' also won. Their official version of the purge presented it as a 'simple choice between the radical, youthful and successful political leadership of the past year, and a group of people who...wanted to ignore corruption and rumour-mongering...and to hamstring the NF with out-dated conservative policies', turning it into 'a reactionary anti-immigration pressure group'. With their eyes firmly on Ulster, the 'political soldier' wing saw the split as 'part of a carefully coordinated campaign of disruption designed to neutralize the NF while Thatcher and co. deal with Ulster and the police try to keep the lid on the simmering pot of racial tension in the inner cities'.

According to this version, at least one 'mole' within the Directorate had disrupted the NF organization and leaked information, whilst MI5 or Special Branch disrupted postal communication with the branches and tapped its phones.[66] The purged opposition members formed their own National Front Support Group, better known as the 'Flag' Group, after their newspaper of that name. Nevertheless, although the Flag group assumed that it had the support of the bulk of the membership, it had no leverage over NF policy, and suspensions and expulsions continued, most notably the suspension of Joe Pearce in August. In January 1987, the Flag group renamed itself the National Front, creating two rival NFs until the official NF was wound up in January 1990.

The constitution of the 'Flag' Front gave autonomy to the branches, 'to organize themselves and their activities according to local goals'; the 'political soldiers' placed ever greater insistence on the threat of state repression and the consequent need to become 'a closed movement where assets, membership records and activities are widely decentralized, but where overall authority and ideological direction are centralized' under a 'unified command'.[67] Recruiting was to be 'highly selective',[68] and the leadership issued what amounted to an ultimatum to the membership: 'The leadership will not compromise with any of our enemies… It will not allow any individual or group of individuals to stand in the way of the NF's progress… If you cannot accept the new direction, do *not* renew [membership].'[69]

The Disintegration of the National Front

Even after this blood-letting, the 'political soldiers' NF failed to hold together and retain the loyalties of the membership, largely because of its altered presentation of the race issue. At the start of the 1980s, *Nationalism Today* had printed the results of surveys that argued that West Indian immigrants had IQs up to 15 per cent lower than native Britons, and concluded that 'Negroes… simply are not fitted to go to White schools or to live in White society.'[70] It linked drugs and crime to the black immigrant population, and wrote of Jamaica that: 'The latest election bloodbath has only confirmed that these people are incapable of ruling themselves and bodes ill for Britain which may one day have more Jamaicans than Jamaica.'[71] As the Strasserites sought to 'build a third way', or 'third position' in the traditional sense of 'neither capitalism nor communism',[72] the economic and social aspects of the programme took greater prominence. Racial separation, national sovereignty and social justice were three sides of a triangle used to explain nationalist ideology at education seminars 'and are inter-dependent'.[73]

But in September 1987 *Nationalism Today* acquired a new slogan. No longer 'The Radical Voice of British Nationalism' it issued 'A Call to Arms, A Call to Sacrifice', proclaimed 'a membership unified around the ideology of the Third Position', identified itself with other Third Positionist regimes and movements abroad, and rejected the old NF as motivated by 'racial hatred and social nihilism'.[74] Central to this change was the realization of the potential of black nationalism. *Nationalism Today* first took note of Louis Farrakhan, then an aide in Jesse Jackson's election campaign, and his anti-semitism in 1984.[75] In 1985, possibly as a result of Nick Griffin's contact with Tom Metzger, the leader of White Aryan Resistance in America and a principal figure in exploring potential cooperation between white and black separatist organizations, a second article on Farrakhan concluded: 'White nationalists everywhere will wish him well for we share a common struggle for the same ends. Racial Separation and Racial Freedom.'[76]

This was followed by a 'photo-essay' on the Nation of Islam and the publication of its programme in November 1986.[77] By issue #42, *Nationalism Today* considered that Farrakhan had 'come to symbolize the new point of departure for the revolutionary forces of the **Third Position**... It is a point where Blacks and Whites meet, not only to combat the greed, exploitation and barbarism of Capitalism and Communism, but also to crush the pernicious ideas of multi-racism and racial intermarriage'. Farrakhan was 'A Godsend to *all* races and cultures...' The comment was made in an article in praise of the founding father of American black separatism, Marcus Garvey.[78]

On race, the Third Positionist objective was thus 'a broad front of racialists of all colours'[79] in a common cause against enforced multi-racialism in the service of capitalist exploitation. The same aim of cooperation applied to other Third Positionist countries, Libya above all.[80] But the NF also praised the third positionist work of Jerry Rawlings in Ghana,[81] noted that 'as Third Positionists we are obliged to support the

Third Way nation of Iran' and wrote an approving obituary of Sankara in Burkina Faso.[82] The ecological and anarchist implications of distributism also took the NF towards Green, animal welfare and anarchist movements, although practical attempts to participate were, as with the miners' strike, regarded as infiltration rather than participation.[83]

These developments, particularly the revised approach to the question of race, alienated the rank and file which had not moved as far from white British nationalism towards the Third Position. Issue 99 of *National Front News*, with the banner slogan 'Fight Racism', provoked an outcry, and the Manchester branch refused to distribute it. Towards the end of 1989 the NF split again, when Griffin, Holland and Colin Todd seceded to form the International Third Position (ITP). In March 1990, the remaining leaders, principally Patrick Harrington, Graham Williamson and David Kerr formed the Third Way, and disbanded the NF. The Flag Group National Front remained in possession of the name and ensured the NF's continued existence.

The factionalism of the NF was costly. As David Kerr recalled, 'I have lived through five splits in the movement myself in 1975, 1979, 1983, 1986 and 1989 and it was very definitely very discouraging to ordinary members.'[84] Membership figures guessed by outside sources are unreliable, but in the mid-1980s appeared to oscillate between two and three thousand.[85] The only consolation was that in the 1980s Conservatism was so strong that the NF could expect to make little headway in any case. Officially, the NF has written off this period of its history: 'the 1980s and early 90s were sluggish',[86] but that was a comment on its political achievement. Ideologically, it was the most innovative period in the history of the British Radical Right since the 1930s.

and echoes are clear within the alt right

Third Positionism and National-Anarchism

The ITP retains much of the doctrine worked out by the political soldiers of the NF during the 1980s. It emphasises the primacy of spiritual revolution and the importance of the New Man embodying that revolution. It is nationalist in defence of the diversity of nations, races and cultures that, in common with much of the recent Radical Right, it sees as threatened by internationalism and enforced muticulturalism and multiracialism. It is accordingly in favour of racial separation, entailing the return of races to their original countries. In its concern for the defence of England as 'Englishness' and of time running out, its outlook

International Third Position

is reminiscent of Joseph Chamberlain. Within the nation, the family forms the basic unit of its society and it stresses the importance of large families. It opposes abortion, artificial birth control, euthanasia, divorce and homosexuality, although it does not condemn, as the Order of the Red Rose did, bachelors and spinsters whom the Red Rose considered to be failing in their social responsibilities.

Like the political soldiers, the ITP is committed to the decentralization of power to the smallest possible unit and building from below, both in its vision of popular self-government in a properly constituted society and as part of the struggle with the existing corrupt system. Creating a counter society, a 'counter-power', from below, again somewhat after the manner of the 1980s NF, will, it argues, ultimately render the system irrelevant. It is strongly committed to distributism and the individual freedom and social justice that distributism sought to secure through widely distributed property. Distributism is the economic corollary and support of political decentralization. In common with earlier Distributists, including the NF of the 1980s, it maintains the superiority of rural over urban living, but seeks a balance between country and town, agriculture and industry. But whilst a guild system would be in place to regulate industry, it evades, as interwar Distributists did, the problem that has always bedevilled distributism, the organization of heavy industry. Here especially, as with Belloc's distributism, it seems that a revolution in values must precede industrial reorganization.

Many of its ideas, the spiritual revolution, the New Man, the need for sacrifice, ruralism and distibutism fall within the traditions of the Radical Right, particularly the anarchist tradition. The insistence that education should go beyond the academic to include the training of character echoes the views of Willoughby de Broke and the Edwardian Right. The enemies also remain the same, Israel and international 'Zionism', international finance and the power of international corporations and media over government. The banking system is condemned, not only for its exploitative practices, but also for its false values, treating money as a commodity rather than as a medium of exchange. But the real enemy is materialism in all its manifestations, including liberalism, capitalism, socialism and, reflecting the later twentieth century shift in attitudes, imperialism. The list also includes anarchism which might be considered a strange position for a Distributist movement.

Where the ITP has developed the ideas of the 1980s is in the more explicit emphasis given to the Christian basis of its spiritual revolution that Steve Brady critizised as religiosity. The Third Position asserts a

'Moral Order' and an 'Objective Truth' which define and delimit the freedom of the individual. The people must live according to the 'Moral Order', their wishes can be deemed invalid despite the commitment to decentralized self-government. The earlier NF belief in a written constitution or a bill of rights has been abandoned, as apparently has the suggestion of an armed people to avert oppression by the state. For the ITP, both the state and the guilds, considered as moral agents, have responsibilities to ensure that the 'Moral Order' is sustained. There exists here a coercive potential at odds with the initial purpose of distributism. Against that, the essence of the ITP position is conversion not coercion.[87] Its English branch has been renamed England First.[88]

Nick Griffin left the ITP not long after its formation, to reappear in 1995 in the BNP. In September 1992, Troy Southgate and others left to form the English Nationalist Movement (ENM) because the ITP refused to continue with the cadre structure, the secessionists disapproved of Roberto Fiore's business operations and above all because they saw in the ITP's leadership an 'increasing obsession with Catholicism and its gradual descent into the reactionary waters of neo-fascism'.[89] Despite the secession, the ENM was still Third Positionist and militant. In 1998, it became the National Revolutionary Faction (NRF), and began to call for 'armed insurrection against the British State in even stronger terms', in contrast to the BNP's 'obsession with marches and elections'. In common with several of the splinter groups since 1990, including the ITP and Blood and Honour/Combat 18, the NRF developed extensive international contacts in what amounts to a 'nationalist international'.

In 2003, the NRF changed again to National Anarchy expressing its rejection of Third Positionism 'beyond Capitalism and Communism' in favour of 'transcending the very notion of beyond'. In place of the state, National Anarchism seeks

> independent enclaves in which National-Anarchists can live according to their own principles and ideals... even after the demise of Capitalism, they neither hope nor desire to establish a national infrastructure, believing that like-minded and pragmatic individuals must set up and maintain organic communities of their own choosing. This, of course, means that whilst the NRF retains its vision of Natural Order and racial separatism it no longer wishes to impose its beliefs on others.'

Nevertheless, National Anarchy also preserves in its outlook many of the concerns of the past. It emphasises again the need for spiritual revolution and the moral vacuum at the heart of western civilization. It believes that

that civilization is doomed to decline and collapse, although unlike social imperialists, including Mosley, it regards that collapse favourably and would hasten its demise to replace it with a more 'natural' way of living. The consequent collapse of western industrial technology is accepted as inevitable, although National Anarchy appears also to favour a far more primitive economy, even one of hunters and gatherers, not least because it sees such a society as enjoying greater leisure. Like Social Credit, it is opposed to the work ethic on which modern industrial society is built.

Its essential position is decentralization in all its forms, political, social and economic, creating self-governing independent village communities in which like-minded people can create their own way of life and defend it as an armed people. Within that framework, however, National Anarchy has its own absolutes derived from its belief in a Natural Order. It is elitist and aristocratic, at least to the point of regarding the emergence of elites and aristocrats, natural leaders, as part of that 'Natural Order'. It is opposed to abortion and homosexuality, and not only opposed to multiracialism, but regards racial miscegenation as inherently dangerous to mankind. To that extent, there is a certain tension arising from the 'Natural Order' and inviolable laws of nature with moral as well as material force on the one hand, and anarchism on the other. Authority remains, even as government is abandoned.[90]

Arguably, by seeing a moral vacuum as the primary problem facing the West, rather than the specifically economic and political problems identified by the Radical Right for much of the twentieth century, both the ITP and National Anarchy have moved beyond the Radical Right.[91] But the spiritual dimension and the need for a revolution in values was the starting point for many of those from Social Imperialism onwards who foresaw the imminent collapse of the empire, or liberalism or Britain's national identity, even if this led them to economic and political rather than moral solutions. In this respect, the ITP and National Anarchy represent a further evolution in the thinking of the Radical Right rather than an entirely new dimension, a response to the new situation of the late twentieth century in which the apparent triumph of materialist international capitalism on a global scale requires a greater assertion of the centrality of anti-materialist nationalism.

The Rise of the BNP

Divisions also afflicted the dissident (Flag) NF. Following the Dublin football riot of 1995, the chairman, Ian Anderson, decided that past associations made the name a liability and transformed it into the National Democrats. Some members remained loyal to the NF name, further dividing the already small group. The National Democrats seem now to be the Campaign for National Democracy rather than an explicit political party. Both the National Democrats and the NF ran candidates in the general election of 1997, and the NF stood again in 2001, but in neither case with any great impact. The NF issued an extensive manifesto in 2001 and claims to be 'back…poised on the brink of the new millennium ready to mushroom once again'.[92] But in course of the 1990s, its leading role on the Radical Right had passed to the BNP.

In contrast to the innovation of the NF in the 1980s, the BNP represented more of a continuation of both the issues and the methods of the 1970s. The combination of a sizeable immigrant community and government attempts to foster a multiracial society enabled it to present the native white population as an oppressed people in their own country. The BNP's 'Rights for Whites' campaign, which took off after a major demonstration in Dewsbury in 1989, marked the beginning of a more active approach. 'The real watershed', as John Tyndall observed, 'signifying the party's determination to enter mainstream politics occurred around 1990'.[93] Although it only contested 13 seats in the 1992 general election and lost all its deposits, extending the 'Rights for Whites' campaign to London began to have an effect.[94] By the end of 1992 the BNP had over 2000 members in over 50 branches. In a local by-election in Tower-Hamlets (Millwall) it secured 20 per cent of the votes cast, and in September 1993, Derek Beacon won the ward with 33.9 per cent of the votes, the first success since the NP in the mid-1970s. The seat was lost in the elections of May 1994, but in those elections the BNP achieved its best results so far. It gained 34 per cent in Newham, and in June, Tyndall won 9 per cent in the Dagenham parliamentary by-election, saving his deposit.

1994 was, however, the peak in the BNP's fortunes in the 1990s. By 1995, it was down to only some 800 members, and fielded only ten candidates in the local elections. In the 1997 parliamentary elections it did slightly better, fielding 55 candidates and saving three deposits, but in the 1998 local elections the party again fought only 34 seats, and in 1999 was still only averaging 7.65 per cent of the votes in the seats it fought, with 17 per cent in Tipton Green the best performance. A full slate of candidates in England and Scotland for the 1999 European elections showed its popular support nationally to be just over 100,000 votes, although membership was again rising,[95] as the asylum seekers factor made its influence felt. The problem from 1994 onwards was pressure from its own creation, Combat 18 (C18), and the internal dissension that this caused.

'Whatever it Takes'

Greater activity by the BNP in the early 1990s revived the perennial problem of security at meetings and thus of recruiting its own stewards. C18 emerged in this way during 1991–92. From the first, however, it was different from earlier stewarding organizations, not least in the experience of its members, despite their relative youth. Gary Hitchcock, who originally devised the name 'Combat 18' had been a member of the British Movement in the early 1980s, as had Adam Butler, Phil Edwards and Charlie Sargent who emerged as the leading figure in the new group.[96] As well as years of street experience, members of C18 already had contacts with football hooligans, Ulster loyalists and the nazi music scene.[97]

The disintegration of the British Movement in 1983[98] may also have contributed to their independent attitude. C18 was aggressive. It produced *Redwatch*, a list of known or suspected anti-fascists, and in 1992 while still formally attached to the BNP attacked left-wing targets, such as the Anarchist bookshop and the offices of the *Morning Star*.[99] An early influence on its thinking was the American, Harold Covington, whose *March Up Country* predicted the extinction of the white race in 50 years, and advocated 'a White Revolution' beginning with a small elite: 'There will be nothing in the way of formal organisation at this stage, just a group of people who hold similar views.' Such informal cohesion remained the essence of C18's operational methods, together with Covington's other recommendation, propaganda. In addition to *Redwatch*, Steve Sargent also produced *Putsch*, John Cato *The Oak* and Charlie Sargent *The Order*.[100]

A white revolution was not part of the BNP's agenda. The Millwall victory indicated electoral possibilities, which dictated respectability. Moreover, there was a strong class element in C18's dislike of the BNP leadership, some members of which Sargent argued, 'view most working class people as scum to be used. Such people can have no place in a National Socialist movement who must be seen to protect and help the White working class of Britain'.[101] The Millwall by-election made no difference to this analysis. Sargent condemned the futility of the BNP's 'tiny "success"' together with the entire democratic approach. 'It is time we faced the truth that elections are a waste of time. ONLY A WHITE WORKING CLASS REVOLT AGAINST THE STATE WILL EVER WIN US ANY FORM OF POWER...'[102] In December 1993 Tyndall pre-empted Sargent and proscribed C18, singling out its ' "class-war" rhetoric... attempting constantly to divide nationalist from nationalist by exploiting differences of social and educational background'.[103]

Beyond tactics and class there was a fundamental ideological divide between the BNP and C18, similar to that between Jordan and Tyndall. C18 was a national socialist movement of white or Aryan rather than British nationalism. The latter it regarded as 'reactionary', whereas national socialism was 'a revolutionary movement which seeks the complete overthrow of the present order and its replacement with a new order: its aim for a complete re-birth, a renaissance...an entirely new type of society, based on noble idealism – and, ultimately seeks to create new ways of living'.[104] In 1994 C18 created the National Socialist Alliance (NSA) with the slogan 'Our race is our nation.' Like C18 itself, this was a loose, umbrella organization of component parts around a central core that widened the split within the BNP between moderates and C18 sympathizers, whilst drawing together a variety of national socialist groups including sections of the British Movement, White Aryan Resistance and subsequently the National Socialist Movement of David Myatt.

Myatt represented a personal link with Colin Jordan and in the early 1970s had been active on behalf of the BM in Leeds.[105] A prolific author, his writings and the *National Socialist* that he launched in 1995 provided C18 with a theoretical basis for their direct action tactics: 'National Socialism means revolution: the overthrow of the existing system and its replacement with a National-Socialist society. Revolution means struggle: it means war...To succeed, such a revolutionary movement needs tough, uncompromising, fanatical individuals.'[106] At the inaugural meeting of the NSA, Charlie Sargent announced 'within a short time we must begin the war'.[107]

Race war was both the means to destabilize the country and overthrow the system, and an end in itself. The ultimate object according to a magazine attributed to a rising figure in C18, Will Browning, was 'to ship all non-whites back to Africa, Asia or Arabia, alive or in body bags...To execute all queers...To execute all white race mixers...To weed out all Jews in the Government, the media, the arts, the professions. To execute all Jews who have actively helped to damage the white race and to put into camps the rest until we find a final solution for the eternal Jew',[108]

▷ these hippy-sounding ideas of distributism

and violence

views with which Charlie Sargent agreed: 'My view is that all blacks should be killed... There is bound to be racial war in Europe – it is only a matter of time and we in Britain are ready.'[109]

With C18, violence entered a new level beyond street politics. Late in 1994, in issue 3 of a new magazine, *Combat 18*, Will Browning included information on bomb making, lists of names and the exhortation, 'Now you have the technology, bomb the bastards.'[110] As a result, early in 1995 the police raided the homes of both Browning and Charlie Sargent, and both were charged with race relations offences. The following month, the Dublin football riot was blamed on C18 by the media.[111] C18 had done what the BUF did in the 1930s with the violence at Olympia and the Battle of Cable Street, aroused so much criticism of its violence that the state was forced to be seen to act. From then on C18 endured increasing surveillance and harassment.

It was also beginning to suffer internal dissent. Music was the one success story of the 1980s. Initially organized around the NF, Ian Stuart Donaldson, the lead singer of the iconic band, Skrewdriver, broke away in 1987 to form Blood and Honour which by the early 1990s was organized by surviving elements of the British Movement. After his death in 1993, C18, which had already been moving into the music scene, took over. Again, its venture was marked by innovation. ISD Records was the first independent nazi CD label realizing profits estimated at over £100,000.[112] In contrast to much of the Radical Right, C18 was comparatively well funded.

The likelihood that Browning and Sargent would be imprisoned for *Combat 18* #3 raised the question of an interregnum to maintain C18 control for the duration. There was discontent within Blood and Honour,[113] the British Movement waited in the wings, and in 1995 the BNP counterattacked with a five page article in *Spearhead* claiming in effect that C18 was a state asset.[114] C18's response incurred the wrath of David Lane, then serving 190 years in the United States for his membership of the American Far Right terrorist group, The Order. Lane, who enjoyed heroic status, damned C18's leadership as 'obviously Zionist agents or they are so ignorant and dangerous that they might as well be. It can no longer be tolerated. For now, the bands will need to provide their own security. At the appropriate time, the enemy amongst us will face a night of the long knives'.[115]

Under pressure from both the police and critics within the Right, C18 did what all Radical Right groups were prone to do, divide into those like Charlie Sargent who wished to compromise rather than alienate more of

Blood and Honour, and those who, like Will Browning, wished to move into active terrorism. The difference in approach was compounded by confusion over ISD accounts and Sargent's accusation that Browning had stolen the ISD money.[116] But the planned letter bomb campaign from Denmark and Sweden, reputedly inspired by Browning, was foiled by police in Denmark on a tip-off from Britain[117], whilst the feud between him and Sargent culminated in the murder of Browning's friend, Chris Castle, for which Sargent and Martin Cross were ultimately convicted. Before then came the long-delayed trial and conviction of Sargent, Cross and Browning for *Combat 18* #3. With its leading figures in prison and its members confused and divided, Steve Sargent was right to conclude: 'The movement here is now in tatters.' An attempt to stitch together those tatters was made with the formation of the NSM in 1998. It was, however, small, with only about 80 members and when it was revealed that David Copeland, who planted three nail bombs in London in 1999, was the Hampshire organizer of the NSM, its then leader, Tony Williams, closed it down.

Combat 18 survived the disruption. On his release, Will Browning continued with a more directly anti-state agenda. 'We are anti-Government, we want to be given our own land where we can govern ourselves. The root of our problem is the Government... It is the Government who try to destroy us, imprison us, murder us. It is the government that floods our nation with non-whites...'.[118] In 2001, C18 was reported as 'closely aligned' with the NF,[119] operating as it has always operated by linking up with football hooligans in a loose informal way. Such methods proved effective in Oldham in May of that year. Riots that the police described as 'sheer carnage' were, according to Nick Lowles, the product of a 'C-18 inspired chain of events'.[120] On 1 July 2001, in an article about the Oldham riots, the *Observer* reported that a new group, the Order of White Knights, had been formed as a result of the riots composed of experienced C18 members, but gave no further information. It also reported metal fences had been put up to separate the rival white and immigrant groups.[121] For a government committed to a multiracial society it was a small but significant admission of failure.

Men in Suits

Despite John Tyndall's claim that the modernization of the BNP began long before the leadership election of September 1999, it is his successor,

Nick Griffin, who has been credited with the rapid transformation of the BNP at the start of the twenty-first century. Griffin returned from the political wilderness in 1995, joining the BNP and becoming editor of the *Rune*, and then of *Spearhead*. His early record in the BNP, as Tyndall has pointed out in a well-documented critique, was not one of a modernizing moderate[122], but that of a hardliner who argued that 'We need to take political people and convert them into thugs.'[123]

Although the BNP has moderated its policy on other issues such as homosexuality, the key area of adjustment is race, combined with a radical change in presentation. Despite using the now common argument that if current demographic trends continue 'we, the native British people, will be an ethnic minority in our own country within sixty years',[124] the BNP has abandoned the central tenet of compulsory repatriation in favour of voluntary repatriation. For Griffin, this is the 'the historically vital switch'.[125] Further immigration would be halted immediately, and voluntary repatriation encouraged by 'generous financial incentives both for the individuals and the countries in question'. Overseas aid would be directed to those countries willing to take back their ethnic population, and the BNP is prepared to spend 'whatever it takes to ensure that Britain once again becomes – and will remain – the fundamentally white nation that it always was before 1948'.

There would be domestic pressures to leave. Non-whites who chose to remain would not have full citizenship status but 'will be regarded as permanent guests', facing 'a continual effort' to convince them to leave, in the context of 'a comprehensive programme of national preference schemes, designed to undo the wrongs of decades of anti-white "positive discrimination"'.[126] Griffin shares Tyndall's view that anything more than this policy would provoke retaliation from abroad, particularly from the United States which 'would bomb this country back into the Stone Age if we gave them the excuse by evicting the last non-white at gunpoint'.[127] He is also reported as wishing 'to shift the focus from race to culture',[128] a more flexible approach that would allow the possibility of the assimilation of a small non-white minority. In the aftermath of the destruction of the world trade centre in September 2001, the immediate threat is seen as 'the fundamentalist wing of militant Islam',[129] and not the black population.

The BNP has not shed its opposition to what it considers Zionist globalization, nor abandoned its commitment to economic nationalism. 'Withdrawal from the European Union', 'selective' protection to ensure 'secure well-paid employment', 'greater national self-sufficiency', 'the *his got a lot of what he wanted...*

restoration of our economy and land to British ownership', and of 'Britain's family and trading ties with Australia, Canada and New Zealand', 'industrial reconstruction' and 'encouraging worker shareholder and co-operative schemes', are all in the party's policy. So, too are its more traditionalist proposals for discipline and the ending of 'politically correct indoctrination' in schools, the reintroduction of national service, but with a strong civilian content, a 'crack down on crime', 'a return to healthy moral values...strengthening the family' including 'financial incentives for women to have children and so offset the present dangerously low birthrate', the guarantee of political freedom through a bill of rights or written constitution, and the devolution of power 'to the lowest level possible'.[130]

The party recognizes the need to get more of these policies across to escape its one issue image, but given the centrality of race to its thinking, this could be difficult. 'Mankind', Griffin argues, 'is divided into races, and those races, while sharing many common features of humanity are innately different in many ways beyond mere colour...The British National Party recognizes such ineradicable facts of human nature and seeks to base its programme on such realities...' Nationality, although influenced by many other factors 'is first and foremost decided by ethnicity', the differences are 'genetically determined'. The fundamental objection to immigrants is not the competition for jobs, houses and services, but because 'their very presence in such numbers will inevitably transform our society, changing Britain and the British peoples into something which is not British'. From this point of view, the 'dogmatic liberal ruling class' is 'steadily destroying the very possibility of preserving racial and cultural differences...in favour of what they call integration, which is something which honest scientists call miscegenation, and which we recognize as a form of genocide...a programme of cultural and ethnic genocide'.[131]

The BNP has attempted to distance itself from the charge of racism, claiming to be opposed to the system 'which imports cheap labour', and that the skills immigrants have acquired in Britain would be better used assisting the development of their own countries. It condemns racist attacks and violence and claims that 'real race-haters...have long been recognized as thoroughly unsuitable as members'.[132] It has a number of subsidiary sections. Its Ethnic Liaison Committee, chaired by the half-Turkish Lawrence Rustem, has been regarded by its critics as a publicity stunt or a devious attempt to exploit divisions between ethnic minorities. F.A.I.R (Families Against Immigrant Racism) has come in for similar criticism, particularly for its methods and claims. Both, however, can be seen in another light as extensions of the commitment of the BNP to the electoral tactic of 'community politics', working at the grass roots and listening to popular anxieties, many of which, rightly or wrongly, are about asylum seekers, race relations and government priorities.

By Radical Right standards, moderation has so far been a remarkable electoral success. In 2000, the BNP won 2.87 per cent of the votes in the party list section of the London Assembly election; in the provinces, where it ran only 17 candidates, the party won 23.7 per cent of the vote in Tipton Green, 21 per cent in one Burnley ward and 16 per cent in Dudley. It was a reasonable showing for a party that was described in *Searchlight* as 'a paper organisation in the vast majority of the country'. At that time, it was believed that 'the results clearly illustrate how the BNP's strength lies among traditional working-class Labour supporters. Like the NF before, the BNP is benefiting from increasing disillusionment in Labour's heartlands'.[133]

By May 2002, the party had built up sufficient support to make the breakthrough at local level, winning 3 seats, all in Burnley. Between then and the elections of May 2003 it won two more seats in by-elections, the Mill Hill ward of Blackburn in November, and Calderdale (Halifax) in January 2003. Victory in Calderdale, where support came from areas that 'normally return a strong Conservative vote', prompted a revision of the party's support. 'Looking down on Armageddon', Nick Lowles noted that Cliviger with Worsthorne, which the BNP had won, was 'arguably the most affluent ward in Burnley'; in Eccleshill (Bradford) the BNP vote came from 'the more affluent areas of the ward'; Royton North (Oldham), where the BNP secured 29 per cent of the vote, was 'a more prosperous ward' than the others contested, and 'one of its best votes' was 'in the Hillingdon ward of Harehills [London], another traditional Conservative area'. The BNP was gaining from 'Tory meltdown'.[134] Accordingly, whilst the BNP formerly expected to win over 'disillusioned Labour voters' and 'there is evidence that it did in many places, the party is now aware that it is the Conservative areas which it should be targeting'.[135]

This analysis was further confirmed by the BNP victory in the local elections of May 2003 in Broxbourne, Hertfordshire, a predominantly white, traditionally Conservative, area with few ethnic or social problems, but in the south.[136] In those elections, the party gained 11 seats to take its national total to 16, which became 17 in August with its by-election victory in Heckmondwike (Yorkshire) where the BNP targeted 'the middle class areas of the ward' as well as areas of social deprivation.[137]

In September, it also won Thurrock (Grays Riverside) in Essex. The racial issue is outside the linear parameters of mainstream politics, and the BNP can reasonably campaign as both the defender of the white working classes in the North and of England's green and pleasant land in the south on the basis that both are threatened by the same enemy, alien immigration. It is a potent issue extending beyond deprived areas. Asylum seekers are the UFOs of the suburbs. Rumours abound, there are reports of sightings, but even the BNP accepts that there are no asylum seekers in Broxbourne. *So what y there are?*

The appeal of the transformed BNP, however, rests on more than immigration and race. The Heckmondwike campaign centred on law and order, and 'there was very little mention of race...'[138] Support for the BNP is also a protest vote by both rich and poor, which has various interconnected elements. At one level, it is a protest inspired by a belief that immigrants receive preferential treatment. As a council worker in Dudley noted, the government not the council sets the standard for asylum accommodation, and some asylum seekers enjoy higher living standards than local people at public expense.[139] The reaction is similar to that of the residents associations and the RPS of the 1960s and 1970s, a combination of fear of 'swamping' and the politics of scarcity in a dependency culture. There is anecdotal evidence that some BNP voters do distinguish between the modernized BNP and more hardline organizations.[140]

But the protest is also against perceived neglect by an apparently remote, uncaring political establishment, fuelled by a sense of powerlessness within local communities. If an area can become sufficiently notorious as a haven of the BNP and thus, according to the national image of the BNP, a hotbed of potentially violent inter-racial tension, then the authorities may pay attention to its deprivation. In Slade Green (Bexley, Kent) the success of Colin Smith, the BNP candidate, in coming second with 27 per cent of the vote in a council by-election in July 2000, stimulated a £1 million local regeneration programme that reassured local residents that they had not, after all, been left to rot.[141] This is a double-edged response, allowing the BNP to argue that without its intervention they would have been.[142] In this analysis, the BNP gains because supporting it is the most dramatic shock that voters can give to the established political parties not only on immigration, crime and the allocation of resources, but on almost any issue that angers them.

The protest element puts Griffin's achievement into context. Although Labour was re-elected convincingly in 2001, it was on a turnout of only 59 per cent, the lowest for 100 years. The hopes of 1997 had vanished, to be replaced by even greater resignation, but the Conservatives were never seen as a realistic alternative. For the first time since Thatcher took office, political space re-opened on the right on a range of issues that the BNP was well positioned to exploit. But as in the 1970s, success awakened the opposition. Since the heady days of the summer of 2003, the BNP has suffered some setbacks. In October, it lost a seat in Burnley, and failed to secure a widely expected victory in Mixenden, Calderdale. In two further council by-elections in November, it once again failed to make a break-through in Oldham, and made little progress in a difficult ward in Birmingham.[143] It remains to be seen whether the BNP will be able to maintain its momentum, still less move beyond protest to support for its own radical policies for social reconstruction.

Conclusion: Past Failures and Future Prospects

The world and Britain's place in it changed during the twentieth century, and the Radical Right responded with changes of emphasis, but the central themes remain central. Edwardian social imperialists feared that racial degeneration would lead to the loss of the empire. In practical terms, it was a largely environmental fear, the impossibility of rearing an imperial race in the slums accentuated by anxiety about decadence in the upper classes occasioned by luxury. At the end of the century, with the imperial 'mission' abandoned and the empire lost, the 'invasion' that titillated the late Victorian and Edwardian imagination had occurred. But it was a different invasion to that imagined by those novelists. The history of the Radical Right hinges around the loss of international power and the arrival of coloured immigrants in the middle decades of the twentieth century. Immigration and its impact on the native population has become the principal fear with the corresponding focus on colour and religion, particularly Islamic fundamentalism. ⟶ _post 9/11_

For some sections of the Radical Right, the idea of 'race' itself had changed from 'British imperial' through 'Nordic' to a far wider white European diaspora. But the primary concern is still nationalism, most frequently based on race, and the threat from internationalism in all its forms, 'globalism', the 'New World Order' and the malevolent machinations of international finance. Overt anti-semitism may have declined, but anti-semitism still lurks behind the opposition to internationalism, immigration and ethnic minorities. The Radical Right's answer remains economic nationalism, even if the insulation has become progressively more insular than imperial.

but same central themes

141

The same can be said of the Radical Right's other core beliefs. The tension between inevitable disaster and potential renaissance has changed from the Chamberlain/Mosley choice between a glorious imperial civilization and impotent insularity, to insularity or racial annihilation through 'passive genocide', but the tension between disaster and action is still present. The Radical Right still hovers between authoritarianism and anarchism; it still believes, though with rather less conviction, that the people are basically 'sound' in contrast to the inadequacies, or worse, of its political leaders; it still sees the need for leadership by 'a new type of man' committed to the virtues of service, sacrifice, honour, loyalty and duty. Whether he is called an 'aristocrat', 'fascist man' or a 'political soldier', the 'new type of man' is a still part of an elite that can recognize and respond to the struggle that is the fate of mankind and the mission of civilization. With the expansion of 'welfare capitalism' in the second half of the century, the Radical Right analysis has increasingly concentrated on the 'servile state' rooted in the materialist base of both capitalism and socialism, and hence the anti-materialist, 'anti-bigness' Distributist response as the 'third way'. The domestic solution to Britain's problems, political, economic and spiritual lies in 'back to the land' mutated at times to 'blood and soil', combined with village communities and workers' cooperatives.

The problem of the Radical Right is that its outlook, whether on race, economic nationalism or 'small is beautiful', runs counter to accepted liberal capitalist orthodoxy at the various levels of government, the media and, for the most part, public opinion. Throughout the twentieth century, the Radical Right has failed to get beyond the political fringe. As a result it has been, and still is, beset by the difficulty of getting its complex message across with the consequent dilemma posed by 'respectable' and 'street' politics. It peaked in 1934 when the BUF had some 50,000 members; in the second half of the century the NF reached only 17,500 in 1974. At its most obvious, it failed because the vast majority of the electorate refused to vote for it, it never achieved anything like the physical force to overthrow the parliamentary system, and despite predictions, that system resolutely failed to collapse economically or politically.

General explanations for this lack of support tend to be negative correlations of what happened elsewhere and apply principally to the inter-war years[1]: the absence of recent foreign invasion or defeat in a major war, to which might be related a strong sense of national identity when threatened by a foreign power; a relatively long tradition of parliamentary government under a flexible elite which adapted to the gradual extension of democracy; a strong Conservative party which worked with democracy rather than becoming isolated and reactionary; a reformist Labour movement, both parliamentary and industrial, that evolved within the liberal tradition, and a self-image of being successful both in acquiring and governing an empire, and in relinquishing it when it could no longer be sustained.

To these could be added more specific factors: the notorious difficulty created for minor parties by the 'first past the post' system; a near boycott and neglect by the media which left the Right struggling for publicity and turning to street marches and demonstrations; the presence of an equally militant and determined Left opposition which challenged it on those streets, and the underestimated residual power of the British state. The Right might, from the 1930s until the end of the century demand the old British 'right' of freedom of speech and assembly, but 'rights' were such as parliament determined. If the Right appeared to be too troublesome, its 'rights' were curtailed by legislation from which there was no appeal.

The absence, in relative terms, of a severe economic crisis is perhaps less significant than the resilience of the political system and identification with it by the vast majority of the population. There were two points at which the British economy appeared to be in sufficient trouble to threaten social and political stability, the first half of the 1930s and the late 1970s/early 1980s. Both moments occurred within a longer period of economic difficulty and both were preceded by trade union activity that amounted to a challenge to the prerogatives of the state. It was during these periods that the Radical Right achieved its peak membership, but in neither case was there any level of support that threatened the major parties, or of unrest with which the police could not deal.

The Radical Right also contributed considerably to its own difficulties, most obviously in the endless succession of splits throughout the century. Divided on tactics, presentation, and policy, riven by bitter internal feuds, the Right was self-destructive. With the exception of a small core, members tended to flow through it rather than remain as a stable base on which to build. Unable to break out of its marginalized position, throughout the century the Right oscillated between electoral politics and 'street politics'. They were not mutually exclusive but they required different approaches and presented different images to different target audiences. The violence of street politics alienated respectable voters; moderation discouraged activists.

The difficulty in getting the policies across tended to disguise the problems inherent in the policies themselves. Arguably, even when Joseph

Chamberlain launched tariff reform in 1903 it was already too late for a beleaguered Britain to find refuge in her empire. Whatever the ties of kinship and sentiment, the self-governing Dominions would not accept the role of granaries, mines and markets for industrialized Britain. It was not until after the Second World War that Mosley belatedly recognized Dominion industrialization, and turned instead to Africa. He failed completely to recognize the strength of colonial nationalism which had been evident even before 1914. Despite the LEL and Tyndall's fantasy of reconquering Africa and reuniting the white empire, the reality that the empire was not an option slowly dawned. The Radical Right had to adapt to a post-imperial and increasing globalized world.

Nor was this the only adaptation required. Both tariff reform and Mosley's programme in the 1930s were radical in their commitment to intervention in the economy. After the Second World War, apart from the brief interlude of the libertarian New Right in the 1980s, intervention was orthodox. At the same time industrial mergers and the attempts by successive governments to find a role for the trade unions brought a degree of corporatism into mainstream economic thinking. With these developments unfettered capitalism, the right–wing pole of the Left-Right polarity that the Radical Right sought to transcend, was partially removed. The taming of the trade unions, the collapse of Soviet power and the advent of New Labour removed the other, international and domestic socialism. By then, however, the Radical Right had redefined its old enemies, capitalism and socialism, as the globalization pursued by the New World Order in the interests of international finance-capitalism.

In the second half of the twentieth century, stripped of its more orthodox economic ideas and moving in a changed world, the Radical Right became identified increasingly, if not entirely accurately, with a single issue, race. There was, however, a degree of change in its outlook even on race. Insofar as coloured races intruded on the thinking of the Radical Right before 1950, and that was little, the feeling was still one of superiority and confidence born of imperial rule. By the 1980s this outlook had changed. As Griffin wrote early in 2003, 'as racial realists we have no choice but to recognize the wealth of scientific data which shows that East Asians – Japanese or Chinese for example – who live in Western societies have lower average crime rates and higher average intelligence levels than us whites, and that these differences are genetically determined even when factors such as social and economic status are taken into account'.[2]

Neither the BNP nor the NF are imperialist, thereby abandoning one of the founding elements of the Radical Right, its conviction that the empire was a formative influence on the character of the British race. Rather, the reassessment of the capacity of other races has reinforced the pessimistic biological determinism of Arnold Leese which led him to advocate retreating behind the Channel to preserve and re-build racial stocks free from contamination. Repatriation is a continuation of the same defensive thinking. The British are an endangered species. The strongest argument of the contemporary Right against a multiracial society is that most of the evidence suggests that such societies dissolve into race war. Even critics of the Right acknowledge a problem with multiracialism: 'It is an idea that isn't sure how to become a reality ... So far no one has come up with a post-imperial identity for Britain that is broad enough to be inclusive but relevant enough to want to be included in. There remains an uncertainty about how to embrace cultural diversity without succumbing to cultural relativism.'[3] As long as that uncertainty remains, there is political space for those who deny the possibility of inclusion.

However, 'failure' for the Radical Right in particular has to take into account not only its electoral performance, but also its ambitions. The Radical Right sought power to transform, revolutionize, society and politics. But it also sought to transform mankind, to create the 'higher type of man', both in terms of physique and, more importantly, attitude, from the self-interest of materialist capitalism to the service of the national community. Such a change was implicit even in social imperialism, the conversion of the urban 'street corner loafer' in his dead-end job into the disciplined worker or farm boy/boy scout through uniformed youth movements, conscription and 'back to the land'. It became explicit in the interwar years as the Fascists argued that the 'modern movement' would be created from 'new men ... free from the trammels of the past'[4] and Distributists awaited a change in outlook to make their system viable. It remained explicit in its austere form in the ideas of the NF political soldiers in the 1980s and the adoption of the cadre structure. It was both a precursor to and part of the process of acquiring power.

But it was also an objective in its own right, an essential element in the realization of the vision of the integrated national community. In this respect, the dispute between respectable 'populists' and doctrinaires extends beyond tactics to encompass fundamentals. The former may achieve power by concessions to prevailing opinion. But if that opinion is decadent, corrupted by materialism to the point that concessions mean the abandonment of radical change to both society and the individual, then electoral success may be bought at the price of ideological failure.

New Century: Old Problems?

Allowing for differences in emphasis and detail, at the start of the twenty-first century there is broad, though not complete, agreement between the major groups on the Radical Right over a range of attitudes, policies and the type of society they would wish to create. The starting point is nationalism, usually race-nationalism, national independence and separate development; the immediate consequences, apart from the repatriation of coloured immigrants and ending or redirecting foreign aid, are withdrawal from the European Union and the North Atlantic Treaty Organisation (NATO) and, by implication at least, from the United Nations, the International Monetary Fund and other international bodies associated with the New World Order. Nationalist Britain would have an independent defence force including nuclear capacity, free of international commitments. Economic policy would be nationalist and independent, protective tariffs and redirected investment to British industries promoting employment, a high-wage economy and self-sufficiency. That economy would be liberated from the power of international banks by restoring the control of credit to the government, explicitly or implicitly nationalizing the banking system, and breaking up multinational and monopolist companies.

'Britain for the British' is understood in class as well race-national terms. Both the BNP and the NF draw much of their inspiration from distributism, the latter being explicitly Distributist. The ideal is that of small businesses, small farms and, where industry remains large-scale, workers cooperatives owned by the workers, restoring ownership as far as possible to the British people. The modern Radical Right is, however, unafraid of the state, and is best described as 'mixed' or 'symbiotic' distributism, retaining large-scale industry where unavoidable, and sufficient state control to ensure the survival of a Distributist economy. But the power of the central state would be limited by a constitution or Bill of Rights and as much power as possible decentralized to local government working through smaller local institutions. Contrary to the projected image of the Radical Right as authoritarian, both the BNP and the NF claim that their political reforms would extend democracy in government.

Insofar as this represents the promotion of family firms and farms, it reflects the importance placed by the Radical Right on the family as the basic institution of its reconstructed society. As a pious aspiration, praise of the family hardly differentiates the Radical Right from the mainstream parties. The Radical Right, however, not only proposes greater financial assistance but would require a positive image of family life in the media, in contrast to what it considers to be the encouragement of alternative life-styles, including homosexuality, to which it is strongly opposed. In education, inculcating a pride in the national heritage goes hand in hand with the restoration of classroom discipline and for post-school youth some form of primarily civilian national service. Comparatively minor in the context of national regeneration, other reforms include the need to improve the NHS and transport and to 'crack down on crime', where the Radical Right would re-introduce capital punishment for serious offences like murder if guilt was beyond doubt.[5]

In this thinking there is a considerable degree of continuity from the past. The 'Strasserite'/Distributist legacy is apparent in both economic and political decentralization. Between the wars the Radical Right was just as suspicious of international organizations such as the League of Nations, and just as determined to 'mind Britain's business'. The critical difference lies in the idea of separate development and the rejection of imperialism, or indeed any blocs, in favour of insularity and such bilateral agreements as would suit Britain's interests. At a time when Britain's military and economic power was far greater, neither Chamberlain nor Mosley believed that Britain could stand alone. John Tyndall cites Sweden, Norway and Switzerland as models of successful non-aligned independence,[6] but the thinking remains defensive.

Broad agreement is not sufficient to overcome differences on key points or promote organizational cooperation. In 2001, Eddy Morrison, a veteran of Radical Right politics, formed Aryan Unity to campaign for the unity of the white races. Aryan nations include almost all European countries east as far as the Urals, together with the white populations of the United States, Australia, New Zealand, Canada and South Africa plus minorities in South America. 'At this time when the whole White World is in mortal peril... the thing for Aryans in all lands is now to UNITE or face extinction.'[7] It is 'supranational' in the Colin Jordan tradition of racially based nationalism, with the goal of 'a linked network of White Nationalist groups all over the globe'.[8] Aryan unity also hoped for at least a linked network of racial Nationalist groups in Britain,[9] but this proved a vain hope.[10]

In May 2002, the White Nationalist Party (WNP) was set up explicitly because 'none of the existing Nationalist groups in Britain offer a full programme of White Nationalism' either 'compromising on major issues', or worse 'prepared to sell out our basic ideologies.'[11] The WNP is the British political wing of Aryan Unity, 'part of a world wide revolt of the White People against the New World Order multiracialists who would see it destroyed.'[12] Its first principle states:

Our race comes above all. Without the solid foundation of a homogeneous race, no healthy nation can be built. We are opposed to mass immigration into our homelands and are opposed to both integration of races and the multi-racial society. We believe that racial integration breeds violence and hatred and is detrimental to all races. Racial separation leads to mutual respect and separate development as each race follows its own unique destiny.[13]

On many issues, the family, crime, withdrawal from the EU, NATO, the UN 'and all other arms of the New World Order'; a strong and independent defence force; economic nationalism; 'nationalization of the banking system...breaking the stranglehold that the international bankers have on the United Kingdom'; 'the encouragement of British agriculture'; rebuilding national pride, reorganizing education, reform of the NHS; ending overseas aid, 'a proper Constitution and Bill of Rights'; the reintroduction of capital punishment, 'a major crack down on all types of crime', and ending abortion, it is broadly in accord with the policies of the NF and even the BNP. Even so, just as the tone of the NF differs from the BNP in its more aggressive presentation of 'a creed of national regeneration' or even 'National Revolution' to determine whether 'a great land and a great people slide with the old parties into oblivion or...once more...scale the heights of greatness',[14] so the tone of the WNP is still more outspoken in its ideological dynamic.

Its inspiration is unashamedly national socialist,[15] and thus in the etatist tradition which sets it slightly apart from the anti-etatist elements of distributism incorporated into the outlook of the NF and BNP. It is 'morally opposed' not just to 'liberal democracy' as 'another form of International totalitarianism' but all democracy as 'a fraud and a sham',[16] and advocates the 'Leadership Principle'.[17] 'We wish to establish a new type of State based on leadership, authority and discipline. There are no rights without duties.'[18] Its object is 'the creation of a morally correct society...' through 'a moral, spiritual and physical revolution in the hearts and minds of the masses so that all become part of a healthy, clean and energetic folk state'.[19] Like the pre-Second-World-War Radical Right, the WNP is prepared to fight elections, demonstrate and march, but it predicts a coming crisis, and expects little change before it.[20]

[Marginal handwritten note:] Believing that other races are inferior whilst also

The WNP remains committed to 'compulsory repatriation of all non-whites'; 'a return to active street politics'; 'total opposition to the pink Mafia of organized homosexuality' and 'total opposition to Zionism and Israel'.[21] It is on these key points that it criticizes the BNP's 'populist nationalism', even while welcoming its electoral successes. Perhaps more significant in activating the WNP is what it sees as the 'weeding out of all veteran "Nazis" who had kept the flame flying for decades'.[22] John Tyndall, who has criticized Griffin both for being the original source of the divisions within the BNP, and for turning his back on his previous principles[23] remains a focal point for discontented hardliners still within the BNP, and has the outside support of the WNP.[24] Those hardliners are still dubious about the new direction of the BNP and how far it will go. Even Griffin concedes that the February 2003 issue of *Freedom*, in which the editor, Martin Wingfield, defended a 'very decent and hard-working BNP activist' and candidate who had mixed race grandchildren, 'struck many experienced and dedicated nationalists like a dead rat in the face'.[25] There have reportedly been resignations and defections to the WNP across the country, but especially in the Northwest and Yorkshire.[26] Tyndall was expelled from the BNP in August 2003, but has since been reinstated.

The WNP was not, however, the only new party to emerge on, or near, the Radical Right in the new century. There are also a number of groups wedged in the narrowing gap between the BNP and the disaffected Conservative Right. The Liberal Nationalist Party, which seems to exist only as a small website, openly expresses its support for the BNP despite some serious policy differences. It opposes 'National Socialist ideals and all other forms of nationalist fundamentals, Christian or otherwise', and projects itself as a party for the working classes 'the everyday victims who simply do not belong to conservatives or Aryan revolutionaries... It is the white working classes condemned to multicultural ghettoes who desperately need our support and attention'.[27]

More significant is the Freedom Party which, according to *Spearhead*, was 'formed from a breakaway from the BNP',[28] but which appears to be more an emanation from the Bloomsbury Forum, a meeting point for dissidents from both the Conservative party and the BNP. It published *Standard Bearers: British Roots of the New Right* in 1999, a book which regards as standard bearers not only Conservative figures, but Blatchford, Belloc and Morris. The Freedom Party includes not only some former members of the BNP who had drifted towards the now defunct Revolutionary

The Freedom Party

Conservative Caucus in the early 1990s, but more recent defectors from the Griffin era, including Sharron Edwards (Deputy Chairman), Steve Edwards (National Agent/Campaign Director), and Michael Newland (National Press Officer). It already has its own candidates in local elections that stand against the BNP, and seems to be making an impact. Sharron Edwards won its first council seat in Wombourne (South Staffordshire) with 40.6 percent of the vote.[29] Like the BNP, it seeks to replace the Conservative party which the chairman, Adrian Davies, believes is 'dying on its feet'.[30]

Future Prospects

The political situation in the early 2000s has given the Radical Right opportunities for expansion. The Conservative party's lacklustre performance in the 1990s culminating in its overwhelming defeat in 1997 partially removed a key obstacle to right-wing credibility. The Labour party is sufficiently at odds with itself for a Labour dissident to split the Labour vote at Heckmondwike, and voter alienation from the mainstream is substantial. The widely publicized issue of asylum seekers has reopened the whole question of immigration and with it 'swamping', preferential treatment and the exploitation of Britain's social services. It is an issue on which all major political parties appear weak and confused, but which, by its very existence, draws attention again to the coloured communities already living in Britain. Fear of crime, especially street crime, is overlain with racial preconceptions. Increasing awareness of international terrorism after 9/11 colours perceptions of all Muslims. In 2001, serious rioting erupted that gave some substance to the Radical Right's critique of multiracialism and its assertion that the consequence will be race war.

Thus far, the BNP, by distancing itself from extremism, has been able to exploit these new circumstances. At present, it is the most viable Radical Right alternative to mainstream politics. The NF appears to have divided, albeit on organizational rather than programmatic grounds, with the Yorkshire NF attacking the Directorate for over-centralization, and adopting the title the United National Front.[31] The WNP has suffered a setback in the rejection by the Electoral Commission of its application for registration as a political party on the grounds that the word 'White' might be considered offensive![32] At the expense of a disagreement with the ITP, its members have since registered the name England

First Party which won 14 per cent of the vote in its first local election contest in Heysham South (Lancashire).[33] The Freedom Party, despite Sharron Edwards' success, has yet to make its mark in contrast to the media coverage that the BNP receives.

There are risks in the central position in which the BNP finds itself within the Radical Right, and with so many parties in so narrow a political space the self-destructive history of the Radical Right over the past century may well repeat itself. In electoral terms, the BNP has achieved more in the first three years of the twenty-first century than the Radical Right as a whole achieved in the previous seventy. Whether that is enough, or whether in becoming 'national populism' the BNP has, as the WNP argues, sacrificed the radical aspiration of a new national community to the exigencies of political pragmatism is another question. The long debate between 'populists' and 'hardliners' continues. By retaining at least strong elements of distibutism and building up from below through community politics, the BNP has added another dimension to working within the system while seeking its radical alteration. The ITP and even more National Anarchy represent a further evolution of the distributist strand in Radical Right thinking, recognizing its anarchist potential. The outlook of the Radical Right remains, as it was throughout the twentieth century, ideologically innovative.

Notes

Introduction: Some Pointers Towards a Definition

1. Martin Walker, *The National Front* (2nd edn, 1978), p. 9.
2. Nigel Fielding, *The National Front* (1981), p. vii.
3. The word 'racist' is used throughout in the specific sense of a belief in racial differences. It is not intended to imply either a belief in the superiority of one 'race' over another, or aggression towards other 'races'. The Right often used the word 'racialist' in a vain attempt to distinguish the idea of separate development from that of racial superiority.
4. 'Spooks' of various kinds have been part of the legend of the Radical Right since J. M. Kennedy was rumoured to have been spying on A. R. Orage's idiosyncratic paper, the *New Age*, before 1914. See Paul Selver, *Orage and the New Age Circle*, (1959), p. 10. Allegations and rumours serve the political purpose of discrediting individuals and spreading distrust, but are hard to substantiate.
5. Nick Ryan's rather startling description of John Tyndall, Nick Ryan, *Homeland* (2003), p. 54.
6. D. S. Lewis, *Illusions of Grandeur. Mosley, Fascism and British Society, 1931–81* (1987), pp. 7–9.
7. Maximilien Robespierre, Report on the Principles of Political Morality, 5 February 1794 in Paul H. Beik (ed.), *The French Revolution* (1970), p. 279.
8. The definition of fascism is still debated. For an introduction see Roger Griffin, *The Nature of Fascism* (1991, 1994); Roger Eatwell, 'Towards a New Model of Generic Fascism', *Journal of Theoretical Politics*, 4, 2 (1992), pp. 161–94; Dave Renton, *Fascism, Theory and Practice* (1999),

Roger Griffin, 'The Primacy of Culture: The Current Growth (or Manufacture) of Consensus within Fascist Studies', *Journal of Contemporary History* 37, 1 (2002), pp. 21–43; 'Comments on Roger Griffin' in ibid., 37, 2 (2002), pp. 259–74; and Robert O. Paxton, 'The Five Stages of Fascism', *Journal of Modern History* 70 (1998), pp. 1–23.

9. Gladstone to Acton, 11 February 1885, in John Morley, *The Life of William Ewart Gladstone* (1903), 3, p. 173.

10. 'The Manifesto of the Enrages', 25 June 1793, in John Hardman, *The French Revolution Sourcebook* (1999), p. 179.

11. E. Bristow, 'The Liberty and Property Defence League and Individualism', *Historical Journal*, xviii, 4 (1975) p. 763.

12. Robert Taylor, *Lord Salisbury* (1975), p. 17.

13. Lord Hugh Cecil, *Conservatism* (1912), pp. 118–9.

14. Ibid., p. 153.

15. Peter Fraser, *Joseph Chamberlain, Radicalism and Empire, 1868–1914* (1966), p. 51.

16. John L. Finlay, *The English Origins of Social Credit* (1972), p. 71.

17. Joseph Chamberlain quoted in Wolfgang Mock, 'The Function of "Race" in Imperialist Ideologies: the Example of Joseph Chamberlain', Paul M. Kennedy and Anthony Nicholls (eds), *Nationalist and Racialist Movements in Britain and Germany Before 1914* (1981) p. 195.

18. Nick Griffin, 'The BNP: Anti-asylum protest, racist sect or power-winning movement?' p. 3. *http://www.bnp.org.uk/articles/racereality.htm* 22/08/03.

Chapter 1: Social Imperialism and Race Regeneration

1. For a survey of invasion literature, see I. F. Clarke, *Voices Prophesying War* (1966).

2. Aaron L. Friedberg, *The Weary Titan. Britain and the Experience of Relative Decline, 1895–1905* (1988), p. vii.

3. See B. H. Brown, *The Tariff Reform Movement in Great Britain 1881–98*, (1943).

4. There were 54 successful 'Labour' candidates in 1906. F. Bealey and H. Pelling, *Labour and Politics* (1958), p. 274.

5. B. E. C. Dugdale, *Arthur James Balfour, First Earl of Balfour* (1936), 1, p. 115.

6. J. W. Mackail and Guy Wyndham, *Life and Letters of George Wyndham* (n.d.) 2, pp. 540–1.

7. Bernard Semmel, *Imperialism and Social Reform. English Social-Imperial Thought 1895–1914* (1960), p. 62.

8. C. F. G. Masterman, *The Heart of the Empire* (1902), quoted in Donald Read, *Documents from Edwardian England* (1973), p. 23.

9. G. R. Searle, *Eugenics and Politics in Britain 1900–1914* (1976), p. 25.

10. Ibid., p. 27.

11. Ibid., pp. 45–66, 71.

12. Ibid., p. 28.

13. Ibid., p. 106.

14. Dan Stone, *Breeding Superman. Nietzsche, Race and Eugenics in Edwardian and Interwar Britain* (2002), pp. 124–34.

15. Searle, 'Eugenics', pp. 92–5.

16. Stone, 'Breeding Superman', pp. 33–61.

17. Searle, 'Eugenics', pp. 107–8.

18. Ibid., p. 23.

19. Semmel, 'Imperialism and Social Reform', p. 63.

20. Sidney Webb, 'Lord Rosebery's Escape from Houndsditch', *Nineteenth Century and After*, September 1901, pp. 366–86.

21. Quotations from Chamberlain's speeches are from C. Boyd, *Mr. Chamberlain's Speeches*, vol. 2 (1914) unless otherwise noted.

22. Wolfgang Mock, *Imperiale Herrschaft und nationales Interesse: 'Constructive Imperialism' oder Freihandel in Grossbritannien vor dem Ersten Weltkrieg* (1982), p. 186.

23. J. L. Garvin, 'The Principles of Constructive Economics as applied to the Maintenance of Empire', *Compatriots Club Lectures* (1905), p. 55.

24. J. L. Garvin, 'The Maintenance of Empire: A Study in the Economic Basis of Political Power', C. S. Goldman (ed.), *The Empire and the Century* (1905), p. 142.

25. Salisbury to Selborne, 10 August 1904, quoted in Alan Sykes, *Tariff Reform in British Politics, 1903–1913* (1979), p. 106.

26. Vct. Milner, *The Nation and the Empire* (1913), pp. 135–52.

27. Ibid., pp. 135–52.

28. Ibid., pp. 196–7.

29. Ibid., pp. 214–5.

30. Proof Copy, House of Lords Record Office, Bonar Law Papers, 28/4/75.

31. *Morning Post*, 19 October 1910.

32. Hilaire Belloc and Cecil Chesterton, *The Party System*, (2nd edn, 1913), p. 59.

33. Ibid., pp. 56, 75–6.

34. Ibid., pp. 113, 115.

35. Ibid., p. 29.
36. Ibid., p. 150, p. 181.
37. Ibid., p. 158.
38. Jay P. Corrin, *G. K. Chesterton and Hilaire Belloc. The Battle Against Modernity* (1981), p. 123.
39. Willoughby de Broke to Law, 11 September 1913, House of Lords Record Office, Bonar Law Papers, 30/2/10.
40. William S. Rodner, 'Leaguers, Covenanters, Moderates: British Support for Ulster, 1913–1914', *Eire-Ireland*, XVII (1982), pp. 68–85.
41. Willoughby de Broke, 'The Unionist Party and the General Election', *National Review*, 63 (July 1914), p. 776.
42. Willoughby de Broke, 'The Coming Campaign', *National Review*, 56 (September 1910), p. 62.
43. Willoughby de Broke, 'The Unionist Party', p. 780.
44. Willoughby de Broke, 'National Toryism', *National Review*, 59 (May 1912), pp. 416–17.
45. Willoughby de Broke, 'The Restoration of the Constitution', *National Review*, 58 (February 1912), p. 869.
46. Willoughby de Broke to Bonar Law, 5 May 1912, House of Lords Record Office, Bonar Law Papers, 26/3/11.
47. Willoughby de Broke, 'National Toryism', pp. 413, 417–18.
48. Ibid., pp. 417–18, 420–1.
49. Chris Wrigley, 'In Excess of their Patriotism': The National Party and Threats of Subversion', C. Wrigley (ed.), *Warfare, Diplomacy and Politics: Essays in Honour of A.J. P. Taylor* (1986), p. 106.
50. Willoughby de Broke, 'The Coming Campaign', p. 67.
51. Willoughby de Broke, 'The Unionist Party', p. 785.
52. Willoughby de Broke, 'The Unionist Position', *National Review*, 62 (October 1913), pp. 214–16, 221.
53. Willoughby de Broke, 'National Toryism', pp. 422–3.
54. Ibid., p. 421.
55. Ibid., p. 424.
56. Ibid., p. 422.
57. Willoughby de Broke, 'The Comfortable Classes and National Defence', *National Review*, 68 (May 1914), pp. 428–9.
58. Willoughby de Broke 'The Unionist Party', pp. 782–3.
59. Ibid., p. 786.
60. Stone, 'Breeding Superman', pp. 69–70.
61. For a survey, see Mark Girouard, *The Return to Camelot. Chivalry and the English Gentleman*, (2nd edn, 1981); for public schools see

D. Newsome, *Godliness and Good Learning* (1961); for the cult of athleticism, J. A. Mangan, *Athleticism in the Victorian and Edwardian Public School*, (1981/2000) and *The Games Ethic and Imperialism*, (1985); for militarism, Geoffrey Best, 'Militarism and the Victorian Public School', in I. Bradley and B. Simon (eds), *The Victorian Public School* (1975), pp. 129–46.

62. See J. A. Springhall, *Youth, Empire and Society. British Youth Movements 1883–1940* (1977).

63. Stone, 'Breeding Superman', p. 37.

64. Alan Sykes, 'Radical Conservatism and the Working Classes in Edwardian England: The Case of the Workers Defence Union', *English Historical Review*, CXIII, 454 (November 1998), pp. 1180–209.

65. For British Syndicalism, see Bob Holton, *British Syndicalism 1900–1914. Myths and Realities* (1976).

66. The following paragraphs are based on the Order of Red Rose pamphlets, nos. 1–3, 5 (1913–14), and W. J. Sanderson, *The Industrial Crisis* (1912).

67. For an overview, see Panikos Panayi, 'Anti-immigrant riots in nineteenth- and twentieth-century Britain' in Panikos Panayi (ed.), *Racial Violence in Britain, 1840–1950* (1993), pp. 1–25.

68. See, B. Gainer, *The Alien Invasion* (1972).

69. Colin Holmes, *Anti-semitism in British Society, 1876–1939* (1979), p. 72.

70. See G. R. Searle, *Corruption in British Politics 1895–1930* (1987), pp. 172–217, Holmes, 'Anti-Semitism', pp. 70–80.

Chapter 2: Patriotic Labour and International Conspiracies

1. Wrigley, 'National Party', pp. 101–02.

2. Ibid., p. 108.

3. Semmel, 'Imperialism and Social Reform', pp. 232–3.

4. Robert Blatchford, *Britain for the British*, n.d., p. 170.

5. Robert Blatchford, *Merrie England*, n.d., pp. 23–32.

6. Semmel, 'Imperialism and Social Reform', p. 227.

7. Blatchford, 'Britain for the British', p. 51.

8. Ibid., p. 18.

9. Semmel, 'Imperialism and Social Reform', p. 233.

10. Barry Doyle, 'Who Paid the Price of Patriotism? The Funding of Charles Stanton during the Merthyr Boroughs By-Election of 1915', *English Historical Review*, CIX, 434 (1994) pp. 1215–22.

11. J. O. Stubbs, 'Lord Milner and Patriotic Labour, 1914–1918,' *English Historical Review*, 87 (1972), p. 723.
12. Wrigley, 'National Party', p. 98.
13. Stubbs, 'Lord Milner', p. 728.
14. Ibid., p. 732.
15. Ibid., pp. 737–8.
16. Ibid., p. 742; Wrigley, 'National Party', p. 108.
17. Stubbs, 'Lord Milner' p. 750; Wrigley, 'National Party' p. 109.
18. Roy Douglas, 'The National Democratic Party and the British Workers' League', *Historical Journal*, xv, 3 (1972), p. 537.
19. William D. Rubinstein, 'Henry Page Croft and the National Party 1917–22', *Journal of Contemporary History*, 9, 1 (1974), p. 132.
20. Ibid., p. 133.
21. Ibid., p. 141.
22. Wrigley, 'National Party', p. 106.
23. Rubinstein, 'Henry Page Croft', p. 142.
24. Wrigley, 'National Party', p. 108.
25. Rubinstein, 'Henry Page Croft', p. 143.
26. Wrigley, National Party', p. 107.
27. Rubinstein, 'Henry Page Croft', p. 143.
28. Ibid., p. 144.
29. Ibid., p. 144.
30. Ibid., p. 145.
31. Ibid., p. 148.
32. Thomas Linehan, *British Fascism 1918–39. Parties, Ideology and Culture* (2000), p. 55.
33. Holmes, 'Anti-semitism', p. 148, 150.
34. Ibid., p. 146.
35. Gisela C. Lebzelter, *Political Anti-Semitism in England 1918–1939* (1978), p. 66.
36. Holmes, 'Anti-semitism', p. 149.
37. Roger Eatwell, *Fascism. A History* (1995), p. 176.
38. Linehan, 'British Fascism', p. 62.
39. Ibid., pp. 124–44.
40. Richard Thurlow, *Fascism in Britain. A History* (1987), p. 71.
41. Linehan, 'British Fascism', pp. 72–3, Lebzelter 'Political Anti-semitism', p. 72.
42. Linehan, 'British Fascism', p. 73. Lebzelter, 'Political Anti-semitism' p. 83 gives figures of 150 and 800. John Morrell, 'Arnold Leese and the Imperial Fascist League: the Impact of Racial Fascism', Kenneth

Lunn and Richard Thurlow, (eds), *British Fascism: Essays on the Radical Right in Inter-War Britain* (1980), p. 72n14 suggests 1000.

43. Lebzelter, 'Political Anti-semitism', p. 70.
44. Ibid., p. 72.
45. Ibid., p. 71, Linehan, 'British Fascism', p. 76.
46. Morell, 'Arnold Leese', p. 68.
47. Lebzelter, 'Political Anti-semitism', pp. 73–4.
48. Lebzelter, 'Political Anti-semitism', p. 74, Holmes, 'Anti-semitism', p. 162.
49. Lebzelter, 'Political Anti-semitism', p. 78, Linehan, 'British Fascism', p. 180, Holmes, Anti-semitism', p. 163.
50. Douglas A. Lorimer, *Colour, Class and the Victorians* (1978), p. 137.
51. Holmes, Anti-semitism', p. 163.
52. Lebzelter, 'Political Anti-semitism', p. 79.
53. Ibid., p. 73.
54. Morrell, 'Arnold Leese', p. 63.
55. Morrell, 'Arnold Leese', p. 61, Holmes, 'Anti-semitism', p. 163.
56. Linehan, 'British Fascism', p. 185.
57. Ibid., p. 186.
58. Morrell, 'Arnold Leese', pp. 61. 63–4; Holmes, 'Anti-semitism', p. 163; Lebzelter, 'Political Anti-semitism', p. 79.
59. Linehan, 'British Fascism', pp. 222–40; Morrell, 'Arnold Leese', p. 66; J. Holmes, 'Anti-semitism', p. 166.
60. Holmes, 'Anti-semitism', p. 167; Morrell, 'Arnold Leese', p. 68.
61. Holmes, Anti-semitism', p. 165.
62. Ibid., p. 165.
63. Ibid., p. 165–6.
64. Lebzelter, 'Political Anti-semitism', p. 77. See also Linehan, 'British Fascism', p. 178; Holmes, 'Anti-semitism', p. 163.
65. Linehan, 'British Fascism', p. 76.
66. Ibid., p. 182.
67. Lebzelter, 'Political Anti-semitism', p. 78; Holmes, 'Anti-semitism', p. 163.
68. Lebzelter, 'Political Anti-semitism', p. 77.
69. Morrell, 'Arnold Leese', pp. 68–9; Holmes, 'Anti-semitism', p. 168.
70. Morrell, 'Arnold Leese', p. 69; Thurlow, 'Fascism', p. 74.
71. Holmes, 'Anti-semitism', p. 169; Morrell, 'Arnold Leese', pp. 68–70.
72. Lebzelter, 'Political Anti-semitism', p. 76.
73. Thurlow, 'Fascism', p. 70.
74. Ibid., p. 73.

75. Holmes, 'Anti-semitism', p. 164.
76. Lebzelter, 'Political Anti-semitism', pp. 81–2; Morrell, 'Arnold Leese', p. 62.
77. Morrell, 'Arnold Leese', p. 70. Holmes, 'Anti-semitism', p. 169.
78. Ibid., p. 163.
79. Lebzelter, 'Political Anti-semitism', p. 82; Morrell, 'Arnold Leese', p. 71.
80. Lebzelter, 'Political Anti-semitism', p. 76.
81. Holmes, 'Anti-semitism', p. 166.
82. Lebzelter, 'Political Anti-semitism', p. 73.
83. Ibid., p. 73.
84. Ibid., p. 72.
85. Linehan, 'British Fascism', p. 75.
86. Thurlow, 'Fascism' p. 75.
87. Morrell, 'Arnold Leese', p. 65.
88. Ibid., p. 70.
89. Ibid., p. 65 and fn 51.
90. Linehan, 'British Fascism', p. 77.
91. For the *Patriot*, see Markku Ruotsila, 'The Antisemitism of the Eighth Duke of Northumberland's the *Patriot*, 1922–1930', *Journal of Contemporary History*, 39, 1 (2004), pp. 71–92.

Chapter 3: Sir Oswald Mosley and British Fascism

1. Thurlow, 'Fascism', p. 96.
2. 'Revolution by Reason', 1925, quoted in Lebzelter, 'Political Anti-semitism', p. 87.
3. Michael Holroyd, *Bernard Shaw* (1989), 2, p. 73.
4. Ibid., p. 13.
5. Ibid., p. 74.
6. Ibid., p. 13.
7. Ibid., p. 77.
8. Robert Skidelsky, *Oswald Mosley* (1981), p. 478.
9. Ibid., p. 167, 178.
10. Ibid., p. 225. See also pp. 134–5.
11. Ibid., p. 232.
12. K. O. Morgan, *Consensus and Disunity: The Lloyd George Coalition Government 1918–1922* (1979), pp. 177–8.
13. Skidelsky, 'Mosley', p. 127.
14. Ibid., p. 146.

15. Ibid., p. 174.
16. Ibid., p. 199.
17. Ibid., p. 204.
18. Ibid., pp. 215–6.
19. Ibid., pp. 226–7.
20. Ibid., p. 233.
21. Ibid., p. 235.
22. Ibid., p. 236.
23. Ibid., p. 237.
24. Ibid., pp. 257–8.
25. Ibid., p. 271.
26. Ibid., p. 276, 280.
27. Ibid., pp. 284–7.
28. Ibid., p. 293.
29. N. Nugent, 'The ideas of the British Union of Fascists', Neil Nugent and Roger King (eds), *The British Right. Conservative and right wing politics in Britain* (1977), p. 148.
30. Skidelsky, 'Mosley', p. 293.
31. Nugent, 'Ideas', p. 136.
32. Lewis, '*Illusions of Grandeur*', p. 33.
33. Nugent, 'Ideas', p. 137.
34. Ibid., p. 137.
35. Ibid., p. 138.
36. Ibid., p. 140.
37. Ibid., p. 139.
38. Linehan, 'British Fascism', p. 89.
39. Nugent, 'Ideas', p. 139.
40. Ibid., p. 140.
41. Ibid., p. 141.
42. Ibid., pp. 142–4.
43. Thurlow, 'Fascism', p. 122.
44. Robert Benewick, *The Fascist Movement in Britain* (1972), p. 174.
45. Dave Renton, *Fascism, Anti-Fascism and Britain in the 1940s* (2000), p. 56. Moore was Conservative MP for Ayr Burghs.
46. Skidelsky, 'Mosley', p. 322.
47. Ibid., pp. 380–3.
48. Stephen Cullen, 'The Development of the Ideas and Policy of the British Union of Fascists, 1932–40', *Journal of Contemporary History*, 22 (1987), pp. 115–36.
49. Nugent, 'Ideas', p. 149.

50. Linehan, 'British Fascism', p. 191.
51. Skidelsky, 'Mosley', p. 381, 386.
52. Christine Bolt, *Victorian Attitudes to Race* (1971), p. 9.
53. Linehan, 'British Fascism', p. 193.
54. Skidelsky, 'Mosley', p. 385.
55. Ibid., pp. 384–5.
56. G.C. Webber, 'Patterns of Membership and Support for the British Union of Fascists', *Journal of Contemporary History*, 19 (1984), pp. 575–606; Thurlow, 'Fascism', pp. 122–7.
57. Thomas Linehan, *East London for Mosley: The British Union of Fascists in East London and South West Essex 1933–40* (1996), p. 302.
58. Thurlow, 'Fascism', p. 133.
59. Thurlow, 'Fascism', pp. 136–9; 177, Skidelsky, 'Mosley' 463–4.
60. For details of factionalism and reorganisation, see Linehan, 'British Fascism', pp. 99–111.
61. Ibid., p. 113.
62. Nugent, 'Ideas', p. 145.
63. Linehan, 'British Fascism', p. 118n63.
64. Skidelsky, 'Mosley' p. 33.
65. Ibid., p. 134.

Chapter 4: Alternative Economics and Peace-Loving Patriots

1. Margaret Canovan, *G. K. Chesterton, Radical Populist* (1977), p. 50.
2. Finlay, 'Social Credit', p. 51.
3. Corrin, 'Battle Against Modernity', p. 110.
4. Canovan, 'Chesterton', p. 89.
5. Corrin, 'Battle Against Modernity', pp. 130–5.
6. Ibid., p. 128.
7. Ibid., p. 140.
8. Ibid., pp. 93–6, 148–59.
9. Canovan, 'Chesterton', p. 92; Corrin, 'Battle Against Modernity', p. 137.
10. Ibid., p. 140, Finlay, 'Social Credit', p. 57.
11. Corrin, 'Battle Against Modernity', pp. 177–9.
12. Ibid., p. 163.
13. Canovan, 'Chesterton', pp. 131–2.
14. Ibid., pp. 137–8.
15. Corrin, 'Battle against Modernity', pp. 188–91.
16. Ibid., pp. 187–8.

17. Ibid., p. 191.
18. Ibid., p. 194.
19. Ibid., p. 200.
20. For a sympathetic view of Social Credit as the alternative to 'debt driven' capitalism, see Frances Hutchinson and Brian Burkitt, *The Political Economy of Social Credit and Guild Socialism* (1997), esp. chs. 2 and 3.
21. Holmes, 'Anti-semitism', p. 209.
22. C. H. Douglas, 'Social Credit Principles'. Swanwick Address, 1924, reprinted in *The Social Crediter*, March–April 1988, *http://cog.kent.edu/lib/DouglasSocialCreditPrinciples.pdf*, 27/03/03.
23. Finlay, 'Social Credit', p. 112.
24. Ibid., p. 108, 112.
25. Ibid., p. 191.
26. Ibid., pp. 107–9.
27. The rather complex argument for eventual collapse is summarized in ibid., pp. 107–111.
28. C. H. Douglas, ' A + B and the Bankers', *New Age*, 22/29 January 1925, p. 4, *http://www.ccn.net.au/socred/lectures.htm*, 28/03/03.
29. Finlay, 'Social Credit', p. 194.
30. W. K. A. J. Chambers-Hunter, *British Union and Social Credit* (c.1938), (2nd edn, 2002), p. 4. Chambers-Hunter was an Aberdeenshire laird, largely responsible with his sister-in-law for Fascist activity in Aberdeen. Nigel Copsey, *Anti-Fascism in Britain* (2000), p. 71.
31. Finlay, 'Social Credit', p. 154.
32. Ibid., p. 207.
33. Ibid., pp. 103–4.
34. This paragraph and the next are based on Philip Coupland, 'The Blackshirted Utopians' *Journal of Contemporary History*, 33 (2) (1998), pp. 255–71. See also the illuminating discussion of the cultural aspects of British fascism in Linehan, 'British Fascism', pp. 201–84.
35. Coupland, 'Blackshirted Utopians', p. 255. For the imagined community, see also Georgina Boyes, *The Imagined Village: Culture, Ideology and the English Folk Revival* (1993).
36. Coupland 'Blackshirted Utopians', p. 257, quoting Julian Huxley, *On Living in a Revolution.*
37. Coupland, 'Blackshirted Utopians', p. 264.
38. Douglas, 'Social Credit Principles', Swanwick Address, 1924.
39. Finlay, 'Social Credit', pp. 208–09.
40. Ibid., p. 213.

41. Douglas, 'Social Credit Principles'. Swanwick Address 1924.
42. Both 'The Age of Plenty' and 'The Leisure Society' were titles of Social Credit journals.
43. C. H. Douglas, *Economic Democracy* (5th edn, 1974), p. 29; Finlay, 'Social Credit', p. 100.
44. Ibid., p. 104.
45. Ibid., p. 171.
46. C. H. Douglas, *The Nature of Democracy*, quoted in Politics and Social Credit, p. 2, *http://www.ccn.net.au/-socred/pol.htm*, 28/03/03.
47. Finlay, 'Social Credit', p. 102.
48. Ibid., pp. 105–07.
49. Ibid., p. 182.
50. For Hargrave and the Kibbo Kift, see Finlay, ch.7, Mark Drakeford, *Social Movements and their Supporters: The Green Shirts in England* (1997), pp. 16–100, John Hargrave, *The Confession of the Kibbo Kift* (1927).
51. Drakeford, 'Social Movements', pp. 47–8.
52. Finlay, 'Social Credit', pp. 149–50, 158.
53. Drakeford, 'Social Movements', p. 20, 44.
54. Finlay, 'Social Credit', pp. 150–2.
55. Drakeford, 'Social Movements', p. 59.
56. Ibid., p. 99.
57. Finlay, 'Social Credit', p. 154.
58. Ibid., p. 156.
59. Ibid., p. 133–4.
60. Drakeford, 'Social Movements', p. 117.
61. Ibid, p. 120.
62. Drakeford, 'Social Movements', pp. 116–43, and 181–2 for details. See also Copsey, 'Anti-Fascism', pp. 23–4, 28.
63. Finlay, 'Social Credit', p. 160.
64. For the Leeds campaign, see Drakeford, 'Social Movements', pp. 165–77.
65. Ibid., p. 161.
66. Finlay, 'Social Credit', pp. 174–7.
67. Richard Griffiths, *Fellow Travellers of the Right. British Enthusiasts for Nazi Germany 1933-9* (1983), p. 351.
68. Ibid., p. 352.
69. Linehan, 'British Fascism', p. 139.
70. See Lothian in Griffiths, 'Fellow Travellers', p. 302.
71. Ibid., p. 304.

72. Ibid., pp. 358–9.
73. For Ramsay and the Right Club, see Richard Griffiths, *Patriotism Perverted. Captain Ramsay, the Right Club and British Anti-Semitism 1939–40* (1998).
74. Thurlow, 'Fascism', pp. 164–5, 174–5.
75. Mosley, *Tomorrow We Live*, quoted in Griffiths, 'Fellow Travellers', p. 355–6.
76. Ibid., pp. 354–5.
77. Ibid., pp. 304–05.
78. Ibid., p. 322. For Lymington, the English Mistery and the English Array, see Dan Stone, 'The English Mistery, the BUF, and the Dilemmas of British Fascism', *Journal of Modern History*, 75 (2003), pp. 336–58.
79. Thurlow, 'Fascism', pp. 170–1.
80. Linehan, 'British Fascism', p. 139.
81. Gateshead, 1924–29 and Peckham, 1929–31.
82. Linehan, 'British Fascism', pp. 139–40.
83. Thurlow, 'Fascism', p. 172.
84. Griffiths, 'Fellow Travellers', p. 353, 325.
85. Thurlow, 'Fascism', p. 172, 170; Griffiths, 'Fellow Travellers', pp. 324–5.
86. Ibid., p. 355.
87. Thurlow, 'Fascism' pp. 180–1.
88. 26 July 1939.
89. Thurlow, 'Fascism', pp. 183–4.
90. Ibid., p. 181.
91. Ibid., p. 179, 191.
92. Ibid., p. 171.
93. Ibid., pp. 194–5, p. 208.
94. The Earl of Portsmouth, *A Knot of Roots. An Autobiography* (1965), p. 197.
95. Morrell, 'Leese', p. 59.
96. Thurlow, 'Fascism', p. 223.

Chapter 5: The Union Movement and the National Front

1. For a recent interpretation, see Tony Kushner, 'Anti-semitism and austerity: the August 1947 riots in Britain', in Panikos Panayi (ed.), *Racial Violence in Britain, 1840–1950* (1993), pp. 149–67.
2. Formerly Tavistock. The BPP was finally wound up in 1954.
3. There are some interesting, if slightly disconnected, observations on Mosley's return in Richard Thurlow, 'The Guardian of the 'Sacred

Flame': The Failed Political Resurrection of Sir Oswald Mosley after 1945', *Journal of Contemporary History*, 33 (2) (1998), pp. 241–54. Nicholas Hillman, ''Tell me chum in case I got it wrong. What was it we were fighting for during the war?' The Re-emergence of British Fascism 1945–58', *Contemporary British History*, 15 (Winter 2001), pp. 1–34 has useful comments on other secondary literature.

4. Skidelsky, 'Mosley', p. 481.
5. Oswald Mosley, 'European Socialism',(n.d.). p. 5. Reprinted from *The European*, May 1956 (first printed May 1956 in *Nation Europa*). As Mosley noted, the concept of European Socialism was continually evolving. An earlier version appeared in *Nation Europa* in June 1951 and *Union* July 1951. (5th edn, 1999).
6. Skidelsky, 'Mosley', p. 485.
7. Mosley, 'European Socialism', p. 5. See also 'The European Situation. The Third Force' (March 1950).
8. Skidelsky, 'Mosley', p. 481.
9. Ibid., p. 484.
10. Mosley, 'European Socialism', p. 5.
11. Ibid., pp. 5–6.
12. Ibid., p. 16.
13. 'Union Movement-Key Issues', p. 3. *http://www.oswaldmosley.com/um/keyissues.html*, 08/05/03.
14. Skidelsky, 'Mosley', pp. 495–6.
15. Mosley, 'European Socialism', p. 4.
16. Ibid., p. 4, p. 6. See Skidelsky, 'Mosley', p. 495 for a 3-stage version.
17. 'European Socialism', p. 14.
18. Ibid., p. 14.
19. Ibid., p. 4.
20. Ibid., p. 4.
21. Ibid., pp. 12–13.
22. Ibid., pp. 9–10.
23. *The European*, July 1954, quoted in Skidelsky, 'Mosley', p. 500.
24. 'European Socialism', p. 13.
25. Ibid., p. 11.
26. Ibid., p. 17.
27. Renton, 'Fascism, Anti-Fascism', pp. 33–41, 134–6, 141–2.
28 Thurlow, 'Fascism', p. 245.
29. Anne Poole, 'Oswald Mosley and the Union Movement: Success or Failure', M Cronin, (ed.) *The Failure of British Fascism: The Far Right and the Fight for Political Recognition* (1996), pp. 70–1 argues that Mosley's racism was biological in the mid-1940s.

30. Skidelsky, 'Mosley', pp. 486–7.
31. Renton, 'Fascism, Anti-fascism', p. 47.
32. Thurlow, 'Fascism', p. 247.
33. Walker, 'National Front', p. 31.
34. Ibid., pp. 33–4.
35. Ibid., pp. 34–5.
36. Ibid., p. 37.
37. Ibid., pp. 38–9, 68.
38. Ibid., p. 41.
39. Ibid., pp. 45–7; Thurlow, 'Fascism', pp. 268–9.
40. Walker, 'National Front', p. 46.
41. Ibid., pp. 51–3.
42. Ibid., pp. 69–71.
43. John Tyndall, *Six Principles of British Nationalism*, http://www.arya-nunity.com/sixprincip. html, 11/06/03.
44. Walker, 'National Front', pp. 62–4.
45. Ibid., p. 67.
46. Rosine de Bounevialle, quoted in ibid., p. 66.
47. See Ken Phillips, 'The Nature of Powellism', in Neill Nugent and Roger King (eds), *The British Right* (1977), pp. 99–129.
48. Walker, 'National Front', pp. 110–13.
49. Ibid., pp. 90–1.
50. Ibid., pp. 98–100.
51. Ibid., p. 104.
52. Ibid., pp. 139–43, 149–50.
53. Ibid., pp. 150–3.
54. Ibid., p. 154.
55. Ibid., p. 147.
56. Larry O'Hara, 'Notes from the Underground – British Fascism 1974–92 (part one) 1974–83', *Lobster*, 23 (June 1992), p. 1.
57. For 'Strasserites', see below p. 116.
58. Walker, 'National Front', pp. 156–7.
59. Ibid., pp. 159–60.
60. Ibid., p. 155.
61. Ibid., p. 159.
62. Ibid., p. 147.
63. Ibid., p. 230.
64. Ibid., p. 151.
65. Ibid., p. 175–7.
66. Ibid., p. 179, 182–3.

67. Ibid., p. 185.
68. Ibid., p. 192.
69. Ibid., p. 193–4.
70. Ibid., p. 184.
71. Ibid., p. 198–9.
72. Ibid., p. 225–7.
73. Ibid., p. 230–1.
74. Stan Taylor, *The National Front in English Politics* (1982), esp. pp. 38–43, 118–31, 173–6. For a complex account of NF support, see C.T. Husbands, *Racial Exclusionism and the City* (1983).
75. Walker, 'National Front', pp. 227–8.

Chapter 6: Warrior Saints and Men in Suits

1. Taylor, 'The National Front', p. 163.
2. Larry, O'Hara, 'Notes' part 1, pp. 5–6.
3. NF Members Bulletin, July 1980, quoted in Ibid., p. 5.
4. 'Organisers Bulletin', 15, 5 (September 1983), quoted in Larry O'Hara, 'Notes from the Underground, part 3: British Fascism 1983–6' *Lobster*, 25 (June 1993), p. 4, p. 11n15.
5. O'Hara, 'Notes', part 1, pp. 5–6. By 'capitalism', the NF meant neither private ownership nor private enterprise but 'big' capitalism, the familiar 'plutocracy'. See Joe Pearce, 'A Definition of Capitalism', *Nationalism Today*, 4, n.d. (1981), p. 8 and 'Communism: The False Alternative', *Nationalism Today*, 13 (n.d.) (February 1983), p. 10.
6. *Nationalism Today*, 1 (March 1980), p. 20.
7. O'Hara, 'Notes', part 3, p. 2.
8. Thurlow, 'Fascism', pp. 296–7, 281.
9. O'Hara, 'Notes', part 3, p. 10n13.
10. Walker, 'National Front', p. 194. *Searchlight* also describes the NP as Strasserite, *From Ballots to Bombs: The Inside Story of the National Front's Political Soldiers* (1989), p. 4. See also Gerry Gable, 'The Far Right in Contemporary Britain', in Luciano Cheles *et al.* (eds), *Neo-fascism in Europe* (1991), pp. 248–9 and the interesting article by David Edgar, 'Racism, fascism and the politics of the National front' *Race and Class*, XIX, 2 (1977), pp. 124–5.
11. Larry O'Hara, 'Notes from the Underground: British Fascism 1974–92. Part 2, *Lobster*, 24 (December 1992), p. 3.
12. O'Hara, 'Notes', part 3, p. 10n13.

13. David L. Baker, 'A.K.Chesterton, the Strasser Brothers and the Politics of the National Front', *Patterns of Prejudice*, 9 (1985), pp. 23–33.
14. Derek Holland, 'A.K.Chesterton: Radical Nationalist', *Nationalism Today*, 12 (November 1982), p. 10.
15. This point is made by Andrew Brons, 'The Roots of British Nationalism', *Nationalism Today*, 26 (n.d.) (January 1985), p. 15.
16. Joe Pearce, 'Communism', p. 10.
17. Dave Stevens, 'The State of Things to Come', *Nationalism Today*, 21 (n.d.) (April 1984), p. 20.
18. 'Joe Pearce: Portrait of a Revolutionary', *Nationalism Today*, 9 (April 1982), p. 10. See also Joe Pearce, 'A Stake In Our Country', *Nationalism Today*, 26 (n.d.) (January 1985), pp. 18–19, p. 22.
19. Joe Pearce, 'Industrial Ownership and Racial Nationalism', *Nationalism Today*, 6 (n.d.) (September 1981), p. 11.
20. Andrew Brons, 'Small Businesses: A Policy for Revival' *Nationalism Today*, 17 (n.d.) (1983), p. 9.
21. For example, Nick Griffin, 'Towards Economic and Social Freedom', *Nationalism Today*, 11 (September 1982), p. 11.
22. See 'A Call for Economic Nationalism', *Nationalism Today*, 5 (n.d.) (1981), p. 20.
23. 'Spotlight on Policy 2, Unemployment', *Nationalism Today*, 5 (n.d.) (1981), pp. 14–15.
24. 'A Call for Economic Nationalism', p. 20.
25. NF News 68, July 1985, quoted in O'Hara, 'Notes', part 3: p. 13n36.
26. Nick Griffin, 'Back To The Land', *Nationalism Today*, 26 (n.d.) (January 1985), pp. 10–11.
27. *Nationalism Today*, 26 (n.d.) (January 1985), p. 23.
28. Larry O'Hara, 'Notes from the Underground, part 4, British Fascism 1983–6 (II), Lobster, 26 (December 1993), p. 1.
29. Nick Griffin, 'Towards Economic and Social Freedom', *Nationalism Today*, 11 (n.d.) (September 1982), p. 11.
30. Nick Griffin, 'Back To The Land', pp. 10–11.
31. Andrew Brons, 'We Are Not Marxists – We Are Not Capitalists', *Nationalism Today*, 7 (n.d.) (November 1981), pp. 11–12.
32. Derek Holland, 'Land for the People', *Nationalism Today*, 9 (April 1982), p. 12.
33. Nick Griffin, 'Policies for National Survival', *Nationalism Today*, 17 (n.d.) (1983), p. 8.
34. Michael Fishwick, 'The Structure of Folk Government', *Nationalism Today*, 36 (February 1986), pp. 14–5.

35. 'People Not Parliament', *Nationalism Today*, 41 (September 1987), pp. 10–11.
36. 'Principles of Democracy', *Nationalism Today*, 42 (1988), pp. 6–7, See also pp. 16–17.
37. Troy Southgate, 'Transcending the Beyond. From Third Positionism to National-Anarchism', p. 2. *http://obsidian-blade.com/synthesis/12/06/03*
38. 'Principles of Democracy', pp. 6–7.
39. Dave Stevens, ' State Of Things To Come', p. 20.
40. Derek Holland, 'The Armed People', *Nationalism Today*, 39 (n.d) (November 1986), pp. 22–3.
41. Nick Griffin, 'The Deadly Trap' *Nationalism Today*, 29 (May 1985), p. 16.
42. O'Hara, 'Notes', part 1, p. 6.
43. Nick Griffin 'The Aftermath of Brixton', *Nationalism Today*, 5 (1981), pp. 12–3.
44. Joe Pearce 'The Way Forward: Comradeship, Commitment and Direction', *Nationalism Today*, 20 (March 1984), p. 12.
45. Souter Clarence was alleged to be connected with the shadowy Column 88. These stories are examined in depth in Larry O'Hara, 'Notes', part 2, p. 10.
46. O'Hara, 'Notes', part 1, p. 4,
47. Joe Pearce, 'Comradeship, Commitment', p. 12.
48. Derek Holland, 'Terrorism: An Enemy Of The People', *Nationalism Today*, 33 (September 1985), pp. 12–13.
49. Steve Brady, 'Why Reds Scab On The Miners', *Nationalism Today*, 24 (September 1984), p. 16.
50. Larry O'Hara, 'Notes', part 3, pp. 6–7, 13; 'A Question of Principle', *Nationalism Today*, 27 (1985), p. 2.
51. O'Hara, 'Notes', part 3, pp. 6–7.
52. Ibid., p. 5.
53. Derek Holland, *What is a Political Soldier: A New Preface* (1994), pp. 1–2. *http://www.politicalsoldier.net/ps-net/whatsaps.shtml*, 29/09/03.
54. Ibid., p. 11.
55. Joe Pearce, 'The Spiritual Struggle', *Nationalism Today*, 32 (August 1985), pp. 12–13; Steve Brady, 'The Real Spiritual Struggle', *Nationalism Today*, 34 (October 1985), pp. 12–13.
56. Hilaire Belloc, *An Essay on the Redistribution of Property*, (1936) (n.d.) (1984), p. 62.
57. Larry O'Hara, 'Notes', part 4, p. 3.

58. Nick Griffin, 'The Way Forward: Training For Power, *Nationalism Today*, 31 (July 1985), pp. 8–9.

59. For example, Nick Griffin, 'The Way Forward: Cadre Hope', *Nationalism Today*, 40 (n.d.) (March 1987), p. 10.

60. Joe Pearce, 'The Way Forward', *Nationalism Today*, 19 (n.d.) (January 1984), pp. 10–11.

61. Pat Harrington, 'The Way Forward. Education For Unity', *Nationalism Today*, 27 (March 1985), p. 8; Ian Anderson, 'The Way Forward. A Constitution For The Future', *Nationalism Today*, 28 (April 1985), p. 9.

62. Griffin, 'Cadre Hope', p. 10; 'Preparing for Power', *Nationalism Today*, 41 (September 1987), p. 5.

63. Nick Griffin, 'The NF Solution', *Nationalism Today*, 37 (March 1986), p. 13.

64. Larry O'Hara, 'The 1986 National Front Split, Part 1', *Lobster*, 29 (June 1995), pp. 1–2.

65. Steve Brady, 'The Real Spiritual Struggle', pp. 12–13.

66. Larry O'Hara, 'The 1986 National Front Split, Part 1' analyses the dispute in detail. The quotations are from p. 5 and p. 4, respectively. For the 'official' version, see Nick Griffin (introd.), *Attempted Murder: The State/Reactionary Plot Against the National Front* (1986).

67. Nick Griffin, 'The Way Forward: Adapt or Die', *Nationalism Today*, 39 (November 1986), pp. 8–9.

68. Nick Griffin, 'Preparing for Power', p. 5.

69. O'Hara, 'The 1986 National Front Split', p. 9.

70. *Nationalism Today*, 7 (November 1981), p. 15. See also *Nationalism Today*, 1 (March 1980), pp. 12, 15.

71. *Nationalism Today*, 4 (February 1981), p. 7.

72. *Nationalism Today*, 37 (March 1986), p. 13.

73. Griffin, 'Cadre Hope', p. 10.

74. *Nationalism Today*, 41 (September 1987), p. 23.

75. *Nationalism Today*, 22 (June 1984), p. 7.

76. *Nationalism Today*, 29 (May 1985), p. 17; See also *Nationalism Today*, 37 (March 1986), p. 7.

77. 'Nation Of Islam: A Photo-Essay', *Nationalism Today*, 39 (November 1986), pp. 16–20.

78. 'Garvey's Vision', *Nationalism Today*, 42 (n.d.) (1988), pp. 20–2.

79. 'Garvey's Vision', p. 20.

80. The NF's Third Positionist philosophy was elaborated in 'Principles of Democracy' (NT42) and 'Revolution and Evolution' (NT43) adapted from Gadhafi's Green Book 'which best outlines this philosophy's **all**

embracing and **universal** nature.' (NT 45, p. 20). 'Libya: A Study of the Third Position in Practise' (sic) appeared in NT. 44.

81. 'Ghana: A Study of the Third Position in Practice – part 2', *Nationalism Today*, 45 (May 1989), pp. 20–1; Ibid., pp. 8–9.

82. *Nationalism Today*, 42 (1988), p. 17.

83. Larry O'Hara, 'Notes' part 3, p. 5, 12.

84. David Kerr reviewing John Bean, *Many Shades of Black; Inside Britain's Far-Right*, Ulster Nation, vol. 2, 25, p. 10 *http://www.ulsternation.org.uk/many_shades_of_black.htm*, 19/05/03.

85. Thurlow, 'Fascism', p. 290; O'Hara, 'Notes', part 4, p. 7.

86. National Front: 'A History of the NF', p. 4, *http://www.natfront.com/history.html*, 14/08/03.

87. The above three paragraphs are based on *The Third Position Handbook*. The Third Position (1997), *http://dspace.dial.pipex.com/third position/*.

88. *http://politicalsoldier.net/efnet.020615-speech.shtml*, p. 3 20/06/03.

89. Troy Southgate, 'Transcending the Beyond', p. 3.

90. Ibid., p. 4; 'Beyond the Fascism of the Right and the Dogmatism of the Left', Folk and Faith, *http://www.folkandfaith.com/anarch.shtml*, 14/03/04; 'Synthesis – Interview with Troy Southgate', *http://www.rosenoire.org/interviews/southgate2.php*, 14/03/04.

91. . Roger Griffin suggests 'the emergence of a new political genus, "the groupuscular right" ', Roger Griffin, 'From slime mould to rhizome: an introduction to the groupuscular right', *Patterns of Prejudice*, 37, 1 (2003), pp. 27–50.

92. National Front, 'History', p. 5.

93. John Tyndall, 'Humbug in the guise of "politics"', *Spearhead*, *http://www.aryanunity.com/humbug.html*, 11/06/03.

94. For the early history of the BNP and the 'Rights for Whites' campaign, see Nigel Copsey, 'Contemporary Fascism in the Local Arena: The British National Party and 'Rights for Whites', M. Cronin (ed.), 'Failure of British Fascism', pp. 118–40, and Roger Eatwell, 'Britain: The BNP and the Problem of Legitimacy' in Hans-Georg Betz and Stefan Immerfall, (eds), *The New Politics of the Right: Neo Populist Movements in Established Democracies* (1998), pp. 143–54.

95. John Tyndall, 'Divisions in the BNP', *Spearhead*, 403 (September 2002) claimed a rise of 90 per cent between 1997 and 1999, *http://www.aryanunity.com/bnpdiv.html*, 11/06/03.

96. Nick Lowles, *White Riot. The Violent Story of Combat 18* (2001), pp. 18–20, 24.

97. For these links, see Ibid., pp. 60–119.

98. It was reformed in 1988 according to *Searchlight*. *Searchlight*, 'The State of the Right in Britain today – April 2001', p. 3, *http://s-light.demon.co.uk/presspack/gh1.html*, 29/08/03. However, Larry O'Hara notes that when Michael McLaughlin, who succeeded Colin Jordan as the BM leader, wound up the movement in 1983, some leading members objected and in 1985 restructured the movement and re-named it the British National Socialist Movement. (O'Hara, 'Notes' part 4, p. 10). The old name 'British Movement' nevertheless continued to be used.

99. Lowles, 'White Riot', pp. 3–4.

100. Ibid., pp. 34–5.

101. Ibid., pp. 40–2.

102. Ibid., pp. 39, 52, 57.

103. Ibid., pp. 56–7.

104. Ibid., pp. 121–2.

105. Eddy Morrison, *Memoirs of a Street Soldier*, part 3, p. 3, *http:// www.wnpuk.org/memoirs3.html*, 11/08/03.

106. Lowles, 'White Riot', p. 131.

107. Ibid., p. 120. For Myatt's writings see the David Myatt Homepage *http://www.geocities.com/davidmyatt*. The substantial 'David Myatt Online Resource' seems to have disappeared, but see *http://david-myatt.cjd–net*.

108. Lowles, 'White Riot', p. 53.

109. Ibid., p. 165.

110. Ibid., p. 117.

111. Ibid., pp. 160–75.

112. Ibid., pp. 100–05, 119.

113. Ibid., pp. 185–97.

114. Ibid., p. 187. This question is discussed by Larry O'Hara in 'Combat 18 and MI5: some background notes', *Lobster* 30 (December 1995), pp. 1–4.

115. Lowles, White Riot', p. 195.

116. Ibid., pp. 199–206, 220–227.

117. Ibid., pp. 206–219.

118. Ibid., p. 289.

119. *Searchlight*, 'The state of the right – April 2001', p. 2.

120. Lowles, 'White Riot', pp. 319–26.

121. *Observer*, 1 July 2001, *http://observer.guardian.co.uk_news/story/ 0,6903,515253,00.html*, 27/08/03. The OWK's policies can be found at *http://www.orderofwhiteknights.org*, 30/07/03.

122. John Tyndall, 'Humbug'.

123. John Tyndall, 'Humbug', p. 2.

124. BNP, 'What we stand for', p. 1. *http://www.bnp.org.uk/policies.html,* 11/06/03.

125. Nick Griffin, 'BNP: Anti-asylum protest', p. 6.

126. Ibid., pp. 7–8.

127. Ibid., p. 7.

128. Andrew Anthony, 'Flying the Flag', *Observer,* 1 September 2002, *http://observer.guardian.co.uk/magazine/story/0,11913,783675,00.html,* 12/08/03.

129. BNP, 'The disturbing story of the appeal of the swastika for many young Britons', *http://www.bnp.org.uk/articles/appeal_swastika.htm,* p. 5, 22/08/03.

130. These two paragraphs are based on 'Our Stance' and 'Frequently Asked Questions', *http://www.bnp.org.uk/faq.html,* 18/08/03.

131. Griffin, 'BNP: Anti-asylum protest', pp. 1–3.

132. Ibid., p. 4.

133. Nick Lowles, 'Election analysis-racism the victor', *Searchlight* (June 2000), *http://www.searchlightmagazine.com/stories/electionanalysisjune 2000.htm.* See also, Nick Lowles, 'The Looming Threat', *Searchlight* (March 2002), *http://www.searchlightmagazine.com/stories/Looming Threat.htm,* 12/08/03.

134. Nick Lowles, 'Looking down on Armageddon', *Searchlight* (March 2003), *http://www.searchlightmagazine.com/stories/032003_story03.htm,* 12/08/03.

135. Ibid.

136. 'Election Overview', *Searchlight* (June 2003), *http://www.searchlight-magazine.com/stories/062003_story01.htm;* Paul Harris, 'Mythical refugees help BNP win white suburb', *Observer,* 11 May 2003, *http://society.guardian.co.uk/localgovelections/story/0,8150,954175,00. html,* 12/08/03.

137. Terry McKay, 'Labour disarray helps BNP by-election victory', *Searchlight,* September 2003, *http://www.searchlightmagazine.com/ stories/092003_story02.htm,* 16/03/04.

138. Ibid.

139. Esther Addley, 'On the stump with the BNP', *Guardian,* 30 April 2003, *http://politics.guardian.co.uk/farright/story/0,11375,946378,00.html,* 12/08/03.

140. Martin Wainwright and Tom Overton, 'BNP win brings council tally to 17', *Guardian,* 16 August 2003.

141. Hugh Muir, 'Community that saw off the BNP', *Guardian*, 27 May 2003, *http://politics.guardian.co.uk/farright/story/0,11375,963959,00.html*; 12/08/03, Nick Ryan, 'Homeland', pp. 164–68.
142. See 'BNP in double election defeat', *Searchlight*, December 2003, *http://www.searchlightmagazine.com/stories/122003_story01.htm*, 16.03/04.
143. 'BNP seen off in Super Thursday', *Searchlight* (November 2003), *http://www.searchlightmagazine.com/stories/112003_story01.htm*, 16/03/04, 'BNP in double election defeat'.

Conclusion: Past Failures and Future Prospects

1. Roger Eatwell, 'Why Has the Extreme Right Failed in Britain?' in Paul Hainsworth (ed.), *The Extreme Right in Europe and the U.S.A*, (1992), pp. 175–91 is a good discussion of support after 1945, but rather evades the question asked.
2. Nick Griffin, 'The BNP: Anti-asylum protest', p. 2.
3. *The Observer*, 'Flying the Flag', p. 9.
4. Coupland, 'Blackshirted Utopia', p. 264.
5. This summary of Radical Right proposals is derived from 'An Introduction to the White Nationalist Party', *http://www.wnpuk.org/wnpintro.html*, 06/06/03; 'The Policies of the White Nationalist Party', *http://wnpuk.org/policies.html*, 11/06/03; 'The National Front Manifesto', December 2001, *http://www.yorksnf.com/nfm.html*, 20/05/03; '100 Questions and Answers About the National Front', *http://www.yorksnf.com/qu.html*, 02/07/03; 'BNP, What We Stand For', *http://bnp.org.uk/policies.html*, 11/06/03; 'BNP, Frequently Asked Questions', *http://www.bnp.org.uk/faq.html*, 18/08/03; Frank Martell, 'Then What Do We Do?' *http://www.bnp.org.uk/policy/martell_economics.htm*, 22/08/03; Nick Griffin, 'The Disturbing Story of the Appeal of the Swastika'; Nick Griffin, 'the BNP: Anti-asylum protest'.
6. John Tyndall, *The Eleventh Hour*, (3rd Edn, 1998), p. 294.
7. 'Wolf88', 'Slavs Are Aryans', p. 1. *http://www.aryanunity.com/slavs.html*, 11/06/03.
8. Aryan Unity, *http://www.aryanunity.com/index2.html*, 11/06/03.
9. *Aryan Unity*, 1 (17 March 2001), pp. 1–2, *http://www.aryanunity.com/arun1.htm*, 9/06/03.
10. 'Wolf88', '2002: A Nationalist Odyssey', p. 1, *http://wnpuk.org/nocompromise.html*, 11/06/03.

11. 'An Introduction to the White Nationalist Party', p. 1, *http:// www. wnpuk.org/wnpintro.html*, 06/06/03.
12. Eddy Morrison, *White Revolution*, p. 1, *http://www.wnpuk.org/ tomorrowintro.html*, 27/08/03.
13. 'An Introduction to the WNP', p. 1.
14. 'NF Manifesto', Section 15, p. 1; 'National Revolution' is from '100 Questions', Section 1, p. 1.
15. Eddy Morrison has charted his own intellectual journey in 'From British Nationalist to National Socialist', c.2001, *http://www.wnpuk.org/ bntons.html*, 22/06/03.
16. 'An Introduction to the WNP', p. 2.
17. 'The Purpose of this Site', p. 1. *http://www.wnpuk.org/purpose.html*, 11/06/03.
18. 'An Introduction to the WNP', p. 2.
19. 'The Policies of the White Nationalist Party', p. 2.
20. 'Wolf88', '2002: A Nationalist Odyssey', p. 2.
21. Ibid., pp. 1–2.
22. 'Aryan Unity/White Nationalist Report' 22 September 2002, *http://www.thebirdman.org/Index/Temp/Temp-BritishNationalist Infighting.htm*, 08/08/03.
23. 'Divisions in the BNP', *Spearhead*, 403, September 2002, *http:// www. aryanunity.com/bnpdiv.html*, 11/06/03, John Tyndall, 'Humbug'.
24. '2002: A Nationalist Odyssey' p. 1.
25. Griffin, 'BNP: Anti-Asylum Protest', p. 5.
26. 'Tyndall's last stand', *Searchlight*, August, 2003, *http://.www.searchlight-magazine.com/stories/082003_story03.htm*, 15/08/03.
27. 'Liberal Nationalist Party', *http://easyweb.easynet.co.uk/goldsmith/ lbnp/lnp. htm*, 20/08/03.
28. 'British National Party. A Night of the Long Knives?', *Spearhead*, 403, September 2002, *http://.www.aryanunity.com/bnprush2.html*, 17/08/03.
29. 'Freedom Party News', 2 May 2003, *http://www.freedompartyuk.net/ public/partynews/index.html*, p. 1, 20/08/03.
30. Ibid., 22 March 2003.
31. 'What is the United National Front', *http://www.yorksnf.com/udi1.html*, 07/08/03.
32. 'Are Your White?' *http://www.wnpuk.org/elect1.html*, 27/08/03.
33. *http://www.white.org.uk/wnpstatement1.html*, *http://www.white.org.uk/ efp1.html*.

Further Reading

The closest to a general history of the Radical Right is Richard Thurlow, *Fascism in Britain: From Oswald Mosley's Blackshirts to the National Front* (1998), a revised and updated version of his *Fascism in Britain: A History, 1918–1985* (1987), or his brief *Fascism in Modern Britain* (2000). As histories of fascism, these concentrate on the interwar period. The essays in Mike Cronin (ed.), *The Failure of British Fascism. The Far Right and the Fight for Political Recognition* (1996) cover the twentieth century, but in disconnected fashion, and the subject is again fascism. Roger Eatwell, 'Continuity and Metamorphosis: Fascism in Britain since 1945' in Stein Ugelvik Larsen (ed.), *Modern Europe After Fascism* (1998) is a very useful brief overview of the second half of the century, whilst Nigel Copsey, *Anti-Fascism in Britain* (2000) is an excellent survey of the opposition which reveals much about the ebb and flow of Fascist popularity.

The easiest introduction to the Edwardian right is David Dutton, *His Majesty's Loyal Opposition: The Unionist Party in Opposition 1905–1915* (1992), the best is E. H. H. Green, *The Crisis of Conservatism* (1995). Alan Sykes, *Tariff Reform in British Politics, 1903–13* (1979) provides more detail on one aspect whilst Bernard Semmel, *Imperialism and Social Reform* (1954) is dated but still inspired. Dan Stone, *Breeding Superman* (2002) has brought new insight into the potentially lethal theory of eugenics without quite replacing Geoffrey Searle, *Eugenics and Politics in Britain 1900–14* (1976). D. S. Thatcher, *Nietzsche in England* (1970) and Wallace Martin, *The New Age under Orage* (1967) discuss the cultural side. Two essays by Geoffrey Searle, 'Critics of Edwardian Society' in Alan O'Day (ed.), *The Edwardian Age* (1979) and 'The Revolt from the Right in Edwardian Britain' in P. Kennedy and A. Nicholls (eds), *Nationalist and*

Racialist Movements in Great Britain and Germany before 1914 (1981) are focused directly on the Radical Right. G. Phillips, *The Diehards* (1979) gives some background to aristocratic revivalism.

There is little on the patriotic labour groups during the First World War beyond the articles cited in the footnotes, except Panikos Panayi, 'The British Empire Union in the First World War' in Tony Kushner and Kenneth Lunn (eds), *The Politics of Marginality* (1990). Alfred Gollin, *Proconsul in Politics. A Study of Lord Milner in Opposition and in Power* (1964) provides some context. Apart from Thomas Linehan, *British Fascism 1918–39* (2000), discussion of the post-war groups most often arises in studies centred on anti-semitism. The standard work is still Colin Holmes, *Anti-Semitism in British Society 1876–1939* (1979), supplemented by Gisela Lebzelter, *Political Anti-semitism in England 1918–1939* (1978) and B. Gainer, *The Alien Invasion: The Origins of the Aliens Act of 1905* (1972), and extended into the Second World War by Tony Kushner, *The Persistence of Prejudice* (1989).

There are several collections of essays on aspects of fascism, racism and anti-semitism, largely before 1945: Tony Kushner and Kenneth Lunn (eds), *The Politics of Marginality* (1990), Tony Kushner and Nadia Valman (eds), *Remembering Cable Street* (2000), Panikos Panayi (ed.), *Racial Violence in Britain 1840–1950* (1993), Tony Kushner and Kenneth Lunn, (eds), *Traditions of Intolerance* (1989), Neil Nugent and Roger King (eds), *The British Right* (1977), which includes Neil Nugent's useful essay 'The Ideas of the British Union of Fascists', and Kenneth Lunn and Richard Thurlow (eds), *British Fascism* (1980).

Mosley's career is discussed in Robert Skidelsky, *Oswald Mosley* (1975, 1981) and D. S. Lewis, *Illusions of Grandeur* (1987); the British Union of Fascists in Robert Benewick, *Political Violence and Public Order* (1972), and of course, Thomas Linehan above. The ideas are put into context by G. C. Webber, *The Ideology of the British Right 1918–39* (1986). Stephen Cullen's articles, 'The Ideas of the British Union of Fascists', *Journal of Contemporary History*, (1987) and 'Political Violence: the Case of the BUF', ibid., (1993), amend conventional interpretations. G. C. Webber, 'Patterns of Membership and support for the British Union of Fascists', *Journal of Contemporary History* (1984) takes the membership question about as far as possible, but see also the more human dimension in Stuart Rawnsley 'The Membership of the British Union of Fascists' in Thurlow and Lunn above. Thomas P. Linehan, *East London for Mosley* (1996) reveals the difficulty of generalization even in a key area. Dave Renton, *Fascism, Anti-Fascism and Britain in the 1940s* carries the story of fascism beyond the 'hinge' of the Second World War. David Baker, *Ideology of Obsession* (1996), a biography of A. K. Chesterton, links the pre- and post-war periods.

For the pluralist and anarchical elements, see S. T. Glass, *The Responsible Society: The Ideas of the English Guild Socialists* (1966) which, provides a brief introduction, and like Frances Hutchinson and Brian Burkitt, *The Political Economy of Social Credit and Guild Socialism* (1997) draws attention to the influence of A. R. Orage and the *New Age*. J. L. Finlay, *The English Origins of Social Credit* (1972) has an extended survey of the intellectual roots, J. P. Corrin, *G. K. Chesterton and Hilaire Belloc: The Battle Against Modernity* (1981) is excellent on the complications of distributism, supplemented by Margaret Canovan, *G. K. Chesterton. Radical Populist* (1977). Amidst the social theory, there is a good history of the Greenshirts in Mark Drakeford, *Social Movements and Their Supporters* (1997). Hilaire Belloc's *The Servile State* (1912) is essential to understand the motivation behind such unorthodoxy, and arguably also that of the NF in the 1980s. Richard Griffiths, *Fellow Travellers of the Right* (1983) remains the standard work on those who sought rapprochement with Germany, together with his study of the Right Club, *Patriotism Perverted* (1998).

After 1945 secondary reading becomes more scarce. The Union movement can be traced in the books on Mosley above. The success of the NF in the 1970s occasioned a flurry of interest at the time: see Martin Walker, *The National Front* (1977), Stan Taylor, *The National Front in English Politics* (1982), Nigel Fielding, *The National Front* (1981) and for the continuing difficulty in identifying support, C. T. Husbands, *Racial Exclusionism and the City* (1983). John Tyndall has written a testamentary autobiography, *The Eleventh Hour* (3rd edn, 1998) and John Bean a more orthodox one, *Many Shades of Black* (1999). Martin Durham, 'Women and the National Front' in Luciano Cheles *et al.*, *Neo-Fascism in Europe* (1991) says much about the NF's racial priorities. Larry O'Hara's articles in *Lobster* 23–6 and Roger Eatwell 'The Esoteric Ideology of the National Front in the 1980s' in M. Cronin, above, introduce the upheaval of the 1980s, whilst Nigel Copsey, 'Contemporary Fascism in the Local Arena: the British National Party and 'Rights for Whites', also in Cronin, gets the BNP off the ground. Nick Lowles, *White Riot. The Violent Story of Combat 18* (2001) and Nick Ryan, *Homeland* (2003) deal fairly sympathetically with the more frightening aspects of the Radical Right. Nigel Copsey's important new study, *Contemporary British Fascism. The British National Party and the Quest for Legitimacy*, (2004) appeared too late to use here.

There is an extensive range of material on the internet, ranging from the programmes and publications of active political groups to the re-publication of original material from the 1930s and even earlier. On the theoretical side, Roger Griffin *The Nature of Fascism* (1991), Roger Eatwell, 'Towards a New Theory of Generic Fascism' *Journal of Theoretical Politics* (1992) and Dave Renton, *Fascism, Theory and Practice* (1999) provide an introduction to the debate on 'generic fascism', whilst Roger Eatwell and Noel O'Sullivan (eds) *The Nature of the Right* (1989) attempts the equally difficult task of identifying the multifaceted 'Right'.

Index